The Writer's Digest Handbook of Short Story Writing Volume II

D0109491

The Writer's Digest
Handbook of Short Story Writing
Volume II

Edited by Jean M. Fredette

Writer's
Digest
Books

Cincinnati, Ohio

About the Editor

Jean M. Fredette was acquisitions editor of the writing books for Writer's Digest Books for four years. Formerly she edited six editions of *Fiction Writer's Market* and assisted Jud Jerome on the first *Poet's Market*. She also edited *Writer's Digest Handbook of Magazine Article Writing* and has written articles for *Writer's Digest*, *Writer's Yearbook*, and *A Beginner's Guide to Getting Published*. As a freelancer she has written ads and brochures. She has also published in *Cincinnati* magazine, trade magazines and other local, national, and international publications. Jean lives in Cincinnati.

THE WRITER'S DIGEST HANDBOOK OF SHORT STORY WRITING VOLUME II. Copyright © 1988 by Writer's Digest Books. Printed and bound in the United States of America. All rights reserved. No part of this book may be reproduced in any form or by any electronic or mechanical means including information storage and retrieval systems without permission in writing from the publisher, except by a reviewer who may quote brief passages in a review. Published by Writer's Digest Books, an imprint of F&W Publications, Inc., 1507 Dana Avenue, Cincinnati, Ohio 45207. (800) 289-0963. First edition. First paperback printing 1991.

Other fine Writer's Digest Books are available from your local bookstore or direct from the publisher

99 98 97 96   10 9 8 7

Library of Congress Cataloging-in-Publication Data

Handbook of short storywriting.
    Vol. 2: The Writer's Digest handbook of short story writing/edited by Jean M. Fredette.
    Includes index.
    1. Short story. I. Dickson, Frank A. II. Smythe, Sandra. III. Fredette, Jean
M. IV. Title. Writer's Digest handbook of short story writing.
PN3373.D5   808.31   73-100315
ISBN 0-911654-15-1 (v.1)
ISBN 0-89879-463-3 (v.2)

The following page constitutes an extension of this copyright page.

PERMISSIONS

Contents

Preface

Short Story Writing

The Importance of Fiction
John Updike   1

Mastering the Short Story
Paul Darcy Boles   5

Anatomy of a Short Story
James Gunn   17

Getting Started

The Carrot and Some (Writing) Tricks
Lawrence Block   19

Notebooks and Lists
R.V. Cassill   23

Getting Ideas
Robert Cormier   29

Short Story Fundamentals

The Finer Points of Characterization
Orson Scott Card   31

What Is Plot?
Ansen Dibell   41

Plot = Motivation = Plot
   Michael A. Banks   52

Call Me Ishmael: Point of View
   Janet Burroway   58

The Secrets of Writing Powerful Dialogue
   Gary Provost   70

"Dialogue," Said the Writer, "Is a Fantastic Tool for
Enriching and Enlivening Your Fiction"
   Robyn Carr   79

Setting
   Rust Hills   86

Craft and Technique

How to Start Smart
   Roy Sorrels   89

High Middle
   Dwight V. Swain   95

End Games
   Esther M. Friesner   104

Making the Scene
   James B. Hall   110

Sensing Extra Perceptions
   Paul Darcy Boles   122

Trouble-Free Transitions
   Jean Z. Owen   132

How to Make Your Fiction Three Dimensional
   Darrell Schweitzer   137

Using Symbols as a Shortcut to Meaning
Rega Kramer McCarty   143

Naming Names: How to Make Your Story
Real and Accessible
Hal Blythe and Charlie Sweet   148

Using Flashback Effectively;
or Is This Trip Necessary?
Will C. Knott   153

What to Leave Out and What to Put In
Kit Reed   159

Style: The Manner of the Telling
Hallie and Whit Burnett   168

Revising and Rewriting

Cut, Carve and Polish Your Story
Barbara Wernecke Durkin   175

The Fiction Writer's Polish Kit
Judith Ross Enderle and Stephanie Gordon Tessler   180

The Break-in: An Inside Look at a First Fiction Sale
Sharon Rudd   184

Writing for Specialized Audiences

The Short Short
Vera Henry   195

The Serious Business of Choosing Literary Fiction
Ben Nyberg   200

Mastering Editorial Requirements for
Writing Young People's Stories
   George Edward Stanley   210

Marketing the Short Story

Submitting Your Short Story—The Waiting Game
   Laurie Henry   219

Tips from a Master
   Adela Rogers St. Johns   226

About the Authors   229

Index   236

Foreword

Once upon a time, in fact, a *very* long time ago by publishing standards, Writer's Digest Books issued the first edition of *Handbook of Short Story Writing*.

It was 1970, and in general, not a good time for fiction. Most of the well-known magazines, such as *Collier's, Story, Look, Life,* and *Saturday Evening Post,* had either gone out of business or discontinued their short fiction. More and more there was a noticeable resistance on the part of editors to publish fiction at all. The heyday of the short story was over.

As the years and magazines came and went, we saw publishing take a different direction. New special interest and genre magazines began to appear; likewise many energetic and individualistic little and literary magazines regularly began to spring up all over the country. Both kinds of publications not only helped fill the void the general magazines had left, but they often *invited* short fiction and *encouraged* new writers.

Then in the late '80s, we witnessed a resurgence of interest in the short story form, a sort of renaissance. The literary/little magazines and a few commercial publications were now by reputation the acknowledged avenue for serious or mainstream fiction; more magazines were reviving both the short and the short-short form; and the small presses and commercial publishers were competing for short story collections.

Throughout these two rather tumultuous decades, our faith in fiction never faltered; we reprinted *Handbook of Short Story Writing* nine times. And now we are back, with our second endorsement in the strength and viability of the short form, *Handbook of Short Story Writing, Volume II*. Again we look toward a bright future for fiction—and hope that your short stories will be a part of it.

—*Jean M. Fredette, Editor*

John Updike

The Importance of Fiction

Well, when the importance of something has to be proclaimed, it can't be all that important. And certainly most of the people in the United States get along without reading fiction, and more and more of the magazines get along without printing it. Even *Esquire,* which used to run short stories as automatically as he-men smoked unfiltered cigarettes, has had to whip itself up and cheer itself on to give us a special fiction issue.

The old throwbacks still producing fiction should be grateful, and we are. It's hard to believe that this fragile business ever had any muscle, but it did. In Gutenberg's Gymnasium, Dickens and Balzac worked out on the high rings and the Brontë sisters did back flips in unison on the balance beam and Harriet Beecher Stowe bench-pressed more kilos than Herman Melville, while Flaubert and Mark Twain were just a double blur on the parallel bars and the bourgeoisie in the bleachers went wild. Even in the days of network radio, fiction put hair on Hemingway's chest and gin in Fitzgerald's glass and that far-off starry look in Faulkner's eye, those days when the mules weren't running. But after Hitler's coonskin was nailed to the barn door and the boys came back to make babies and put on gray flannel suits, something went out of fiction. Those good folks who sat around in the kitchen near the wood stove reading about Mr. Tutt and Perry Mason in the *Saturday Evening Post* had slipped out the back door and bought oil burners and television sets, and the aura of the party being over was so pervasive that Norman Mailer tried to be a party all by himself. Saul Bellow kept winning the prizes, but there was something effete and professional about his appeal, compared with the way Sinclair Lewis and John Steinbeck had reached down and given Main Street a shake, and the way those two-dollar books of theirs had stood fading on the sunny windowsills of every small-town piano teacher's front parlor.

Dearth Mother and Beautiful Bards

The '60s were when the demise of fiction became something to crow about. Philip Roth told us that life in America had become so barbaric and bizarre that no fiction could hold a candle to the grotesque truth. Truman Capote allowed as how he had invented a new kind of narrative treat, the nonfiction novel, that made the un-non kind as obsolete as hand-churned ice cream. Tom Wolfe (the younger) let us ineluctably know that his New Journalism was zippier, grabbier, funnier, wilder, and truer-to-life than any old wistful bit of fiction published by, say, those tiny giants over at *The New Yorker.* Even in *The New Yorker,* as the old two-column departments died off and were replaced by learned specialists whose exhaustive poop overflowed the narrow columns like freshly singed popcorn, there was less space for fiction than there had been in the days of Bob Benchley or even the days of Nat Benchley. The Revolution had little use of fiction: Fiction was sublimation, it was Leavis and Trilling, it was graduate school; it was the civilization and its discontents, it was the lonely crowd. Fiction was how you consoled yourself in the dark ages before love beads and "Lucy in the Sky With Diamonds." A revolution sings songs and trashes chain-store windows; it does things in a bunch, and nothing is more antisocial and nontribal than one individual sitting in a quiet room coding make-believe for another individual to decipher in a quiet room maybe tens of years and thousands of miles away.

Accordingly, the Revolution left us rock music and co-ed dormitories but not much in the way of fiction. Who now remembers Marge Piercy's *Dance the Eagle to Sleep* and Gurney Norman's *Divine Right's Trip?* I do, because I reviewed them. Otherwise, there were Pynchon and Kesey, who have subsequently tended to imitate the sound of one hand clapping. The postrevolutionary anticlimax, though, has not lacked for bards, beginning with the beautiful Ann Beattie, who found the right filtered tone to let the lack of sunshine in, and who, young as she is, has played dearth mother to a vast, fresh bevy of delicate/tough female talents, such as Bobbie Ann Mason, Laurie Colwin, Elizabeth Tallent, T. Gertler, Andrea Lee, Deborah Eisenberg, to name but a few. The young males haven't been quite so vivid, since having made their entry splash, they tend to sink into full time extraliterary employment or to sidestroke toward Hollywood, like John Sayles. But even the most diffident such inventory insults the intelligence and the fundamental wonder of fiction, its fundamental irresistibility even in an age when the very sidewalks are heated by television cables. Its fundamental importance, I suppose one has to say.

Fiction is nothing less than the subtlest instrument for self-examination and self-display that mankind has invented yet. Psychology and X rays bring up some portentous shadows, and demographics and stroboscopic photography do some fine breakdowns, but for the full *parfum* and effluvia of being human, for feathery ambiguity and rank facticity, for the air and iron, fire and spit of our daily mortal adventure *there is nothing like fiction:* It makes sociology look priggish, history problematical, the film media two-dimensional, and the *National Enquirer* as silly as last week's cereal box.

Humility on Eternal Record

In fiction everything that searchers for the important tend to leave out is left in, and what they would have in is left out. Stendhal had served devotedly under Napoleon and was one of the most lucid thinkers in Europe, but what Fabrizio, in *The Charterhouse of Parma,* makes of Waterloo is sheer confusion, highlighted by a conversation with a *cantiniére* steering her cartful of brandy through the thick of the battle. For Tolstoy, Napoleon was an excuse for the Moscow aristocrats to gossip and to push on with their spiritual searches; for Jane Austen, Napoleon was the reason the English countryside was so sparsely equipped with prospective husbands. Thus a vast historical presence refracts down into little lives that are precious only because they resemble our own. Kutuzov, Tolstoy's splendidly fictionalized version of an actual Russian general, reads French romances while the steppes around him tremble at the approach of the superman, the master strategist, the general of supreme genius. Romances safeguard the importance of our sentiments, our spiritual dignity, amid the uncontrollable large-scale surges that constitute history; the inner lives of the obscure, as Erich Auerbach points out in his *Mimesis,* have been from the New Testament on the peculiar and precious burden of the Western narrative imagination.

The fiction writer is the ombudsman who argues our humble, dubious case in the halls of eternal record. Are defecation, tipsy bar babble, days of accumulating small defeats, and tired, compromised, smelly connubial love part of our existence? Then put them into literature alongside Homer, says *Ulysses.* Has a life been ill-spent in snobbery, inaction, neurasthenia, and homosexual heartache? Then make that life into a verbal cathedral, says *Remembrance of Things Past.* Do pathetic and senseless-seeming murders appear daily in the newspapers? Then show the humble aspirations and good intentions and small missteps that inexorably lead to such ruin, say *Tess of the D'Urbervilles* and *An American Tragedy.* Feeling nervous and as though things don't quite add up? Then write like Virginia Woolf, and give us actuality in its sliding, luminous increments. Feeling worse than nervous, and certain that the world is a mess? Then write like Céline, and wake up the French language. Want a taste of Latin American backcountry blues? Try Graham Greene or Gabriel Garcia Márquez. Want to know what goes on in those tacky developments just beyond the cloverleaf? Let Raymond Carver or Bobbie Ann Mason tell you. Curious about the condo life in the new, homogenized Deep South? Here comes Frederick Barthelme. No soul or locale is too humble to be the site of entertaining and instructive fiction. Indeed, all other things being equal, the rich and glamorous are less fertile ground than the poor and plain, and the dusty corners of the world more interesting than its glittering, already sufficiently publicized centers.

Fiction's Shapely Lies

Yet we do not read fiction for information, informative though it can be. Unlike journalism, history, or sociology, fiction does not give us facts snug in their accredited truth, to be accepted and absorbed like pills, for our undoubted good; we *make* fiction true, as we read it. Fiction can poison our minds, as it did those of Madame Bovary and Don Quixote. It extends our world, and any extension is a risk. The self we are left with when we close the book may not be a useful, marketable one. Fiction offers to enlarge our sense of possibilities, of potential freedom, and freedom is dangerous. The bourgeois capitalist world, compared with the medieval hierarchies it supplanted and with the communist hierarchies that would supplant it, *is* a dangerous one, where failure can be absolute and success may be short-lived. The novel and the short story rose with the bourgeoisie, as exercises in democratic feeling and in individual adventure. *Pamela, The Pilgrim's Progress, Robinson Crusoe*—what do they tell us but that our entrepreneurism, on one level or another, may bear fruit? If fiction is in decline, it is because we have lost faith in the capacity of the individual to venture forth and suffer the consequences of his dreams. Myself, I feel that this most flexible and capacious of artistic forms still holds out its immense space to our imaginations, still answers to a hope within us of more adventure. What is important, if not the human individual? And where can individuality be better confronted, appraised, and enjoyed than in fiction's shapely lies?

Paul Darcy Boles

Mastering the Short Story

The short story has as many definitions as the blind men had for their fabulous elephant.

Its bright and buoyant virtue is that it's traditionally short.

Somerset Maugham said that it must have a beginning, a middle, and an end.

But some beautiful stories are as long as young novels.

And some excellent stories have no more beginning, middle, and end than a plate of lasagna.

Its forward motion may be like the catapult, sudden and fierce and moving from *here* to *there* in a parabola of impact that hits the reader straight between the eyes.

Or it may be artfully slow, rising around the reader in a tide of sensation and revelation.

The best all-around description of the short story was given by Stephen Vincent Benét: "Something that can be read in an hour and remembered for a lifetime."

Writing the marketable story can't be taught.

It can be guided.

If you have talent, your talent can be sharpened toward the making of stories which will have a fighting chance with a magazine editor. Your special fund of emotion and skill can be channeled into the story that gets the editor's attention and starts you on a published career. There is no mystery about this. There are no tricks to it.

There is a lot of work, coupled with the joy of mastering an art almost as old as time—one which many believe to be the most rewarding of any.

Your story will stand a far better chance in today's market if it can be told in 3,000 words or less. This is ten pages, double-spaced. If this restriction bothers your sense of story-values, cheer yourself by reflecting that the Gettysburg Address is very brief, and that the Song of Solomon takes up only modest space in the Bible.

The days of voluminous magazine-room for short fiction are over. Thinking in story-space will encourage you to trim your story as you plan it—to leave out the fat, eliminate side trips, and hold back your self-indulgence for other pursuits.

It will cut down on characters, help you to aim in the manner of a rifle rather than a scattergun, and bring in focus what was fuzzy.

It will eliminate all the dreary padding by means of which so many former long-winded tale-tellers gave the effect of importance by loading their work with detail.

Your detail will improve simply by being vital to the story and not dragged in by the heels.

If you throw up your hands in alarm and say that these artificial boundaries stifle you, that you need room to let the story breathe, and that *Reader's Digest* condensation is a curse meant to squeeze decent prose into palatable capsules, perhaps you were a novelist all the time and shouldn't come near the story except to sneer.

But if you rise to the challenge of capturing on paper a story strong enough to compete with television, movies and radio for the attention of the much-assaulted general reader, you will teach yourself economy.

By doing so, you will improve your writing in all other forms.

Thinking Story

The novel has an up-and-down motion. It goes in a series of wave crests and troughs. It moves with undulance. Even in the pared-down, almost bald novels of the late James M. Cain, which are restricted to action and dialogue whittled to their simplest elements, the movement is Alpine, roller-coaster, rising, falling and rising.

The story is a straight line. The marketable story is nearly always held in tight reins of time. The time elapsed in most stories is at most a season, usually a few days or hours. Chekhov's marvelous observation, "The art of writing is the art of abbreviation," applies to the commercial story of today more than it ever did.

Abbreviation is not private code. It is the clarification of the complex. In the story, large ideas are briskly implied. What is between the lines looms as large as what appears on the page. But there can be no cryptic semaphoring, no messages held so close to the chest they're unreadable. The modern story is like the modern poem in that it relies on the reader's informed imagination much more than did the stories of Sir Walter Scott or Thomas Hardy or Robert Louis Stevenson. Today's reader simply doesn't need excessive explanation—he can see clearly when he is given a few clear-cut hints. But the modern story is not dense and it doesn't require footnotes or translators. Its words may be simple in the extreme, as in the stories of Hemingway. (His story vocabulary has been estimated at about 800 words—that of an average high school sophomore.) A story's words may glitter with light and allusion, as in tales by John Cheever and J. D. Salinger. They may be serviceable earthenware with flashes of gold, as are Scott Fitzgerald's. They may be as full of fireworks as Faulkner's. But their common ground is that they are intensely readable.

The more you train yourself to think in terms of the story, the more readable your stories will be.

You can save yourself extra hours of editing grief by building a few dams in your mind at the start. This doesn't mean that you'll "write short" for the sake of shortness alone, or leave out anything vital that you'll have to insert later with a shoehorn.

It means you'll write in a controlled state of mind, conscious with part of yourself that the market won't stand for self-indulgent excess, and caring enough about your story to make it occupy a tidy pace at full strength.

Kipling said he never "wrote short"—that he'd tried it, and found the story weakened by too much vigilance. His way with a story—and it was quite a way—was to drift until it was ready, then to let it come out, then to set it aside—sometimes for months, in a few cases for years—and, at intervals, have at it with black India ink and a brush, until he'd cut out everything extraneous and the story spun like a top in righteous balance.

Saying enough is as necessary as not saying too much.

Skimping during the composition of a story is slow death. Stopping after every sentence for arduous stock-taking, asking yourself "Did I need that?" instead of "What comes next?" is a strong indication that you haven't spent enough time testing the story before you began it, that you're not yet involved enough to know, emotionally, where you're going, and that you're making a formidable mountain out of the process of creation when you should be skipping along the hills.

Knowing emotionally where you're going is different from knowing mentally where you're going.

Fitzgerald—who should be quoted, daily, by every working story writer as a matter of habit—said that *all good writing is swimming under water and holding your breath.*

Pronouncing Sentence

A story is *not* putting one sentence after another.

It's a series of aimed sentences.

The opening of James Joyce's "Two Gallants" is a series of nearly protoplasmic impressions, floating like light above tepid water, breaking most of the "rules" and leaving the reader puzzled as though he had been dipped in a murky bath, yet intrigued and even entranced.

> The grey warm evening of August had descended upon the city and a mild warm air, a memory of summer, circulated in the streets. The streets, shuttered for the repose of Sunday, swarmed with a gaily coloured crowd. Like illumined pearls the lamps shone from the summits of their tall poles upon the living texture below which, changing shape and hue unceasingly, sent up into the warm grey evening air an unchanging, unceasing murmur.

Reading that, even casually, you'll be struck by an apparent laziness, a repetition of such words as *grey, warm,* an inner chiming and murmuration that sounds a bit like an elderly lady talking in her sleep. It is one long metaphor of sleepwalking, and it sets the scene as nothing else could.

There is no repetition, no incantation, only a direct series of extremely vivid pictures, all in flowing motion, in the opening paragraph of E. M. Forster's "The Story of the Siren":

> Few things have been more beautiful than my notebook on the Deist Controversy as it fell downward through the waters of the Mediterranean. It dived, like a piece of black slate, but opened soon, disclosing leaves of pale green, which quivered into blue. Now it had vanished, now it was a piece of magical India rubber stretching out to infinity, now it was a book again, but bigger than the book of all knowledge. It grew more fantastic as it reached the bottom, where a puff of sand welcomed it and obscured it from view. But it reappeared, quite sane though a little tremulous, lying decently open on its back, while unseen fingers fidgeted among its leaves.

The sentences in both of those stories are aimed at what the story wants. For all its seeming amorphousness, the Joyce story exerts a powerful mood like a rising fog in which specific people will presently be encountered. The Forster story has a sliding, plunging underwater motion which follows that lost notebook like the eye of a whimsical god and gives it specific personality—"quite sane though a little tremulous"—as it rests in sight but drowning.

Your sentences are servants of your story mood, each pulling its proper weight as it enters and makes way for the next, and each related to the other by more than the mere fact that the same person is writing them. Get and read Flannery O'Connor's "A Good Man Is Hard to Find" and notice that in its commentary on good and evil—and the fatuous helplessness of mankind when faced by pure evil—it's as succinctly told as though a lucid stream of icy air had been turned on and then off. Look up Eudora Welty's "Powerhouse" and see how the sentences jump into the skin of a black musician—Fats Waller—seeing him from the inside as a bolt of lightning might be felt. Take any Damon Runyon story and hear in it the stylized voice of a professional Broadway "character" speaking nasally and from a guarded mouth-corner.

Good sentences pace in step with their story.

If you're writing a light story about a mother's struggle with her eight-year-old daughter who wants to enter a dubious neighborhood theater beauty contest, and is asking for the ten-dollar entry fee, your sentences won't be heavy and overdramatic. They'll be humorous, straightforward, concerned. A story about a husband and wife on the verge of breaking up because he's a slipshod driver will have its contemporary pulse in every sentence, using brief description and dialogue to bring out what they're really fighting about—which may not be his driving at all. If your story is told by a young woman and concerns a radio announcer in love with his own chest tones, its sentences will be crisp, sardonic, pungent.

In ten years of reading stories by beginners, I have come across too many in which the sentence is regarded as a slack noose, aimlessly thrown in the hope of surrounding a story.

If you stiffen up and go cold in your center when you think about aiming a sentence, look on it as malleable, fluid, subject to your will. The poor thing needs your direction. It wants to say as much as it can for the story you have in mind. It's waiting to be modeled into kindness, curtness, flexible grace, gleaming steel. It asks to be fitted into your story—to be part of the ambience. Give it a nudge here and there until it's part of the crowd, feels at home. If it opens your story on too high a note, tone it down. If it's flabby, make it work until its muscles show. If it's just a wrong sentence and belongs in some other story you may write later, set it aside with a good word.

All good sentences are organic, belonging in their stories as cherries grown in the same orchard have the same family taste.

In most stories, you'll want to keep the sentences short. The attention span of the reader of marketable short stories varies from the flick of an eyelash to the dart of a lizard. Most readers aren't familiar with the long, looping and wonderfully prolix sentences of Proust, and Faulkner even at his most intense and grand makes them itchy. They're conditioned to television, in which images flitting by keep the eye in a steady state of daze and semi-stupor. By asking them to read a story, you're taxing them with the job of cooperating with you. Brief sentences insult nobody's intelligence. Nor do they have to be in baby talk to be immediately comprehended. Maupassant's stories, even in so-so translations, clip along with the eagerness of horses heading for a stable. He was the short story writer most in demand in his time.

The Fat and the Lean

The story itself, like the sentences that comprise it, must also be aimed. Keep it lean and uncluttered.

First stories can, like Christmas geese, be packed with too much stuffing. There is sometimes a pressing need to get everything in, to make a story overflow its space by holding more than it comfortably can. The old and pleasantly ribald anecdote about the *Reader's Digest* editor who wanted a tale which would be All Things to All Men, and came up with the man who assaulted a bear in an iron lung for the FBI and found God, is a good case in point. So is the apocryphal story sometimes called "Lincoln's Doctor's Wife's Dog," which was wonderfully calculated to please everybody, but which would be too much for mortal readers to accept.

So look around your story for too much obvious meaning. Meaning in a story is not injected with a hypodermic needle, but issues from it after it has been written. It's highly doubtful that Aesop ever said to himself, "Now I shall produce a profound fable upon the subject of Envy, and I think I'll call this one 'The Fox and the Grapes.' " Meaning lurks inside a story, between the lines; it is not always completely clear to the writer while the story is being written, or for that matter afterward. He or she leaves meaning to perceptive readers to interpret for themselves.

Similarly, stroll around your story plot. Study it with narrow eyes and critical objectivity. If it has a rococo touch—if there appears, already, to be too much detail in it, too many possible side shows—clear them away. If it still seems amorphous, merely a fuzzy far-in-the-distance suggestion of two or three characters thrown together, start focusing on just one of the people, and ask what is making this person tick.

When you think you know, begin plumbing the depths of your other protagonists. You may well find that you have imagined a straw doll for your more real people to react to.

The first draft of my short story "Sweet Chariot" was not lean and uncluttered; it was 24 pages long. It was all there, complete, making its point without shouting at the reader; but it was also too leisurely in rhythm, and self-indulgent when it came to halting the forward motion and giving the reader a guided tour of scenic wonders and outside appearances of people. At one juncture, its main character was described as if he weren't inhabiting a *short* story at all, but happened to be in a roomy Sir Walter Scott sort of novel:

> Journey was a looming, rangy man with the high cheekbones of middle Appalachia, descended from hunters, ballad-singers, keepers of their own secret counsels. His eyes, the color of very good, sun-faded denim, sometimes held hints of wildness—of wanting to rush away, like a deer startled from dreaming.

That is passable character-drawing; but it stands by itself without any kinship to the quick, demanding music of character-in-action called for in a short story. It's a trifle show-offy, like a set piece meant for recitation rather than reading in silence. In the process of cutting the first draft from 24 pages to 10, it was thrown out without a qualm. All that remained in the final draft was:

> His eyes held hints of wildness and rushing away.

That line does the job, summarizing everything in the original windy passage and allowing the story to move on without hanging fire.

Let's assume, for a moment, that part of your story is about the reaction of a woman to a snake. (Excellent stories along this line have been done—in the King James version of the Old Testament, for instance; and in more recent times by John Steinbeck.) Your task, to be performed in a minimum of words and space, is to make your reader know the essence of snakedom, the elixir of the woman. You may have read half a hundred volumes about herpetology; you may have spent an instructive summer working in the snake-house at your local zoo. But in your story what you're after is the valid center of the experience—the point, for instance, that dormant snakes smell like new-cut cucumbers; that they inspire atavistic fear, even though they're amazingly sentient, easy to handle and over-maligned. And without doing an essay on it, you will need to quickly interpret the woman's reaction to the encounter; to tell how she takes it, what she does, which will give immediate insight into the middle of her character. This is a section from a short story of mine, which was later, with slight changes, incorporated into a novel, *Glory Day*. Among other things, I wanted to show the impeccable calm of the woman, Phyllis, in a moment of natural crisis. The writing comes in on a slant, by indirection, embedded in the action so that inside and outside factors are working in harness. The reader sees what is going on, and feels it at the same time:

> She took hold of another weed; this one deep, calling for a side twist to bring the root webs out. When she had tossed it back and was reaching for another, she saw the intruder. It was uncoiled, a flake of sun touching

the triangular, turned-away head. The serrate, arid scales looked as though, if touched, they would whisper like autumn leaves. The body of the copperhead was a thick single muscle, relaxing. She sat back, hand hanging in air, then withdrew it gradually, from shade to sun.

Woman and snake are somehow together; the confrontation is mysterious and double. Here, the word *description* is misleading as a cover-word for what is actually happening. The eye sees, the ear listens, the skin feels; the hand of the woman becomes the hand of the reader as it is drawn back from the shadow into the sunlight. The inwardness of snake and woman are respected and let alone to be themselves. There are just sufficient words to allow the reader to participate wholly in the experience.

And here, for full contrast, is a sample from Elizabeth Bowen's short story "Maria." The story is one of the funniest ever written, and the intricately horrible character of young Maria comes through without one extraneous label offered by the author:

> "I can't tell you what I think of this place you're sending me to," said Maria. "I bounced on the bed in the attic they're giving me and it's like iron. I suppose you realize that rectories are always full of diseases? Of course, I shall make the best of it, Aunt Ena. I shouldn't like you to feel I'd complained. But of course you don't realize a bit, do you, what I may be exposed to? So often carelessness about a girl my age just ruins her life."
>
> Aunt Ena said nothing; she settled herself a little further down in the rugs and lowered her eyelids as though a strong wind were blowing.

A thousand labored "signpost" sentences couldn't tell you more about Maria, or more about Aunt Ena's stoic endurance. Their inwardness has been expertly and beautifully externalized.

What I am calling inwardness here—a certain center of withinness in all people, and in animals and birds, and in sunlight and rain—is nearly always seen and simultaneously felt in what we name, too lightly, "good story description."

This withinness, insideness, is there in so-called inanimate objects as well as in the obviously living and breathing. An awareness of it informs the story (even a fantasy) with reality, and it can make the *unsaid* more potent than what is put on paper, and richer than if it were stridently spelled out. When you admire understatement in a story, this is what you are admiring. You are praising considerably more than good taste, which, like fastidiousness, is not a particular virtue when it stands alone; you are impressed by the author's constant consciousness of the entire world of people and things, as well as that author's ability to suggest these in microcosm without turning up the volume.

The In-ness of Things

So for a minute now, consider: Going into a raw, newly constructed house which nobody has lived in, touching the fresh wood, sniffing the plaster, you feel neither alien nor at home. You are in the no man's land of the untenanted.

But after a few years, when the house has been occupied and rubbed by humanity, it gains a special aura, even when its occupants are not at home. A quality more important than furniture or familiar belongings or food and light is there. People have brought to things a felt impact of themselves.

The lived-in story is very like this. Each corner of it reflects, refracts and responds to the tone of whoever lives there . . . whoever wrote it with innate understanding of its inmost character.

There are stories which have never been lived in. They may be built of the most durable material; their authors may have applied every rule laid down by generations of good, indifferent and long-retired or de-funct teachers, and still have produced handsome and hollow shells.

Stories such as this are sometimes published—but when they lack the heat that lies outside technique, readers forget them. They suffer in silence from a need for the character of people *and* things.

The things of a lived-in story don't have to be "described"—some-times they don't even require mentioning. Yet during the writing they were known by the writer as familiarly as his or her hands and feet and heart and bloodstream; they were *felt all through*.

In the paragraph about the discovery of the snake by the woman, while she was weeding an onion patch, I left out the intense fury of the late-afternoon, Fourth of July heat above the simmering Ohio River, the arcade of sun-stunned, leaf-drooping oaks in the near distance, the musky smell of the riverbank, the friable, powdery touch of the baking earth. But they are there. They're in the silence around the snake, around the woman.

And the in-ness of Things is present to a touchable degree in "Maria," whose voice needs no description because we know it is pinched, haughty and insufferable, from hearing it on the page in her words, which characterize her completely—as do Aunt Ena's eyes, barely visible above the rugs as she lowers her eyelids "as though a strong wind were blowing."

Your story's foreground, and the people in it, should be lighted by your feeling for background—the shape and presence of Things.

Now, this so-called background is no stage flat, put there to give an audience the easily destroyed illusion that it is looking at a drawing room or a doctor's office. Its windows are real. Its walls have substance. It is never merely imagined. It is made of your ability to bring out the whole solidity of place. It reminds the reader of *something she or he has known;* and it influences the depth of a story as well as its topsoil. In many commercial stories of the kind published up through the '20s and into the '30s, such background was as bulky as a horsehair sofa, dominating the induction of a story while its characters, and its readers, waited for the action to start. Dress styles were lingered upon, furnishings were depicted at paragraph-length, fabrics were named and sometimes priced. This opulent sandbag approach to a story is no longer necessary or at all desirable—but without *some* fragrance of background reaching the reader, the story will hang in the air, a depthless and curious mobile.

Place is the Greek *Locus*—creator of the atmosphere where drama happens.

Bringing it closer, it's your own hand gripping the rocks of a gully down which your chief character is perilously moving; your observation that these rocks are stippled with tiny deposits of quartz, which glitter in late sun beside the shadow of the mountains; your nostrils expanding to smell time-worn stone; your eye catching the light on a circling hawk's wing; your ear listening to the shuffle of pebbles as they slide below you with the sound of snare-drum brushes; the taste of danger drying the roots of your tongue. Even a story delivered entirely in dialogue—an experiment not to be encouraged—should have this thereness, withness, the felt knowledge of background beating behind the words.

But background is double-edged. When it begins to take over, it can slowly swallow up and cover what began as a story with a clean line of action and event. A story drenched in background is always on the verge of becoming an essay. Every writer, has, inside, a pendulum that swings toward background and foreground—and if you allow this to linger in the direction of mood and scene, you'll discover that your main character has turned into an observer and *only* an observer; that his or her vitality has become muffled.

Keeping the character alive to the least hair in her or his eyebrows, neither dominating the background nor subservient to it, but *in* it, is one of your primary concerns. At this point, if I believed in illustrative charts—which I do not—I would draw one, splitting the page in halves, and at the top of one half I would inscribe BACKGROUND, while at the top of the other I would write CHARACTER. I'd much rather you would imagine this; as a writer, it's considerably more healthy for you to think in words than in geometric designs. But consider the chart as limned in your head. The moment you feel yourself spending too much time, too many sentences, on one side or the other, go back to using your personal pendulum in steady balance; back to the rhythm of Background Place and Foreground Character.

But we are not clocks, we are people, and to point out this necessity for balance between human character and the character of place, a story of mine, "The Thief," is useful. This one depends more than most of my work on a careful division of character and a full realization of background, for the background becomes a "character" in its own right, yet it cannot be allowed to obliterate or even slightly to dim the reader's understanding of the boy, Raoul.

Unravel the Mystery

"The Thief" begins with Raoul awkwardly shoving open the screen door of the summer cabin he shares with his father on the Altamaha River in lower Georgia. He carries a rod, a reel, a creel. It is a blue-hot morning. His father, a judgmatic sportsman-broker on vacation, nods over his first gin and tonic of the day and wishes him luck. The saturating heat and quiet mystery of the morning take over; Raoul is a noticer, a see-er of the small and the large; he appreciates the minuscular flowers that go to make up a bed of moss; the enormity and silence of the river. As he comes to the river, the reader enters its aura of mysticism—and is reminded, in a few lines, that once, before General Oglethorpe's men drove them away, elk roared along its banks, and that until naturalist and explorer William Bartram discovered it, it was known only to Indians and wild animals. The river is, in essence, a god.

As he casts and waits for a strike, Raoul breathes into himself its agelessness, its biding self against his puny humanity. Yet his humanity is important; he is more alert than ever before in his brief years to the presence of the Things—to being watched, perhaps judged. Seeing an egret on the far bank of the sun-mirroring water, he recalls that egrets are called cowbirds by farmers—considered pests and casually shot as such. He has started on this morning to become someone else—someone who was waiting within him to appear . . . older, more alive and aware. And what he wants, tangibly and terribly, is to catch just one decent fish, to carry it back to his father and remark offhandedly that it isn't such a bad catch.

And then he has his strike—a respectable trout of about two pounds. It fights with fury, and for the first time in his life he remembers to apply the controlled skill his father has tried to teach him, to play it as an old hand would; almost miraculously, he lands it, swinging it over his shoulder and back in a shining arc to the firm sand beach. But before he can touch it, a red-tailed hawk is upon it and has snapped the line and sailed to the mesa-like top of a sandstone-and-shell cliff. The cliff is sheer, 30 feet almost straight up, appearing to be unscalable. But in his stricken, ice-hard rage, Raoul climbs without real consciousness of anything but raw injustice. He finds barely enough handholds to keep moving, but never pauses to look down. Attaining the tabletop ledge where the hawk's nest is built, he dives at the hawk, finds his hands around its thin throat, its life under his fingers. The hawk's wings, its crazed and courageous saffron eyes, with their own rage like a lion's, and its searching beak, are all demonic. And in one blinding second, impossible to sustain but only to recall later and to keep with him perhaps to his own death, Raoul understands that the hawk's need is infinitely greater than his own. He drops it. He looks at the already torn, diminished trout, its live river-self faded and gone, its colors paling semblances of what they were. With strong caution, going slowly and nursing his bloody scratches, he makes his way down the side of the cliff. He gathers his snarled gear, and starts back; the revelation he has experienced stays with him, invisible, but as hoary and intense as the river and the heat; he knows an exaltation he will never be able to speak completely.

At the cabin, he merely mentions to his father that the line got tangled in brush, and that he was scratched getting it out. But he has changed completely, and we feel he will forever be.

Keeping Raoul in balance, never allowing him to be subsumed under descriptions of Nature, or the story—which was only seven pages long—to turn into a "nature study" piece of charm, were the only recognizable problems at the time of writing. The rest was swimming under water—perhaps the water of the Altamaha. So far as I know, "The Thief" has no easily explicable theme. It would be simple to say "A ten-year-old child becomes a discerning man," but it wouldn't be true. The internal wrestling in Raoul is strong, and it is brought to an end by his recognition of the purer and more violent wrestling in the hawk, yet there are overtones there which I can only hear, not define.

All of which tells us that mystery is at the heart of many stories, and that unraveling the mystery as far as words can is one of the challenges that keep writers of stories young in their nimble minds.

James Gunn

Anatomy of a Short Story

Five classical terms describe the parts of a short story, and you must know them and know how those parts fit together before you can write readable short stories. The five parts are:

Situation
Fiction has been described as "interesting people in difficulties." The situation is the difficulty the interesting person is in. The description of the characters and the presentation of the situation are called *exposition.* The events of the story, called the *plot,* are brought about by the efforts of the main character, called the *protagonist,* to resolve the situation.

Complication
The situation moves the protagonist to action (if it does not, it is not a suitable situation; if the protagonist is incapable of being moved by it, he or she is not a suitable protagonist, at least for this situation). The protagonist's efforts to resolve the situation create the complication, worsening the situation and making it unendurable; the situation may get worse through the actions of the *antagonist* or through natural processes. Complication also is called *the rising action,* and sometimes is compared to the tying of the knot that is untied in the resolution.

Climax
Generally, the climax is the point of highest interest, where the reader responds most emotionally; it is the turning point in the action—the rising action changes direction and becomes the falling action. At this point, the protagonist must do or die, succeed or fail; the pressures of the situation have reached their peak. Climax also is called *crisis.*

Resolution
After the climax comes the resolution, the resolving of the situation established early in the story, the solving of the problem. The situation should be resolved by the actions of the protagonist, not by an outside

agency; and the situation resolved must be the situation that launches the story. The protagonist can fail or succeed or, in more sophisticated stories, both fail and succeed, and the story can be a tragedy or a comedy, or something in between. The resolution also is called *the falling action*.

Anticlimax

Everything that follows the climax is called the anticlimax (the *anti* here means *opposite* or *reverse of*, but also carries the connotation of *disappointing* or *trivial* or even *unnecessary*). For the best dramatic effect, the anticlimax should be as short as possible, or even be eliminated when the resolution occurs simultaneously with the climax

Arranging the Short Story

The classical elements of the short story may not always arrive in such a neat arrangement, although this is the natural order (because it is the order in which the reader naturally becomes involved in the story through caring what happens to the characters). Sometimes the situation may be revealed as part of the complication, of the climax, or even of the resolution. In the old pulp action stories, the complication, or part of it, often came before the situation; such action was called "the narrative hook." In some cases (usually *tours de force*), the climax, or even the resolution, comes first. The more sophisticated the story, the more the parts of the story are likely to be out of order or hard to recognize, and the reader is compelled to suspend judgment (and work harder at putting the pieces together) until the situation is only implied, or is even omitted.

You should view all such alterations as risks deliberately assumed, since the emotional basis for the reading of fiction has been violated. Readers may not always be sufficiently sophisticated to understand such experiments; such readers are sacrifices to the author's art. In some cases, the piece of fiction does not offer sufficient rewards that will motivate readers to work hard to understand the experiment; those readers will be lost, too. Only when the story will not respond, or will not respond as well, to the normal pattern of reader involvement is alteration justified. Your boredom with easy challenges is not enough.

Sometimes (though not as often as writers like to think), the reader is at fault, in that rewards *are* available for working harder both at learning how to read difficult fiction and at actually reading it. If sufficiently challenged and rewarded, readers will learn to read unusual forms and different patterns of fiction, though the process may take generations. Only writers who can afford to wait, have something to impart that transcends natural reading patterns, should apply. And they shouldn't complain about being unread or misunderstood.

Lawrence Block

The Carrot and Some (Writing) Tricks

I've found over the years that the mechanics of writing appear to be end-lessly fascinating to writers and non-writers alike. Perhaps because the creative process is so utterly incomprehensible, even to those of us who are personally involved in it, it is easier for us to focus on more tangible aspects of writing. Do we write in the morning or at night? At the type-writer or in pencil—or with a crayon, for those of us who are not allowed to use anything sharp? Do we outline in advance or plot things out as we go along?

Somewhere in the course of this sort of conversation, one is apt to be asked just how many hours a day he tends to put in. The answer, whether it's two or twelve hours a day, is apt to be followed by a qualification. "Of course that's just time spent actually writing. Of course that doesn't include the time I devote to research. Of course, when you come right down to it, a writer is working from the instant the alarm clock goes off to the moment when he goes to bed. For that matter, the process doesn't stop when I'm asleep. The old subconscious mind takes over then and sifts things around and sets the stage for the next day's work. So I guess it's safe to say that I actually practice my craft twenty-four hours a day, seven days a week."

I suppose most of us deliver some variation of that speech at some time or other, and I suppose some of the time we even believe it. A cer-tain part of me, however, does not buy this load of pap for a minute. As far as that stern writer's conscience of mine is concerned, I'm only real-ly working if I'm sitting at my desk tapping my typewriter keys and turning out pages of finished copy. Thinking about writing isn't work, and research isn't work, and reading proof isn't work, and meeting with publishers isn't work, and talking on the phone isn't work, and not even rewriting and editing are work. Unless I can actually see a manuscript of mine getting further from the beginning and closer to the end because of what I'm doing, I'm not entirely capable of regarding the task I'm per-forming as work.

50-50

Understand, please, that I *know* better. I realize intellectually that the non-writing chores I've enumerated above are directly related to my profession, that they take time and energy, that I can't slight them without adversely affecting the quality and/or quantity of my writing. But this knowledge doesn't seem to help me much. Unless I've put in my daily stint at the typewriter, and unless I've got something to show for it, I feel as though I've played hookey.

This attitude probably serves a purpose. My mind is sufficiently fertile that I can almost always dream up some worthwhile occupation which will keep me away from my desk. There's always a book it would pay me to read, a neighborhood I could profitably explore, a person whose expertise I should seek. None of these extramural activities is as hard as actually sitting down and writing something; thus, but for the conscience that hounds me, I could happily go months on end without wearing out a typewriter ribbon.

Sometimes, though, I find myself backed into a corner, locked into a no-win situation, damned if I do and damned if I don't. This happened quite vividly when I was working on *The Burglar Who Liked to Quote Kipling*. Bernie Rhodenbarr, the burglar of the title, had just hied himself off to Forest Hill Gardens, an upper-middle-class enclave in the borough of Queens. It occurred to me that I had not been to Forest Hill Gardens in over 20 years, at which time I had visited it very briefly. I had only dim memories of the neighborhood and had no way of knowing if it had changed in the intervening years.

I had two choices. I could trust my memory while taking comfort in the fact that every work of fiction takes place in its own alternate universe anyway. Or I could spend an afternoon zipping out there on the F train and walking aimlessly around to see what I could see.

Either way I was determined to feel guilty about it. If I stayed home and worked, I'd beat myself up for slacking on research. If I went out there, I'd accuse myself of wasting time on pointless research when I might have been tapping typewriter keys and producing finished pages. Once I was able to see that I was in a double bind, I tossed a mental coin and went to Forest Hill Gardens.

As it turned out, my memory was sound and the place hadn't changed a bit. But I felt my time had been profitably spent; I'd refreshed my impressions, picked up a little local color, and certainly enabled myself to write the scene with increased confidence.

It doesn't always work out that way. Sometimes hours devoted to this sort of research are a waste, and sometimes there's no way to determine in advance whether this will be the case. American Tobacco's George Washington Hill used to say that fifty cents of every dollar he spent on advertising was wasted. The trouble was, he went on to explain, that there was no way of knowing which fifty cents it was, so he'd go on spending the whole dollar all the same. It's that way with research, and with all the other tasks that take me away from my desk.

Woolgathering into a Yarn

One factor in the operation of my personal Jiminy Cricket mechanism is, I'm sure, that I *don't* spend all that many hours at my desk. Years ago I was given to putting in long stretches at the typewriter; I was younger then, which may have had something to do with it, and I was a less meticulous writer, which must have had plenty to do with it. In any event, I could work effectively for five or six or eight hours at a clip.

I can't do that now. I don't structure my work in terms of hours, finding it more useful to aim at producing a certain amount of work, usually somewhere between five and ten pages depending on the sort of material I'm working on, the deadline I'm facing, and phases of the moon. My work usually takes me somewhere between two and three hours. If I'm done in an hour, I'm delighted to call it a day. If I'm not done in three hours, I generally call it a day anyway, though I'm by no means delighted about it. There's a point at which it becomes counterproductive for me to continue to work, on a par with running a car's ignition when the gas tank's empty. You don't get anywhere and you just run down the battery.

Most workers, I've been told, don't really spend more than two or three hours a day actually doing anything. They take breaks, they file their nails, they daydream at their desks, they talk baseball, and two hours get stretched into eight. It's comforting to know this, but it doesn't change the fact that I think of myself as putting in a shorter working day than the rest of the world.

I've found a couple of things I can do to make my writing life as guilt-free as possible, and I pass them on for whatever they're worth:

1. *I Make Writing The First Thing I Do.* Over the years, I've written at every possible time of day and night. For some time now I've written immediately after breakfast, and it's by far the best system for me. There are several advantages—I'm freshest then, my batteries recharged after a night's sleep—but the most important reason for me is that once I've got my day's work done, I'm able to give myself permission to do as I wish with the remainder of the day.

2. *I Try to Work Seven Days a Week.* Again, there are other reasons why this is useful. With a novel, for example, working every day keeps the book from slipping away from my subconscious mind. Whatever I'm working on, novels or short stories, daily production helps me keep from feeling profligate over working so few hours per day. By the same token, when I do take an unscheduled day off, I can do so with a clear conscience; after all, I'm still working six days that week.

3. *I Save Routine Work for Later.* I'm frequently tempted to answer my mail the minute it arrives, to proofread galleys as soon as they hit my desk. These chores enable me to be practicing my profession without actually having to write anything. But they're of secondary importance, and I don't have to be at my sharpest to deal with them. They'll still be around when I've got my daily five pages finished. Lately, for example, I've been getting packages, parcels chock-full of entries in a short story contest. My natural inclination is to drop everything and read these stories as they appear, but instead I stay at my typewriter and save those stories for late at night when I can't sleep. After I've read a couple dozen, I sleep like a baby.

Finally, I allow myself to make occasional use of that old reliable copout—i.e., that writers are really working 24 hours a day. Because in certain respects it's undeniably true. Just the other day, for example, I did my daily quota of pages in the morning, spent the afternoon in the gym lifting heavy objects, and then wandered around for an hour or so. In the course of my wandering I watched a car enter an apartment building's underground garage, and it suddenly occurred to me how Bernie Rhodenbarr could get into an otherwise impregnable apartment building by first locking himself in an automobile trunk.

Will I ever use that little bit of business? I probably will, as it happens, but almost every walk I take produces some comparable bit of woolgathering, and most of the wool I gather never gets spun into a yarn. Is it work? And does it matter if it is or not?

R. V. Cassill

Notebooks and Lists

It should go without saying that fiction writers keep notebooks. They may also keep files where fragmentary bits and unfinished manuscripts are systematically saved, along with stories due for revision and tear sheets from various publications that may come in handy someday.

But notebooks are not just portable filing systems—or, at least, they should not be. They ought to be *work* books where the entries are constantly amended, developed, and put in new combinations. They are, for the writer, what sketchbooks are to the painter—a place to begin and continue the labors of composition before one is quite sure what stories may emerge from the compositional process.

Coming across material and retrieving it in verbal form for your notebook is an act of the imagination—an incompleted act without the subsequent labors of combining your discoveries into a unified form, but one of the most crucial steps in assuring that your fiction will have the throb of life. Gather into your notebook the concrete data of colors, shapes, names, and the way things work. Seize the overheard lines of dialogue that characterize and evoke the essence of a person, a situation, a time, a place, a moral climate. Sift incidents from the evening news, from gossip. (How many of the tales of Henry James grew from the germs of ideas picked up as anecdotes in dinner conversation!) Enter the words and phrases that seem to rise of themselves from the stimuli of nature, play, parties, ceremonies, and manual labor. In *Ulysses* the young writer, Stephen Dedalus, walking on the beach, draws forth from his verbal savings account the phrase, "a day of dappled, sea-borne clouds." Accumulate a list of such phrases to match the days when the weather you walk in somehow matches the weather of memory and feeling.

Only—be sure that what you put into your notebooks really has grabbed your imagination. Don't let your notebooks (or your filing system, for that matter) turn into wastebaskets glutted with indifferent and inert trash of merely "interesting" or titillating appeal. As a rule of thumb we might say that whatever seems as striking as part of a dream surely must be entered—stuff that seems to be simultaneously familiar and strange. And for that matter, a journal of your actual dreams might well be interspersed with your other gleanings.

Writers work *from* their notebooks when they begin or when they flesh out their stories. The stuff that has been sifted into a notebook is already half fictionalized. But it is more important to realize that writers also work *in* their notebooks, constantly shifting and combining, reviewing and recombining what their observant senses have found. They are constantly asking, "What goes with what?"—as they recopy and repaste material until, sometimes, a major new idea springs from a lucky combination of items gathered from an unplanned variety of sources. ("Unplanned"?—the lower levels of your consciousness plan more honestly than the upper levels; that is why dreams are so trustworthy when one has learned to interpret them well.)

Perhaps it will help to think of your notebooks as incubators. The fertile, isolated entry you made on Tuesday may be an intuition of some crucial theme you are not yet ready to contemplate in its entirety. Perhaps you have not yet seen enough of the world to make it fully comprehensible. Save it and wait. Have faith that what seemed initially a single glimmer may, in the course of your further work, be part of a continuous series of illuminations.

Many writers have left us notebooks that are at least comparable in merit to their more formal publications. I have particularly cherished those of Chekhov, Hawthorne, and Virginia Woolf. Take a look at one of these if you want a model. Cyril Connolly's best book, by far, is a sort of notebook—*The Unquiet Grave*. It is lovingly, scrupulously cultivated and polished so that every entry enriches and is enriched by all the others. And W. H. Auden's *A Certain World* is another example that falls within my definition of a writer's notebook. He calls it a "commonplace book." It contains his gleanings from many years of reading. By whatever name, it is a shining revelation of the poet's imagination in play—in the play of discovery—and that is what you must try to make of your notebook.

Teasers

A writer's life is a long training in observation and in his notebook the material of observation undergoes part of its transformation into the syntax of sentences, the shapes of paragraphs and the larger units of finished composition. It is natural enough that at some stage of the transformation the material should appear in the form of lists. Lists are a sort of presyntactical ordering and clustering of things caught up in the net of our concerns. Emerson told us that "bare" lists of words are enough to set off the imagination and control its direction. You can prove the truth of this easily by making lists of people who have frightened you, of sensations that induce sleepiness, or of words you associate with war.

See? A story begins to form around the items in the list—and if you continue the experiment by changing the sequence of items, you will see that the ghostly story begins to change in quality. If you were to explain in detail what the separate items in your list had to do with each other, you would be going one step farther in storytelling.

To increase your awareness of how "bare" lists continue to function according to their qualities and sequence when they are incorporated in the finished syntax of prose, jot down the list of nouns or verbs you find on any page of any story in this book and read it over a day after you have read the story, noting the way in which your imagination is stimulated and controlled. Remember that many of the poems of Walt Whitman owe their majesty to the fact that they are essentially lists—catalogings—of the occupations, delights, anxieties, memories, origins, creeds, and triumphs of the Americans he celebrated *en masse* and as individuals. The lists in *Ulysses* provide endlessly varied comic effects as Joyce piles them up to the point of absurdity and tunes them with surprising shifts from realism to improbability. Vladimir Nabokov said— and you'd better believe him—that the part of *Lolita* which gave him the most satisfaction was the *list of the names* of Lolita's classmates.

To get you started with the assembling and manipulating of lists for your own writer's notebook, let me illustrate how three lists of concrete elements provide much of the organic substructure of my story "In the Central Blue." Note that each list has a flavor of its own, while there is some variation in flavor of the elements in each list. As you reflect on the finished story, you will realize that it is the interplay of these three clusters of reality that provides the conflict of emotions in the central character.

List I

Wings (a movie first released about 1930)
spring thaws
gravel road
model airplanes
grain elevator
Steven's Crackshot (a cheap, singleshot .22 rifle)
titless cousin
Essex (an automobile no longer manufactured)
moon-glinting railroad tracks

mother's perfume
War Aces (a magazine)
spatsies (a slang term for sparrows)

The list suggests the observable life of a boy in a rural community of the 1930s. Some of the elements faintly suggest the quality of his imaginative life—it is impossible to make any list of things in his environment that would not—but yet, by and large, these are the mundane exterior trappings of his existence. The list might have been jotted down by a very detached observer who knew and cared little about the boy's passions or fantasies.

List II
Luger
fuselage
Zeppelin
London
spring offensive
Lt. Frank Luke
negligee
Spad
Krauts
flight leader
Sam Browne belt

By itself, this list is a suggestive sampling of the actual historic circumstances of World War I. There really was a Lt. Frank Luke, an American aviator famed as "the Balloon-buster." German Zeppelins raided London and dropped bombs on that city. The macrocosm of history exists as part of the environment within which the boy in the story has to define himself and live. And yet, of course, historic reality comes to the boy, as it comes to most of us most of the time, by reports which are not easy to distinguish from fantasy. These reports are transformed into fantasy by such popular entertainments as the movie *Hell's Angels,* which figures so importantly in the story.

How did the word *negligee* get into this list so obviously dominated by masculine and military concerns? I put it there, as I put it into the story—so that its erotic and nostalgic connotations would startle and amuse you *because* it is "out of place." It is the teaser in the list. In the movie, worn by Jean Harlow, it was the teaser.

List III
tickles
kisses
silks

cleavage
"doing intercourse"
ravish
buttons
quick feel
Silver Screen (magazine)
hot breath

This third list is evidently unified by its exclusive concentration on the erotic concerns of a boy in his early teens. As you see from reading the story, there is a hopeless confusion among these elements in his mind. He can't reasonably distinguish between the promise of Jean Harlow's cleavage, proffered by the movie and the movie magazine, and the flat bosom of young Betty Carnahan. He isn't sure just what sort of ravishment he might be capable of in any event. What he can lay hands on is altogether incommensurate with the magnitude of yearning that has been stirred up inside him by the incitements of his world.

Inventive Variations

The story I wrote is not quite "all there" in these three lists. But I hope the dynamics of conflict that make it exist as a story are more readily discernible when these concrete elements are separated from the syntax and the voice of the narrator.

Actually, I did not set down these lists in my notebook before I wrote this particular story. But I might have. The story might have come more easily if I had. And I am convinced that in my mind as I wrote, or before I wrote, the lists were present. Insofar as I can understand my own compositional processes, I'd say that some sort of clustering of elements (which is the same thing as listing) always precedes any actual writing.

Therefore my recommendation follows with inevitable logic: Make lists as a preparation for writing. Experiment in your notebook by changing the order of elements in your lists, adding items that may at first seem incongruous, for the sake of surprise and irony. Draw on your memory. Draw on immediate observation. Draw on such sources of information as reading, lectures, television.

Set two or three lists in arbitrary combination on a single page. What stirring of your imagination toward a story begins when you note possible conflicts or harmonies among these words that you have forced into proximity without any preconceived plan?

Perhaps the true value of this exercise is to thwart preconceptions and permit the emergence into consciousness of things we didn't know we knew. For surely much of our capacity for observation is inhibited by rigidities of expectation. We report what we are trained to report—until we invent capricious ways to ease ourselves out of our blinders.

I have sometimes asked students to make, and then combine, (1) a list of verbs that pertain to eating a meal, (2) a list of adjectives descriptive of their classmates, and (3) a list of well-loved places. Arbitrarily or on inspiration they string verb-adjective-noun combinations from these juxtaposed lists after the subject pronoun *I*.

Examples:

I savor elfin Portsmouth.

I salt intemperate Bristol.

I sip lazy Vermont.

Perhaps these examples seem merely freakish to anyone reading them cold. But surely they are better than: *I enjoyed picturesque Vermont.* And for the student who made them according to the playful method of shuffling lists together they may draw after them strings of suggestion attached to chunks of remembered observation that precedes and follows when they are socked into a paragraph.

All word games, like this one, are potentially valuable to the writer willing to play them with zest. No doubt a fondness for such verbal sport is one of the earliest and surest symptoms of literary promise. And sometimes from the random combinations thus produced will come glimmering hints of the bedrock analogies that link all our responses of preference, action, and interpretation. Metaphors both natural and fresh may rise to the level of consciousness in the midst of sport. Words will seem to choose themselves, and in matters of diction there is nothing better than that.

The search for the right word that honestly represents our best and fullest perceptions will, of course, go beyond the sometimes arbitrary results of verbal gamesmanship. The delight one takes in all inventive variations is very important in advancing the search.

Robert Cormier

Getting Ideas

The question I hear most often when the subject of writing comes up is "Where do you get your ideas?" No doubt that's the question all writers hear most frequently.

Every writer has his or her own answer, of course. I tell people that my ideas usually grow out of an emotion—something I have experienced, observed, or felt. The emotion sparks my impulse to write and I find myself at the typewriter trying to get the emotion and its impact down on paper. Out of that comes a character and then a plot. The sequence seldom varies: character, plot. Each element contributes to the whole. Which brings up further questions. Where do the characters come from? Are they made up? And where do you get your plots?

For example, my story "Mine on Thursdays" came into being on a Sunday afternoon in the fall some years ago when I accompanied my daughter Chris, who was then about ten years old, to Whalom Park, an amusement park a short distance from our home. On this particular Sunday, I was under assault by a migraine headache: a riveting pain in that vulnerable spot above my left eyebrow in partnership with nausea sweeping my stomach. But I'd promised to take her to the park and did so, pretending, to myself and to her, that I felt fine, just fine.

Our forays into the park were almost but not quite timid. She never showed any inclination to go on the more spectacular rides. For which I was grateful, having long ago lost any inclination toward those rides, if any inclination had ever existed.

What If . . .

That day, Chris was content to stroll the park, go on the merry-go-round and some of the other innocent rides while I watched as usual, delighting in her delight. We then wandered toward a new ride, something called the "Trabant," located near the Ferris wheel and midget motor cars. The Trabant was obviously a popular ride: The line was long. And Chris obviously wanted to try it. She said the kids at school thought it was "super." "But it's a little scary," she said. In repose, the Trabant looked docile enough, although she said the cars went "up, down and around." I remember thinking that a ride that went up, down and around would devastate me completely that day.

"Want to give it a whirl?" I asked, tentatively.

She looked brave in that heartbreaking way kids look when they are attempting to be brave but aren't really.

"Do you want me to go with you?" I asked, hoping she'd say no.

She shook her head. Then, sighing deeply, she took the plunge and we rushed for her ticket. The line had diminished, the attendant called "Hurry, hurry." We bought her ticket; she took her seat and strapped herself in. I almost joined her at the last minute. But didn't. Then the ride started.

The next few minutes were excruciating. The ride was a whirling, tilting nightmare. Dizzying, dazzling. And unending. I caught occasional glimpses of Chris's face as her car shot up and down and around. She held on for dear life. Sometimes her eyes were tightly closed, other times they were wide with horror. I stood helplessly by, trying to hurry time along. Once, our gazes held for a split second, and it seemed to me that I saw betrayal in her eyes. My betrayal of her. A father wasn't supposed to abandon a child like that. Would she ever forgive me?

The ride finally ended and she disembarked. She came toward me on fragile legs, as if she were walking a tightrope. Her hand trembled as I caught it. Was she avoiding my eyes? I told her I was sorry, that I should have gone with her, that I didn't think it would be so terrible. She assured me that it wasn't that bad. She'd been a little scared but it was nothing, really. We both knew this was a gentle lie. For my sake.

As we walked along hand in hand, the idea for the story that eventually became "Mine on Thursdays" came forth. I had been thinking how lucky I was that our love for each other was so simple and secure that my betrayal—if that was the word—of her a few moments before did not threaten us. Yet, what if our love wasn't secure? What if that small betrayal in the park was only one more of many betrayals? What if it had been a final betrayal?

What if? What if? My mind raced, and my emotions kept pace at the sidelines, the way it always happens when a story arrives, like a small explosion of thought and feeling. What if? What if an incident like that in the park had been crucial to a relationship between father and daughter? What would make it crucial? Well, what if the father, say, was divorced from the child's mother and the incident happened during one of his visiting days? And what if . . .

Orson Scott Card

The Finer Points of Characterization

All I have to say is "Uriah Heep," and many of you immediately think of a man constantly rubbing his skinny-fingered hands together, talking about how 'umble he is, and preparing to stab you in the back at the first opportunity.

Or Miss Havisham—you know her, don't you? She's the old woman who wears a tattered bridal gown and lives in a house filled with decorations for a wedding that never took place. Can't you see her sitting by the dust-covered, cobwebbed wedding cake? Can't you hear her gleefully asking a weeping young boy, "Did she hurt you?"

Both these unforgettable characters—and hundreds more—came from the pen of Charles Dickens. He was a genius at creating memorable characters. Some were so exaggerated that they were almost caricatures—but never quite. Instead, he made them more real to us than most of the people we meet in our own lives.

Even if you're not as brilliant a storyteller as Dickens, you can still bring your characters to life; you can still put memorable, powerful people into your storytelling. After all, if your characters aren't memorable, you *have* no story.

Who Is This Guy?

Have you ever watched a movie and had trouble telling some of the characters apart? There's a beautiful woman putting something behind the clock on the mantel. Now, was she the wife of—no, not the wife, the cousin visiting from the country—but it can't be her . . .

And you turn to the person next to you and say, "Who was *that*?"

I had that problem the time I watched *Dallas*. The show had already been running for a couple of years and had a large, loyal audience. Millions of people had spent so many hours with these characters that they knew them on sight—knew not only their names, but also their past experiences, their relationships, their moral character.

The show's writers know that their regular audience has memorized this stuff; consciously or not, they take advantage of it. They don't set up the characters every week. The result was that I, a newcomer to the show, had a terrible time telling all those beautiful men and women apart. Well, I *could* tell the men from the women, but that was about it.

Whether you're using narrative or dramatic form to tell your story, you face the same problem. Your characters must be memorable, or each time you bring them back into the action a large portion of your audience will have forgotten who they are.

And that's bad. Any character who can't be remembered from scene to scene is almost useless to the writer. Let's say you have a story in which Pete and Nora are talking together quietly on a park bench. Suppose someone is calmly walking toward them down the path behind them. If we don't know this person, and Pete and Nora are not doing something that no one should see, there is no particular tension. It happens all the time in film. The person behind them is merely a passerby. He's there for "color," because the scene is in a park and a park, to be believable, has people in it.

But what if the audience *recognizes* the man walking toward them? What if he is Nora's husband, and we know he's intensely jealous?

What if we have already seen him murder someone and know he is looking for Pete?

What if he is a foreign agent who is supposed to get something from Nora, and she can't give it to him because Pete is talking to her?

What if we know the man is Pete's father, who he hasn't seen in 20 years, but he doesn't know what Pete looks like, while Pete, who *would* recognize his father, just doesn't see him?

In every one of these cases, that man walking along behind them adds tremendously to the tension of the scene. But *only* if the audience already knows who he is, and *only* if they remember him. If he is forgotten, the scene fails.

I faced that problem in my novel *A Woman of Destiny*. My main characters were siblings: Robert, Dinah and Charlie. All three were vital to the plot. But their youngest sister—whose name I now forget—was not all that important. As I wrote, I kept realizing that I had forgotten to mention her for hundreds of pages. There was nothing to make her memorable, even to me. Finally, editorial wisdom prevailed—I removed her entirely from the novel.

The Hierarchy of Characters

Every story or novel you read and every film or play you see depends, in scene after scene, on the writer's—or actors'—ability to create characters that hold a place in your memory.

But you don't want *all* your characters to stick in the mind, and not all should be memorable to the same degree. That's because the same devices you use to make a character memorable *also* signal to the audience that the character is *important*.

Every character who makes an appearance can't be just as important as every other. A crucial scene in your story is when Nora must rush the antidote to the hospital before Pete dies. Nora is much more important than the cabdriver who's taking her. And the cabdriver is more important than the guy driving the delivery truck that almost crashes into them.

If you set up that scene by spending two pages—or two minutes—showing us what the delivery truck driver's life is like, the audience will expect him to do a lot more than just slam on the brakes as Nora's cab races by. They'll wait to see what the truck driver does next. If he does nothing at all, if we never even see him again, the audience will be frustrated. "What was that all about with the delivery truck guy?" they'll ask.

When you make a character too memorable, your audience assumes he will matter more than you intend him to. It's just as harmful when your readers expect something to happen with a character you want them to forget as it is when they have forgotten a character you need them to remember.

So the tools you use to make your characters memorable also tell your audience about the hierarchy of your characters. That hierarchy ranges from the central characters, the ones the audience should care deeply for, to the vanishing characters, the place-holders who are forgotten even before they leave the scene.

Unless your story takes place in a hermitage or on a desert island, your main characters are surrounded by many people who are utterly unimportant in the story. Here are a few samples that show what I mean.

Nora accidentally gave the cabby a twenty for a five-dollar ride and then was too shy to ask for change. Within a minute a skycap had all the rest of her money.

Pete checked at the desk for his messages. There weren't any, but the bellman did have a package for him.

People started honking their horns before Nora even knew there was a traffic jam.

Apparently some suspicious neighbor had called the cops. The uniform who arrested him wasn't interested in Pete's explanations, and he soon found himself at the precinct headquarters.

Notice how many people we've "met" in these few sentences. A cabby, a skycap, a hotel desk clerk, a bellman, horn-honkers in a traffic jam, a suspicious neighbor, a uniformed policeman. Every one of these people is designed to fulfill a brief role in the story and then vanish completely.

How do you make people vanish? That's what stereotypes are for.

Good Stereotypes

You've probably heard that stereotyping is a bad thing, but it just ain't so. Even in stories by the best writers of all time, most of the people who appear are stereotypes and nothing more.

A *stereotype* is a character who is a typical member of a group. The readers already know what this group is like, and they'll understand a character who's a member of that group as long as he does nothing but what the group is expected to do. That is, as long as the policeman arrests Pete in the normal manner, perhaps a bit officiously, there is nothing unusual about him. He has behaved exactly according to his role. He is not just forgotten—he is never noticed. He never takes the focus of the audience's attention away from Pete.

The most common stereotypes are occupational: cabdriver, cop, waitress, mugger, telephone operator, dishwasher, lawyer, doctor, politician, prostitute. Other stereotypes are racial or ethnic: the Italian who can't hold his hands still when he talks, for instance. Some are based on age and sex: the bratty little boy, the crusty old lady. Some are based on family role: the maiden aunt, the tattletale sister, the cookie-baking grandmother.

As ordinary human beings, we may not *like* a particular stereotype if we happen to be a member of a group we think is viewed unfairly. But as writers, writing to our own community, we cannot help but be aware of and use our community stereotypes in order to make place-holding characters behave exactly according to expectations.

By definition, place-holders do their job and disappear. Often, though, you'll want a character to do more. He won't get involved in the action, but his individuality will set a mood, add humor, or make the milieu more believable. The way to make such characters instantly memorable without leading the audience to expect them to do more is to make them *eccentric* or *obsessive*.

Remember the movie *Beverly Hills Cop*? There were hundreds of place-holders in that film—thugs who shot at cops, cops who got shot at, people milling around the hotel lobby, people at the hotel desk. They all acted exactly as you would expect them to act. They vanished. Unless you know an actor who played one of the walk-ons, you don't remember any of them.

But I'll bet you remember the desk attendant in the art gallery. You know, the one with the effeminate manner and the Israeli accent. He had absolutely nothing to do with the story. If he had been a mere placeholder, you would never have noticed anything was missing. Why do you remember him?

It wasn't his foreign accent. In Southern California, a Spanish accent, for example, would merely have stereotyped him; he would have disappeared.

It wasn't his effeminacy. The audience would merely see him as a stereotypical homosexual. Again, he would disappear.

But the effeminacy and the accent were combined—the "foreigner" stereotype and the "effete homosexual" stereotype are rarely combined, and so the audience was surprised. What's more, the accent was an *eccentric* one, completely unexpected. The Israeli accent is so rare that few people in the audience would recognize it. It was a novel way to speak. He was not just a foreigner, he was a strange and effeminate foreigner. And his reactions to Eddie Murphy—the hint of annoyance, superiority, snottiness in his tone—made him even more eccentric. Eccentric enough to stick in our minds.

And yet we never expected him to be important in the story. He existed only for a few laughs and to make Eddie Murphy's Detroit-cop character feel even more alien in LA.

Let's go back to Nora's cabby, the five-dollar ride she gave a twenty for. The stereotypical reaction—"Hey, thanks, lady"—is so ordinary we can omit it entirely. But what if the cabdriver is eccentric?

"What is it, you trying to impress me? Trying to show me you're big time? Well, don't suck ego out of *me*, lady! I only take what I *earn!*"

Nora had no time for this. She hurried away from the cab. To her surprise, he jumped out and followed her, shouting at her with as much outrage as she'd expect if she hadn't paid him at all. "You can't do this to me in America!" he shouted. "I'm a Protestant, you never heard of the Protestant work ethic?"

Finally she stopped. He caught up with her, still scolding. "You can't do your rich-lady act with me, you hear me?"

"Shut up," she said. "Give me back the twenty." He did, and she gave him a five. "There," she said. "Satisfied?"

His mouth hung open; he looked at the five in utter disbelief. "What *is* this!" he said. "No tip?"

Now that's eccentric. If you saw that scene in a movie or read it in a novel, chances are you'd remember the cabdriver. Yet you wouldn't expect him to be important in the plot. If he showed up again it would be for more comic effect, not for anything important. For instance, when the story is all but over and Nora is coming home with Pete for a well-earned rest, it could be funny if they get in a cab and it turns out to be the same driver. The audience would remember him well enough for that. But they would be outraged if the cabdriver turned out to be an assassin or a long-lost cousin. Eccentricity is enough for a minor character, but not a character that *matters*.

Eccentricity doesn't have to be comic. It can be menacing. Let's say we're watching a movie. We see several murders committed, but never see the killer's face. What we *do* see is that after every murder, when he's away from the scene of the crime, the killer pulls out a cigarette and then tears it in half before lighting it. Later, Nora meets a really sweet guy; she likes him, and so do we. But after she's agreed to go somewhere with him, we watch him take out a cigarette and tear it in half. He grins. "I'm trying to cut down on my smoking." Then he lights up.

In that example, the eccentricity has done exactly what we want it to do. It has differentiated the murderer from all the other people in the film. When that eccentricity shows up in someone else, we recognize it and so recognize the character. Instead of disappearing, he has become memorable.

Remember, though, that eccentricity, taken to extremes, always leads to farce or melodrama. And the more you emphasize a character's eccentricity, the more you elaborate on it, the more time you spend with him, the more the audience begins to expect important things from him. Molière's comedies, such as *The Imaginary Invalid,* rely on a character with an obsession that is carried so far that the story must be *about* the eccentricity. If a character is to remain minor, you must keep his oddities under control.

It's easy to make a minor character memorable. You use him once and throw him away.

But developing your major characters requires a different set of techniques than those you use for minor characters. Your major characters—those who move the action forward, whose choices determine the events of the story—usually can't be wildly eccentric, or your audience won't believe them.

In Stephen King's *The Dead Zone,* a traffic accident puts the main character in a coma for many years; he loses his career, the woman he loves, and precious years of his life. When he finally recovers from the coma, he remains in constant pain. The magnitude of his suffering makes readers care about him deeply and see him as a hugely important character—great enough, in fact, to sustain the weight of a novel.

Last month I discussed how to make minor characters come alive. But making major characters memorable requires a different method of depiction. Although minor characters can stick in readers' minds simply by being colorful or eccentric, the characters who actually move the action forward, whose choices determine the events of the story, must be made both important and sympathetic in readers' eyes. If readers are not made to feel that the characters are important—if they don't care what happens to the characters—will they care enough to keep reading?

Let's look at three tools you can use to lend stature to your major characters, and see just how vital it is to a successful story that your readers feel sympathy for the people your story is about.

The Sharp Edge of Pain

Pain is a sword with two edges. The character who suffers pain and the character who inflicts it are both made more memorable and more important.

Of course, not all pain is alike. A cut finger doesn't particularly magnify a character. But, as I mentioned, the main character in *The Dead Zone* suffers terribly. Notice that his pain is both physical and emotional. The loss of a loved one can weigh as heavily in the mind of the audience as the loss of a limb. However, *physical* pain is much easier to use because it doesn't have to be prepared for. If a character is tortured, readers will wince in sympathetic agony even if they have never seen the character before. Emotional loss does not come so easily. In *The Dead Zone,* King devoted several pages to creating a warm, valuable relationship between the main character and the woman he loves. His terrible traffic accident occurs at a vital moment in their relationship. Now when he discovers that she married someone else during his coma, readers know how much he loved her, and so the pain of losing her actually outweighs the physical pain he suffered.

Pain loses effectiveness with repetition. The first time a character is hit in the head, the pain raises his importance; the third or fourth time, the character becomes comic, and his pain is a joke.

You increase the power of pain not so much by describing the injury in greater detail as by showing more of its cause and its effect. Blood and gore only make the audience gag. But watching the character try to cope with his pain can heighten the audience's identification with and sympathy for the character.

Even more powerful is the character's degree of choice. Suppose Pete has broken his leg on a hike, and Nora must set it for him. That scene will be painful, and will certainly magnify both characters as they cause and suffer pain. But Pete's pain will be far more powerful if he is alone and has to set the leg himself. As he ties a rope to his ankle, passes it around a tree trunk, braces his good leg and pulls on the end of the rope, the agony he inflicts on himself will make the scene unforgettable, even if we never see his face, even if his agony is never described at all.

And when one character willingly inflicts pain on another, the torturer becomes as important, in our fear and loathing, as the victim becomes in our sympathy.

Jeopardy

Jeopardy is anticipated pain. As anyone who has been to a dentist knows, the anticipation of pain is often more potent than its actuality. When a character is threatened with something bad, the audience automatically focuses its attention on him. The more helpless the character and the more terrible the danger, the more importance the audience will attach to the character.

That is why children in danger are such powerful characters—so powerful, in fact, that some films become unbearable to watch. The film *Poltergeist* was strong stuff for that reason. Some horror-movie buffs pooh-poohed the film because "nothing really happened"; nobody got killed. But a dozen creative slashings of teenage kids in a splatter movie don't equal the power of a single scene in which children are being dragged to terrible deaths while their mother struggles vainly to try to reach them in time.

In the TV movie *The Dollmaker*, the threshold was crossed for me. Perhaps before I had children I could have borne it; but I have children now, and when the mother runs, screaming, to try to snatch her little girl before her legs are run over by a moving train, the tension builds beyond what I can bear. When the wheels finally reach the girl before her mother does, the girl's pain, combined with the climactic release of the exquisite jeopardy, is more than I can stand.

Why did this moment of jeopardy in *The Dollmaker* affect me so strongly? The writer had set up this jeopardy to be as powerful as it could be. The little girl and the mother had already suffered so much emotional pain in the film that the audience cared deeply about them both. And the girl was off by herself because of a painful emotional confrontation. So the audience's stake in these characters was already strong.

As the jeopardy develops, the girl is absolutely helpless—she has no idea the train is about to move. The mother is powerless to rescue her—how can she stop a train? And the power of the train is like the fist of God, irresistible, uncompromising.

As a result, during the seconds—it feels like half an hour—when the mother is struggling to get into the train yard, racing to try to reach her daughter, the jeopardy made the characters more important to me than any characters in my experience of reading and seeing stories. I could not bear to watch that scene again. I don't have to. I can relive every moment of it in my memory.

This particular example is more powerful than most jeopardy situations, of course, but it shows how jeopardy works. Jeopardy magnifies the stalker and the prey, just as pain magnifies the sufferer and the tormentor. Jeopardy also magnifies third-party characters who get involved trying to save the victim or help the stalker.

Remember the old man Sweet-Face in *Butch Cassidy and the Sundance Kid?* Butch and the Kid are upstairs in a whorehouse when the Pinkerton men ride in. Sweet-Face points on up the road—the men ride on. That act of helping the heroes makes him somewhat important. Then the Pinkerton men come back, and, terrified, Sweet-Face points at the whorehouse. The character probably doesn't have more than 20 seconds of screen time. But because of his involvement with jeopardy, he is far more memorable than time would suggest.

Bigger Than Life

Major characters must be extraordinary in some way. We must believe them to be special, even unique. That gives far more importance to their story, makes them far more important in the audience's eyes.

How do you make a character bigger than life? How do you establish this kind of heroic proportion? William Goldman's solution in *The Princess Bride* was simply to say so. In a marvelous comic passage, he tells us that the girl becomes the tenth most beautiful woman in the world at, say, age 13; by 15 she is the second most beautiful. Later, as she falls in love, and still later, as she suffers pain, she becomes the most beautiful woman that ever lived.

But that's in a novel where the narrator's voice is intrusive. When the narrator's voice cannot simply state that she is beautiful, the task is quite different; in film it's harder yet, since you have to cast a real actress in the part. There's a limit to what make-up, lighting, and gauze on the lens can achieve.

It's not enough for the woman in the movie *Body Heat* to be pretty.

She must be so beautiful that a sensible man could lose his mind over her. Now, it helped to cast Kathleen Turner in the role; but pretty women have been cast in other roles, and the audience hasn't found their beauty unforgettable. What worked in this case—and in every case where we believe a character is bigger than life—is that the other characters *responded* to her as the most beautiful woman imaginable.

Even in *The Princess Bride,* Goldman doesn't just leave us with his bald assertion that a girl is the most beautiful woman and a man is the greatest swordsman of all time. Instead we see how women and men respond to her beauty with envy or desire; we watch him in his obsessed struggle to acquire his skill, and see what happens when he meets the first opponent really worthy of his skill.

Why This Isn't Enough

What I've described so far—pain, jeopardy and heroic proportion—is the stuff of romance. Not the commercial romance genre, of course. I'm speaking of the romantic tradition that began in western Europe with the Charlemagne stories and the tales of King Arthur. Fielding and Austen wrote partly to satirize the excesses of the romantic tradition; Louisa May Alcott, Charles Dickens, Mark Twain and Margaret Mitchell arose from that tradition and in many ways epitomize it; Stephen King and William Goldman are, in my opinion, the best of our romanticists today. In fact, most contemporary fiction is romance in this sense.

But romance has gotten a bad name. This is because pain, jeopardy and heroic proportion are easy techniques to learn—and easy for unskilled writers to overuse. As they are used without restraint or inspiration, they become steadily less effective. When they are used again and again, the reader begins to recognize them the moment they appear. Ah, another "most beautiful" woman. Oh, here comes the car chase. Hack, spatter, slash—all the blood looks alike. Readers start longing for a woman who isn't the most beautiful. Let her be ugly.

Your major characters must be unique and important if you expect your audience to care enough to keep reading.

Ansen Dibell

What Is Plot?

The common definition of plot is that it's whatever happens in a story. That's useful when talking about completed stories, but when we're considering stories being written, it's about as useful as saying that a birthday cake is a large baked confection with frosting and candles. It doesn't tell you how to make one.

Plot is built of significant events in a given story—significant because they have important consequences. Taking a shower isn't necessarily plot, or braiding one's hair, or opening a door. Let's call them incidents. They happen, but they don't lead to anything much. No important consequences.

But if the character is Rapunzel, and the hair is what's going to let the prince climb to her window, braiding her hair is a crucial action. If the character is Bluebeard's newest wife, opening the forbidden door which reveals the corpses of her predecessors is a pivotal point. Taking a shower is, in *Psycho*, considerably more dramatic and shocking than the theft of a large sum of money, both in itself and in terms of its later repercussions. By the way they're weighted and presented, by what they lead to, these events are transformed from incident to plot.

A grammar school play in which a little girl dresses up in a frame of chickenwire and canvas to portray a ham, representing Pork, could be trivial, a mere incident; but in Harper Lee's *To Kill a Mockingbird*, the chickenwire costume is what prevents Scout Finch from being stabbed by a man with a murderous grudge against her lawyer father.

The wearing of the costume has important consequences and makes a meaningful difference in the story's fictional world. It's a cause that has significant effects. Cause and effect: That's what makes plot.

The Border of Actuality
Plot is the things characters do, feel, think, or say, that make a difference to what comes afterward.

If you once thought about dying your hair pink but never acted on the thought, that tells something about your psychology, but it's not a potential story plot. If you really went ahead and *did* it, that not only tells about your psychology but creates repercussions, like a stone tossed in a pond. *That* might become the basis for a story like Fitzgerald's "Bernice Bobs Her Hair."

Thought or emotion crosses the line into plot when it becomes action and causes reactions. Until then, attitudes, however interesting in themselves, are just potential, just cloudy possibilities. They're static. They're not going anywhere. Nothing comes of them.

No thought, in and of itself, is plot. No action, however dramatic, is plot if the story would have been about the same if it hadn't happened at all. Any action, however seemingly trivial, can be vital and memorable if it has significant consequences and changes the story's outcome.

Plotting is a way of looking at things. It's a way of deciding what's important and then *showing* it to be important through the way you construct and connect the major events of your story. It's the way you show things mattering.

What's at Stake?

For a reader to care about your story, there has to be something at stake—something of value to gain, something of value to be lost. Paul Boles, in his book *Storycrafting*, called it "wrestling," and I like that image because, unlike "theme" or "message," it doesn't imply something that could be painted on a billboard or winkled out of a fortune cookie. Wrestling is something specific happening: two strong forces are meeting, one of them triumphing over the other—for better or for worse.

One of the forces may be external to the main character (protagonist): a villain, an opponent, a set of circumstances, a feature of the environment or of the landscape. Or both forces may be within the protagonist: the fear of doing something wrestling with the need to do it; a sense of injury wrestling with love or admiration, as with a person of any age trying to come to terms with a demanding parent.

Bringing out the importance of seemingly small things leads to subtlety, drama; showing large things grappling and clashing is melodrama.

You have to convince the reader not only that something is happening, but that what's happening matters intensely—not just to the writer, but to the characters involved.

In Golding's *Lord of the Flies*, what's at stake is survival itself. A group of boys are trying to stay alive, solely by their own efforts, on an otherwise uninhabited tropical island. At least, that's the external form of their struggle. Internally, it's the battle between fear and courage, distrust of the unknown and the will to find out, as played out within individual characters like the protagonist, Ralph; visionary Simon; and Jack, leader of the hunters. It's not only survival at stake, but a particular, civilized kind of survival.

In other words, there can be an outer plot and an inner one which in some sense mirrors and reinforces it, or conflicts and contrasts with it. Or either outer plot or inner plot may stand alone as the main focus of the necessary struggle played out in actions, through scenes.

Making a Scene

If you've been to a writer's conference or a creative writing class, or if you've read any books on fiction writing, you've already heard the major principle that older writers are always telling younger writers: SHOW, DON'T TELL. It's an important concept that's *very* risky not to take very seriously indeed.

Showing, in fiction, means creating scenes. You have to be able to cast your ideas in terms of something happening, people talking and doing, an event going on while the reader reads. If you're not writing scenes, you may be writing fine essays, or speeches, or sermons—but you're not writing fiction.

A definition: A *scene* is one connected and sequential action, together with its embedded description and background material. It seems to happen just as if a reader were watching and listening to it happen. It's built on talk and action. It's dramatized, *shown*, rather than being summarized or talked about. In some ways, it's like a little independent story; some short stories, in fact, are all one single scene.

A scene isn't a random stretch of action. It arises for a reason, and it's going somewhere. It has meaning. It has a point: at least one thing that needs to be shown or established at that spot in a story. That can be something as basic as the fact that your main character wants, this once, to walk his dog in peace without being pestered by an amorous neighbor or something as subtle as your main character's realization that the tolerance she has prided herself on is really just a mask for indifference. Attitudes turning into motives, meeting resistance, creating conflict, and leading to consequences—becoming plot.

A scene can convey many things: moods, attitudes, a sense of place and time, an anticipation of what's to come, a reflection of what's past. But first and foremost, a scene must advance the plot and demonstrate the characters. You may not fully know what a given scene's job is, whether simple or complex, until you've written it. You may need to go back then and cut away the things that would mislead a reader, and add things to support, lead into, and highlight that scene's special chores in the context of the whole story. But when the story is finished, no matter how many rewrites it takes, you ought to be able to name to yourself what each scene brought out, how it developed the characters, how it showed action or led toward consequences.

Scenes can be long or short—just a paragraph, or a dozen pages or more. Creating scenes means finding ways for your story to show itself, rather than ways for you to *tell* it.

Is It a Fair Fight?

Your story's scenes are going to be the specific stages by which your main character's motivations are enacted against opposition, internal or external or both. A motivation against no opposition is boring. How somebody always got everything he wanted, was successful in every task, conquered every girl in sight, and never met a comeuppance, wouldn't have any drama. A chronicle of Don Juan's amorous exploits would be dull (even if pornographically dull) without the avenging paternal statue to send the don gibbering off to a well-deserved damnation.

Likewise, opposition without determined contrary motivation, pure victimization, is not only dull, but depressing. This is true even when, as with Oedipus and with Romeo and Juliet, the protagonist's motivation ultimately ends in tragedy. The protagonist of Lovecraft's "The Shadow Over Innsmouth" may end up a part of the horror he tried to escape; Ahab may be the victim of the White Whale he desired to destroy; but each fought all the way through the shadows into the eventual dark.

A narrative of Dracula's slaughters during the centuries before he met his determined and ultimately successful adversaries, Van Helsing and the thoroughly modern Mina, would be about as engrossing as feeding time at the zoo. Dracula is pure appetite, and his victims merely food, if there is no involving battle between predator and prey.

Incidentally, Ann Rice's effective reinventions of the vampire legends (*Interview with the Vampire* and *The Vampire Lestat,* as of this writing) concentrate on the aspirations of the vampires themselves as individuals, and dwell very little on the neck-biting or on their victims. The resulting stories, because the vampires are the protagonists, tend to be surprisingly upbeat in spite of the implied body count.

"Bambi Meets Godzilla": a Cautionary Tale
Some of you may have seen or heard about a short satirical film called

Bambi Meets Godzilla. While the opening credits are rolling, we see the terminally cute little fawn nibbling and gamboling in a leafy clearing. Then a big reptilian foot comes down and squashes him. Splat. End of movie. It's startling and funny, in a gruesome sort of way, the first time. But a whole hour of buildup, followed by that expressive splat? A whole novel, even? It would be dreadful.

Anytime you're tempted to write a pure-victim story, in which the protagonist doesn't have a chance, think about *Bambi Meets Godzilla* and try something else.

An Even Battle Is More Fun to Watch

Whether the ending is happy or unhappy in the traditional sense, any story needs to be founded on an effective and strongly-felt conflict, in which the opposing forces—whether people, ideas, attitudes, or a mix—are at least fairly evenly matched, enough so that the final outcome is in doubt. If anything, the forces opposing the protagonist ought to seem the stronger, to create drama and suspense. But not an utter mismatch. Oedipus was doomed from the beginning; but he didn't know it, and he was fighting all the way. The emphasis was on the fighting, not on the doom. That's what makes the fighting, the wrestling, become engrossing narrative.

It's been said that happy families don't make good stories. Only unhappy families, or people who for whatever reason are discontented with their current circumstances, give rise to good fiction. If Scarlett O'Hara had easily forgotten Ashley and been rapturously married to an easily-domesticated Rhett Butler early in the novel, if the Civil War hadn't intruded to complicate their unvarying domestic bliss, if their child had grown happily into adolescence and beyond, who would want to read *Gone With the Wind*?

Struggle, conflict, dissatisfaction, aspiration, choice: These are the basis of effective plots.

How to Test a Story Idea

If you're like most of the writers I've run into, you have more story ideas than you know what to do with. They're popping into your mind faster than you can jot them down in your handy bedside notebook.

And how could it be otherwise? Things have been happening to you, and to everybody you know, all your life. You've been reading, and absorbing stories, almost that long. The newspapers and the evening news offer conflicts galore, and memorable people, events of apparent importance. Once you've been writing awhile, people will start forcing stories on you, claiming that they were always going to write them themselves but somehow never got the time. They'll insist the stories are just the thing for your next fiction, and you may even agree with them.

There is no shortage of story ideas that might even *become* stories in the right hands.

Truman Capote took a news account of a brutal and apparently senseless multiple murder and developed it into the nonfiction novel, *In Cold Blood*. Mary Shelley's *Frankenstein* was reportedly based on an alarmingly vivid dream. I took a speculation on the nature of emotion, combined it with some unpleasant childhood memories, and found in the mix the basis for a five-book science fiction series.

Story ideas are everywhere. Finding ideas isn't the problem. Your problem is every writer's problem: figuring out which, of this barrage of fragmentary ideas, is a potential story; and, even more difficult, a story *you* care about and can tell well.

There are four basic questions you should ask of any new story idea you come up with to decide whether or not it's ready to be developed, or whether it needs to mature awhile longer in your notebook.

1. Is It Your Story to Tell? All ideas can't become stories *for you*. I could no more write a story about magic than I could sprout wings, or roots. I've realized that, on some fundamental level, I don't believe in magic. Although I heartily enjoy reading stories about witches and occult happenings, I can't really imagine magic and don't take it seriously, not with the fundamental seriousness needed to write convincingly.

I'm interested, I'm willing to play that game with another writer for awhile; but I don't *really care*. Not about magic, anyway.

And most of the ideas that come to you, from whatever source, are going to be like that. They won't be things of profound importance to *you*. And if they're not, how are you going to persuade a reader to care about them? It will all be forced, mechanical, intellectualized, unconvincing. That's even more true if they are things you uncomfortably think you *ought* to care about, like cruel parents, faithless lovers, The Bomb, World Hunger, or the Heartbreak of Psoriasis.

I think that's what the traditional advice to "write what you know" really means: To choose things that matter enormously to you, things you have a stake in settling, at least on paper.

I've never been aboard a spaceship, but I've lived in cramped quarters, and I can project an experience I've known on one I've only imagined. So I can honestly say that I know what it *could* be like to be the sole crew of a one-man scout ship traveling on a long haul between the stars. And I care how it would feel: It seems worth trying to imagine myself into. I've never been a serious sculptor, but I know something of the way any artist can get lost in his work—perfectly normal, experienced from the inside, but often laughably odd, observed from the outside. So I was able to write, with conviction, a story about a sculptor who carves bas-relief horses out of botched tombstones she calls 'meat' and who loses track of the hours and even the days.

I'm not saying that these were the most wonderful story ideas ever concocted, just that they were *my* stories to tell. They had a special resonance. I could imagine my way into them, from things I've known about, first-hand. And they had a dynamic: They seemed to be going somewhere from the first moment they came into my head. They felt as if they had little hooks built in that refused to let go until I had the whole puzzle solved, the thing written in the form it seemed to want to go into.

Most often these valid, dynamic story ideas won't be things that you already know and have settled. Settled things make for explanations, not for absorbing fiction. Instead, they'll be situations or people or memories that are troubling you, things you want, for yourself, to work out and understand. Explorations, not explanations.

That's the first criterion: *Is this something I really care about, something I partly understand, something that seems to want working out?*

2. Is It Too Personal For Readers to Become Involved With? The second criterion has to do with the purpose of writing. Partly, it's self-expression. But partly—and increasingly, the more and the longer you write—it's communication. You want what you say to reach, and move, a reader. You want to share the exploration. You want to have fun writing your story so that readers can have fun reading it. Maybe you even want it to sell, and to help you become famous. Those are valid reasons too, provided they're not the main or the only ones. (If the results are more important to you than the process, if you don't want to write but only *to have written*, you're in trouble.)

So the second thing you need to ask yourself, about any story idea, is whether it's something that's *too* personal, something that's very important to you but would justifiably bore a stranger sitting next to you on a cross-country bus.

Some experience is too close to us. We feel deep emotion about it, but haven't digested it yet and aren't able to put it in perspective for somebody else to view. Or maybe it's too exotic, like a specialist on the intimate habits of the Amazonian tree snail assuming the subject is going to be fascinating to vast numbers of people.

Personal blind spots.

It's understandable, if mildly tedious, from people waving around pictures of their kids or wanting us to pore through snapshots from their vacations or sit through their home movies of the family washing the dog. From a writer, it's unforgivable—and probably unpublishable.

For such highly personal subjects, the context that would make them meaningful would just take too much explaining for somebody else to understand.

That's a particular problem, by the way, with autobiographical or fact-based fiction. You have to be able to distance it. You not only have to care about it but care just the right way, ruthlessly cutting this incident, changing this character, altering this reaction in the interests of good fiction, regardless of what *really* happened. You have to be, in some meaningful sense, *free* of it before you're ready to write about it. You have to be willing to look at it through a stranger's eyes—the eyes of your potential readers.

But don't underestimate your own experiences as a source of story ideas, either. Tiny, vivid impressions—the feel of new sneakers, sunlight through a colored window, getting up in the middle of the night when it's dark and scary, being the only pedestrian on an empty street—have been the basis of wonderful, imaginative short stories by Ray Bradbury. Coveting an overcoat was the basis of a classic story by Gogol. A chickenwire costume can be life-saving armor. Small things can have immense impact, if you give them a context that brings out their importance.

Your own experience is an inexhaustible mine of fiction ideas, provided only that you can make readers see the experience as important and applicable to their own experience and lives.

You can never know this for sure. You can only recognize the problem and do your best to strike a balance between the personal and the universal. Then, the story has to take its chances, as all stories must.

And always bring, to whatever you write, everything you've known, felt, experienced, imagined. Like Tolkien's Elves of Lorien, put something of what you love in everything you make. If you're cynical or want to escape sentimentality, put in something that you loathe, too. Such first-hand direct experience is the main and invaluable source of the kind of immediately convincing, personal, vivid details that flesh out a plot and make it seem real to a reader.

Dickens, in particular, was a master of this. Joseph Heller's *Catch-22* is another good source for precisely observed detail. Read some of these authors' work and learn the kind of specific detail you should be observing in daily life and jotting in your notebook for later use in fiction—a face, a phrase, a scene. Sometimes the simplest, most personal things are those that can speak direct to the heart.

And the job of distinguishing between the merely personal and the vividly personal is one nobody can do but you. So your second criterion should be: *Can I work with this idea in a caring but uncompromising way to make it meaningful to somebody else?*

3. Is It Going Somewhere? The third criterion has to do with the nature of the material itself. Supposing the first two criteria have been met, is this an idea with a dynamic? Has it got an engine, or could you put one into it? You could attach a motor to a tree, but it wouldn't go very far. A motor-powered bathtub is still a bathtub.

Does your idea divide itself into a vivid opening, one or more specific developments, and a solid ending? Can you block out in your mind a beginning scene, intermediate scenes, a final confrontation or resolution of some kind?

It doesn't matter if the actual scenes you end up writing are different from the ones you imagine at first. The important thing is that the subject you care about, the subject you think you can make immediate and important to readers, lends itself to being cast into scenes of any kind.

Make a poster and put it up where you write: PLOT IS A VERB.

If what you're writing is nounish or adjectival, a thing or a description, or if it's essentially a lecture or an essay, it's going to be static. It may still be a story, but a relatively formless one aimed at a narrow spectrum of readers. If your story happens over a period of years, with nothing much happening in between, and if you can't see a way to compress the action into a single compact tale, even one as long as a novel, you'll have to split out a smaller piece of it to be your story. If it involves a vast number of people or several major changes of locale, it may be a novel, but not a short story. If it's all beginning, a problem you can show but not resolve to give the story a conclusion (even an unhappy one), it's not going to work. If it's a sudden turn of events that nothing seems to lead into, like lightning in the middle of a bullfight, pure ending, it won't make satisfying reading.

Ask yourself, *Can I dramatize this in a series of scenes with a minimum of explanation? Does it have a plot, or can I create a plot for it?*

4. What's at Stake? Finally, ask yourself: *Is there something quite specific and vital at stake—not just to me, but to one or more of the char-*

acters involved? Ask yourself what the central conflict is, the struggle that's the basis of plot. Ask yourself how you can *show*, rather than tell, why this is so important to the character, make the reader understand, empathize, and care about what happens.

If you're writing experimental or literary fiction, you can allow yourself a little more latitude about what's at stake. It can be the impact of a memory of aesthetic ecstasy experienced in a time of artistic dryness, as in Thomas Mann's *Death in Venice*. It can be the downward progress of a deteriorating, obsessive consciousness, as in Poe's "The Fall of the House of Usher." That it's harder to make such things seem vital issues to the general reader doesn't mean they're not worth doing. But neither does it mean that you can ignore the issue and just have meandering ruminations about Life and the World.

It's quite possible to make bread with something other than crushed grain and produce food that's tasty, nutritious, and solid enough so that you know you've eaten something. But whatever your fondness for carrot cake or corn muffins, it's plain old bread, plot, that's been part of human culture since the beginnings of things. We know plot when we meet it: It's in our bones. Maybe even in our genes. We say, "But what's it *about*?" and expect a reasonably concise answer. We want verb bread or we're sure we'll be hungry an hour later.

Any fiction, however literary, still has to possess some dynamic tension, even if it's one of irony, or a surprising contrast. Something has to be seen to matter, and to change—even in a mood piece. The story has to move. If you choose not to have traditional plot, you're going to have to work twice as hard to make your chosen alternate work as compellingly.

If, however, you're writing mainstream or genre fiction intended for a wide readership, it's absolutely crucial that you have and develop a plot and that something quite concrete and definite be at issue. It's what your story is going to be perceived to be "about." Your protagonist wants to gain possession of a ruby approximately the size of New Jersey, become a first-class hockey player, escape from an unsympathetic spouse, get one word of praise from a stern and disapproving parent, or rescue turtles from the zoo and set them free in the all-forgiving sea.

Ideally, you should be able to express the core plot in a sentence or two, in about the same space and style as program listings in *TV Guide*. In fact, it might help to study a few issues of *TV Guide* and one of the several paperback guides to movies on TV, and see how such capsule summaries are done. Practice writing a few about things you've read recently. ("The police chief of a New England vacation community, al-

though terrified of the ocean, sets out to destroy a huge killer shark"—
Jaws; "A group of British schoolboys, attempting to survive after their
plane crashlands on a tropical island, begin reverting to savagery"—
Lord of the Flies.)

See how brief and direct you can make your summaries. The basic
plot of a story (unlike its meaning) ought to be directly expressible in
very few words, though playing it out in scenes may take a dozen or a
thousand pages.

If the summary of your own story turns out to be one you haven't already seen fifty times, so much the better. If not, don't worry: All the
love stories haven't yet been written, nor anything close. And there will
be growing-up stories as long as there are people.

Ready, Steady, Go!

If you test your ideas against these four criteria, a lot will be tossed out,
or saved in your handy notebook for later. Don't let that upset you.
There are a lot more where they came from, and some of them will pass
the test with bells ringing and flags flying.

All you need is one solid story idea at a time to keep writing produc-
tively, successfully, your whole life. Use these criteria and you'll have
the confidence of knowing you're starting with good material from the
very beginning, material worth the thought and energy of developing,
stories that have the potential of reaching readers. You'll hardly be able
to wait to start working out your ideas on paper, embodying them in
scenes, listening to your characters talk.

Michael A. Banks

Plot = Motivation = Plot

You're a detective with the homicide squad, working a tough case. There are few clues, and no "official" suspects. Your instinct, developed over years of investigating similar cases, tells you that the victim's neighbor is the killer. Unfortunately, you can't arrest a suspect on instinct, and this one is "clean." Besides, the prosecutor is tough to convince, so you must build an airtight case.

Where do you start?

You first ask yourself, "If he did it, *why*?" What were his motivations? You can't very well convince anyone of your suspect's guilt without a complete analysis of his motives.

You list possible motivations, and then seek facts to back up your theories. A few questions to other neighbors and some inconspicuous poking around yield some results. The suspect is married to the victim's ex-wife. The suspect is also an unstable, jealous type. Now you have a motive, and it's time to go digging for facts to support your case.

Or put yourself into this scenario: Your sister and her husband have just left your home after a friendly game of cards. After seeing them to the door, you remember to put away the expensive antique watch left to you by your late mother. You had removed it from the wall safe to show it to your brother-in-law, who had never seen it, at the request of your sister. After this, the party had moved into the living room, and you hadn't given the watch another thought.

Now it's gone. You search the house. Nothing. It's beginning to look as if your sister and/or brother-in-law took the watch.

You're shocked because neither of the two had any reason to take it. You've always gotten along well with your sister and her husband, so they certainly wouldn't have taken it out of spite. And, since both of them work and earn a *very* comfortable living, they wouldn't have taken the watch for its monetary value.

But, you think, there must be a reason. *Something* motivated either or both of your relatives to steal the watch. You begin creating possible situations that could have resulted in the need to steal the watch. There *must* be a motivation. There's always a motivation . . .

Believing Is Seeing

These two scenarios (or, if you wish, story situations) are preoccupied with motivations, and in each case, the thought-processes taking place are similar to those taking place in the mind of a reader as he reads your story. The reader is not *consciously* seeking motivations, but he will know if they aren't there. He will be dissatisfied with your story, mainly because what your characters are doing just isn't *believable*.

Readers, you see, must be convinced that your story can happen, otherwise your story is damaged, perhaps even rendered worthless. Like the detective, readers want to know *why* a character does something, along with how he does it. And, like the homeowner with the missing watch, they want to understand your characters.

Writers cannot manipulate characters as they would hand puppets; puppeteers are not concerned with realism. Characters are living, *thinking* creations, and they have reasons for doing what they do. (If you think otherwise, perhaps you should be a puppeteer.)

You should not, of course, baldly state that "Benny's sister had long been jealous of him, but was the type to hide her emotions at any cost, preferring 'getting even' to getting mad, and this is why she stole the watch." That approach is the easy way out, and would probably ruin your story. You must, instead, *show* all of this information—through the eyes of your protagonist as he discovers it.

Motivation—like characterization and plot—must emerge gradually in your story, as part of a well-coordinated effort. If you dump all the information at the feet of your reader right away, he will probably reject it. You must wrap it up nicely within the story and, in aid of realism, let your reader discover the facts bit by bit.

You must also back up the protagonist's discoveries with believable characterization. The character (in this case, the sister who is suspected of stealing the watch) not only must be capable of doing the necessary acts, but also must be capable of having the necessary motivations. So, you must set up your characters and their traits from the very beginning of the story, and build them throughout the plot in such a way as to support their personalities, the required motivation and the plot.

On the surface, motivation may seem to be tied strictly to characterization, in the supporting role of adding realism. The effects of character motivation in a story go far beyond this, though. Plot, theme, character, conflict and motivation—basic elements of fiction—are tightly intertwined, and interact strongly. A change in one element may dictate major changes in all the others, or may prove impossible because of the requirements of other elements.

For example, you may have developed a plot that requires a character to lose her temper over seemingly minor matters. Right away, the plot dictates the need for a certain type of character—one who loses her temper easily. Fine. You think of such a character, and begin working her into the story. As you write, you may well find that the plot has also dictated the character's motivations, if the incidents involving her temper are tied to the conflict of the story, or if the character is your protagonist.

If, however, you are relying heavily on character development in your story, a rigid set of limitations is already established for this character. In this case, you must either change the character—from the beginning of the story—or adjust the plot.

It's a two-way street. In a successful story, these sorts of interactions rumble back and forth all through the story's development, until everything is moving in a synchronized manner, just like city traffic during rush hour, with you as the traffic cop.

As a more specific example, consider John Higgen, a character who appears in a series of my science fiction short stories. Higgen is a huckster in the business of marketing inventions. He is primarily motivated by greed (his percentage of profits) and sometimes by curiosity and survival. Since his primary motivation is greed, I must develop the plot of each story to use this greed.

This sometimes establishes restrictions on plot development. I could not, for example, take the easy way out in the second story of the series, "The Big Black Bag." In this story, Higgen represented the inventor of a device that could instantaneously transport an object from one location to another. I had developed the plot to the point where the only apparent resolution was to have Higgen give the secret of the device to the general public, gratis. Higgen had failed miserably in attempting to sell the device, and having the thing around was dangerous, so there was some motivation to support simply dumping it. I wrote the story that way, and it was rejected. I then realized that, because I had already established Higgen as a greed-motivated individual (in this story and the first one), he couldn't give up that easily. What I had Higgen do was unreasonable, within the motivational framework I had established.

Convincing with Consistency

Since the personality and motivations for Higgen were so strongly fixed, I rewrote the story so that Higgen did profit from the device, instead of attempting to change his motivations. The rewritten version sold.

Higgen's motivation has, in other stories, helped *create* the plot. In another Higgen story, "Horseless Carriage," the plot practically created itself. Faced with the opportunity to sell a workable "anti-gravity" device, Higgen's greed drove him to more and more desperate action (and more and more problems!) as he attempted to overcome potential buyers' beliefs that the invention was a hoax. I concentrated on Higgen's personality and motivation, along with the story conflict, and the necessary scenes suggested themselves.

Since the gadget in the story was one with apparently unlimited money-making potential, it was easy to see Higgen trying almost anything to "cash in." His motivation forced him to believe that there *had* to be a payoff. He tried the obvious markets—toy and novelty manufacturers, and filmmakers—and eventually invested all his savings in the manufacture of 50,000 of the devices. In the meantime, he lied to the inventor about his progress in marketing the device.

All of this occurred in support of his greed, and each event in the story is rendered believable by this same greed. As Higgen summed it up near the end of the story, "I was so damn set against letting anyone else get ahold of the idea that I would have told Epworth [the inventor] *anything* to keep the contract."

None of this would have been believable, of course, without the proper motivation, properly presented. If Higgen were merely in business to make a living and represent his clients, the plot wouldn't have been believable; the average businessman is too conservative. Too, if Higgen had not been so strongly motivated, the plot would have been quite different, and perhaps more difficult to develop.

Your characters will either restrict or support and dictate your plots. Keep this in mind as you write, and be ready to make sacrifices on the part of your characters' motivations or your stories' plots, depending upon which element (motivation or plot) is of more importance.

As I mentioned earlier, the interaction of the various elements of a short story is a two-way street. Just as character motivation can restrict or support plot development, so can the requirements of plot dictate the need for a certain set of character motivations.

Each requirement of plot should be supported by the proper character motivations. Or, to look at it from another viewpoint, *your characters should be capable of doing what you want them to do,* or you will lose any illusion of realism that you may have created. You can *force* your characters to do what is necessary, but the reader won't accept such manipulation.

So, if you need a character who will run from the slightest danger, even though doing so endangers his family, make sure that you have presented that character as at least something of a coward earlier in the story. Don't expect a noble person to do such a thing for you just because your plot requires it.

Because motivations affect a character's personality, you will frequently find that you must alter your characters in response to changing motivations, as dictated by plot events. Such alteration will not be limited to "on the spot" changes, though. Any changes in a character that will affect the plot, or that are dictated by plot, *must* be made at the beginning of the story, and must be consistent throughout the story. Otherwise, your repairs will be visible to the reader, and distracting.

For example, your protagonist may be an elderly, chronically ill man. Because of his condition, the man has plenty of motivation for despising younger, healthy people. (He would have this motivation *if* you developed his personality in that direction, of course.)

As the plot develops, however, you find that your protagonist must perform an act of physical violence that would be impossible for an elderly man to perform. What can you do? If you want to preserve your plot, you'll have to back up and start from scratch, creating a new character who can do what you want and *still* be properly motivated, per the plot requirements. Perhaps a young, strong, hypochondriac woman will do.

I faced a similar dilemma in a recently completed story. In the manuscript, my young female protagonist worked fine until I reached a point in the plot where the protagonist had to protect her "political" tenure in a military research establishment. As I began this portion of the story (one required by the plot), I realized that neither a young nor a female protagonist would do, because a young woman would not—*could* not—have reached a high position in such a male-dominated hierarchy. (To have attained the necessary position, my protagonist had to have begun working in the early 1940s, which ruled out a young person, and the male-dominated military of the 1940s would have ruled out a female in a leadership position.) Thus, because of plot requirements, I had to replace a young woman with an older man, even though the motivations were unaltered.

I ended up with a totally different character, and I had to rewrite much of the story to accommodate him, but the story was improved immensely.

Uncovering a Plot

Just as believable motivations are necessary for realism in fiction, consistency is also essential. Consistency in a short story may be defined as following a set of rules, created by an author, that govern what may and may not exist or occur within a story. You may not be aware of it, but as you write a story, you are creating your own "universe," with a rigid set of laws. Violating these laws is a capital offense, resulting in sudden death for your story, in the eyes of the reader. You can no more violate the laws of your story "universe" and retain realism than you can violate the laws of the real universe by stepping off the edge of a cliff and flying.

For example, if you set your story in a small town, you have created a law that rules out the existence of any "big-city" trappings such as 70-story skyscrapers. Thus, if you have a character take an elevator to the 69th floor later in the hypothetical story, you have violated one of the laws of the story universe and achieved inconsistency.

Similarly, if you create a character who is the most violent, unreasonable person you can imagine, you can't get away with using this character in a scene that calls for a tender, self-sacrificing act (unless the plot events cause the character to undergo a serious character-change).

So, imagine again that you're the detective described at the beginning of this article. Your job is to uncover plots, to analyze the motives of the characters involved in the plots, and finally to integrate plot and motivation into a presentation that will convince the most demanding of judges: your readers.

Janet Burroway

Call Me Ishmael: Point of View

Point of view is the most complex element of fiction. Although it lends itself to analysis, definitions, and diagrams, it is finally a question of relationship among writer, characters, and reader—subject like any relationship to organic subtleties. We can discuss person, omniscience, narrative voice, tone, authorial distance, and reliability; but none of these things will ever pigeonhole a work in such a way that any other work may be placed in the exact same pigeonhole.

The first thing to do is to set aside the common use of the phrase "point of view" as being synonymous with "opinion," as in *It's my point of view that they all ought to be shot.* An author's view of the world as it is and as it ought to be will ultimately be revealed by his or her manipulation of the technique of point of view, but not vice versa—identifying the author's beliefs will not describe the point of view of the work. Rather than thinking of point of view as an opinion or belief, begin with the more literal synonym of "vantage point." *Who* is standing *where* to watch the scene?

Better, since we are dealing with a verbal medium, these questions might be translated: Who speaks? To whom? In what form? At what distance from the action? With what limitations? All these issues go into the determination of the point of view. Because *the author inevitably wants to convince us to share the same perspective,* the answers will also help reveal her or his final opinion, judgment, attitude, or message.

Who Speaks?

The primary point-of-view decision that you as author must make before you can set down the first sentence of the story is *person.* This is the simplest and crudest subdivision that must be made in deciding who speaks. The story can be told in the third person *(She walked out into the harsh sunlight),* the second person *(You walked out into the harsh sunlight),* or the first person *(I walked out into the harsh sunlight).* Third- and second-person stories are "told" by an author; first-person stories, by a character.

Third Person

Third person, in which the author is telling the story, can be subdivided again according to the degree of knowledge, or *omniscience* the author assumes. Notice that since this is a matter of degree, the subdivisions are again only a crude indication of the variations possible. As an author you are free to decide how much you know. You may know every universal and eternal truth; you may know what is in the mind of one character but not what is in the mind of another; or you may know only what can be externally observed. You decide, and very early in the story you signal to the reader what degree of omniscience you have chosen. Once given, this signal constitutes a "contract" between author and reader, and it will be difficult to break the contract gracefully. If you have restricted yourself to the mind of James Lordly for five pages, as he observes the actions of Mrs. Grumms and her cats, you will violate the contract by suddenly dipping into Mrs. Grumms's mind to let us know what she thinks of James Lordly. We are likely to feel misused, and likely to cancel the contract altogether, if you suddenly give us the thoughts of the cats.

The omniscient author, sometimes referred to as the *editorial omniscient author,* because she or he tells us directly what we are supposed to think, has total knowledge. As omniscient author you are God. You can:

1. Objectively report what is happening;

2. Go into the mind of any character;

3. Interpret for us that character's appearance, speech, actions, and thoughts, even if the character cannot do so;

4. Move freely in time or space to give us a panoramic, telescopic, microscopic, or historical view; tell us what has happened elsewhere or in the past or what will happen in the future.

5. Provide general reflections, judgments, and truths.

In all these aspects, we will accept what the omniscient author tells us. If you tell us that Ruth is a good woman, that Jeremy doesn't really understand his own motives, that the moon is going to explode in four hours, and that everybody will be better off for it, we will believe you. Here is a paragraph that blatantly exhibits all five of these areas of knowledge.

(1) Joe glared at the screaming baby. (2) Frightened by his scowl, the baby gulped and screamed louder. I hate that thing, Joe thought. (3) But it was not really hatred that he felt. (4) Only two years ago he himself had screamed like that. (5) Children can't tell hatred from fear.

This illustration is awkwardly compressed, but an author well in control of his craft can move easily from one area of knowledge to another. In the first scene of *War and Peace,* Tolstoy describes Anna Scherer.

> To be an enthusiast had become her social vocation, and sometimes even when she did not feel like it, she became enthusiastic in order not to disappoint the expectations of those who knew her. The subdued smile which, though it did not suit her faded features, always played around her lips, expressed as in a spoiled child, a continual consciousness of her charming defect, which she neither wished, nor could, nor considered it necessary to correct.

Here in two sentences Tolstoy tells us what is in Anna's mind and the expectations of her acquaintances, what she looks like, what suits her, what she can and cannot do, and he offers a general reflection on spoiled children.

The omniscient voice is the voice of the classical epic (*And Meleager, far-off, knew nothing of this, but felt his vitals burning with fever*), of the Bible (*So the Lord sent a pestilence upon Israel; and there fell 70,000 men*), and of most 19th-century novels (*Tito put out his hand to help him, and so strangely quick are men's souls that in this moment, when he began to feel that his atonement was accepted, he had a darting thought of the irksome efforts it entailed*). But it is one of the manifestations of literature's movement downward in class from heroic to common characters, inward from action to the mind, that authors of the 20th century have largely avoided the godlike stance of the omniscient author and chose to restrict themselves to fewer areas of knowledge.

The limited omniscient viewpoint is one in which the author may move with some, but not all, of the omniscient author's freedom. You may grant yourself the right, for example, to know what the characters in a scene are thinking but not to interpret their thoughts. You may interpret one character's thoughts and actions but see the others only externally. You may see with microscopic accuracy but not presume to reach any universal truths. The most commonly used form of the limited omniscient point of view is one in which the author can see events objectively and also grants himself or herself access to the mind of one character, but not to the minds of the others, nor to any explicit powers of judgment. This point of view is particularly useful for the short story because it very quickly establishes the point-of-view character or *means of perception.* The short story is so compressed a form that there is rarely time or space to develop more than one consciousness. Staying with external observation and one character's thoughts helps control the focus and avoid *awkward point-of-view shifts.*

But the form is also frequently used for the novel, as in Gail Godwin's *The Odd Woman.*

It was ten o'clock on the evening of the same day, and the permanent residents of the household on the mountain were restored to routines and sobriety. Jane, on the other hand, sat by herself in the kitchen, a glass of Scotch before her on the cleanly wiped table, going deeper and deeper into a mood she could recognize only as unfamiliar. She could not describe it; it was both frightening and satisfying. It was like letting go and being taken somewhere. She tried to trace it back. When, exactly, had it started?

It is clear here that the author has limited her omniscience. She is not going to tell us the ultimate truth about Jane's soul, nor is she going to define for us the "unfamiliar mood" that the character herself cannot define. The author has the facts at her disposal, and she has Jane's thoughts, and that is all.

The advantage of the limited omniscient over the omniscient voice is immediacy. Here, because we are not allowed to know more than Jane does about her own thoughts and feelings, we grope *with* her toward understanding. In the process, a contract has been made between the author and the reader, and this contract must not now be broken. If at this point the author should step in and answer Jane's question, "When, exactly, had it started?" with, "Jane was never to remember this, but in fact it had started one afternoon when she was two years old," we would feel it as an abrupt and uncalled-for *authorial intrusion*.

Nevertheless, within the limits the author has set herself, there is fluidity and a range of possibilities. Notice that the passage begins with a panoramic observation (*ten o'clock, permanent residents, routines*) and moves to the tighter focus of a view, still external, of Jane (*sat by herself in the kitchen*), before moving into her mind. The sentence "She tried to trace it back" is a relatively factual account of her mental process, whereas in the next sentence, "When, exactly, had it started?" we are in Jane's mind, overhearing her question to herself.

Although this common form of the limited omniscient (objective reporting plus one mind) may seem very restricted, given all the possibilities of omniscience, it has a freedom that no human being has. In life you have full access to only one mind, your own; and you are also the one person you may not externally observe. As a fiction writer you can do what no human being can do, be simultaneously inside and outside a given character; it is this that E.M. Forster describes in *Aspects of the Novel* as "the fundamental difference between people in daily life and people in books."

In daily life we never understand each other, neither complete clairvoyance nor complete confessional exists. We know each other approximately, by external signs, and these serve well enough as a basis for society and even for intimacy. But people in a novel can be understood completely by the reader, if the novelist wishes; their inner as well as their outer life can be exposed. And this is why they often seem more definite than characters in history, or even our own friends.

The objective author. Sometimes the novelist or short-story writer does not wish to expose any more than the external signs. The *objective* author is not omniscient but impersonal. As an objective author, you restrict your knowledge to the facts that might be observed by a human being; to the senses of sight, sound, smell, taste, and touch. In the story "Hills Like White Elephants," Ernest Hemingway reports what is said and done by a quarreling couple, both without any direct revelation of the characters' thoughts and without comment.

> The American and the girl with him sat at a table in the shade, outside the building. It was very hot and the express from Barcelona would come in 40 minutes. It stopped at this junction for two minutes and went on to Madrid.
> "What should we drink?" the girl asked. She has taken off her hat and put it on the table.
> "It's pretty hot," the man said.
> "Let's drink beer."
> "Dos cervezas," the man said into the curtain.
> "Big ones?" a woman asked from the doorway.
> "Yes. Two big ones."
> The woman brought two glasses of beer and two felt pads. She put the felt pads and the beer glasses on the table and looked at the man and the girl. The girl was looking off at the line of hills. They were white in the sun and the country was brown and dry.

In the course of this story we learn, entirely by inference, that the girl is pregnant and that she feels herself coerced by the man into having an abortion. Neither pregnancy nor abortion is ever mentioned. The narrative remains clipped, austere, and external. What does Hemingway gain by this pretense of objective reporting? The reader is allowed to discover what is really happening. The characters avoid the subject, prevaricate, and pretend, but they betray their real meanings and feelings through gestures, repetitions, and slips of the tongue. The reader, focus directed by the author, learns by inference, as in life, so we have the pleasure of knowing the characters better than they know themselves.

For the sake of clarity, the possibilities of third-person narration have been divided into the editorial omniscient, limited omniscient, and objective authors, but between the extreme stances of the editorial omniscient (total knowledge) and the objective author (external observation only), the powers of the limited omniscient are immensely variable.

Because you are most likely to choose your authorial voice in this range, you need to be aware that you make your own rules and that, having made them, you must stick to them. Your position as a writer is analogous to that of a poet who may choose whether to write free verse or a ballad stanza. If the poet chooses the stanza, then he or she is obliged to rhyme. Beginning writers of prose fiction are often tempted to shift viewpoint when it is both unnecessary and disturbing.

> Leo's neck flushed against the prickly weave of his uniform collar. He concentrated on his buttons and tried not to look into the face of the bandmaster, who, however, was more amused than angry.

This is an awkward point-of-view shift because, having felt Leo's embarrassment with him, we are suddenly asked to leap into the bandmaster's feelings. The shift can be corrected by moving instead from Leo's mind to an observation that he might make.

> Leo's neck flushed against the prickly weave of his uniform collar. He concentrated on his buttons and tried not to look into the face of the bandmaster, who, however, was astonishingly smiling.

The rewrite is easier to follow because we remain with Leo's mind as he observes that the bandmaster is not angry. It further serves the purpose of implying that Leo fails to concentrate on his buttons, and so intensifies his confusion.

Second Person

First and third persons are most common in literature; the second person remains an idiosyncratic and experimental form, but it is worth mentioning because several twentieth-century authors have been attracted to its possibilities.

Person refers to the basic mode of a piece of fiction. In the third person, all the characters will be referred to as *he, she,* and *they.* In the first person, the character telling the story will refer to himself or herself as *I* and to other characters as *he, she,* and *they.* The second person is the basic mode of the story *only when a character* is referred to as *you.* When an omniscient author addresses the reader as *you (You will remember that John Doderring was left dangling on the cliff at Dover),* this does not alter the basic mode of the piece from third to second person. Only when "you" become an actor in the drama is the story or novel written in second person.

In *Even Cowgirls Get the Blues,* Tom Robbins exhibits both of these uses of the second person.

If you could buckle your Bugs Bunny wristwatch to a ray of light, your watch would continue ticking but its hands wouldn't move.

The *you* involved here is a generalized reader, and the passage is written in the stance of an omniscient author delivering a general "truth."

But when the author turns to address his central character, Sissy Hankshaw, the basic mode of the narration becomes that of the second person.

You hitchhike. Timidly at first, barely flashing your fist, leaning almost imperceptibly in the direction of your imaginary destination. A squirrel runs along a tree limb. You hitchhike the squirrel. A blue jay flies by. You flag it down.

The effect of this second-person narration is odd and original; the author observes Sissy Hankshaw, and yet his direct address implies an intimate and affectionate relationship that makes it easy to move further into her mind.

Your thumbs separate you from other humans. You begin to sense a presence about your thumbs. You wonder if there is not magic there.

In this example it is a character clearly delineated and distinguished from the reader who is the *you* of the narrative. But the second person can also be used as a means of making the reader into a character, as in Robert Coover's story, "Panel Game."

You squirm, viced by Lady (who excites you) and America (who does not, but bless him all the same), but your squirms are misread: Lovely Lady lifts lashes, crosses eyes, and draws breath excitedly. . . . Audience howls happily the while and who can blame them? You, Sport, resign yourself to pass the test in peace and salute them with a timid smile, squirm no more.

Here again the effect of the second person is unusual and complex. The author assigns you, the reader, specific characteristics and reactions and thereby—assuming that you go along with his characterization of you—pulls you deeper and more intimately into the story.

It is unlikely that the second person will ever become a major mode of narration as the first and third are, but for precisely that reason you may find it an attractive experiment. It is startling and relatively unexplored.

First Person

A story is told in the first person when it is a character who speaks. The term "narrator" is sometimes loosely used to refer to any teller of a tale, but strictly speaking a story "has a narrator" only when it is told in the first person by one of the characters. This character may be the protagonist, the *I* telling *my* story, in which case that character is a *central narrator;* or the character may be telling a story about someone else, in which case he or she is a *peripheral narrator.*

In either case it's important to indicate early which kind of narrator we have so that we know who the story's protagonist is, as in the first paragraph of Alan Sillitoe's "The Loneliness of the Long-Distance Runner."

> As soon as I got to Borstal they made me a long-distance cross-country runner. I suppose they thought I was just the build for it because I was long and skinny for my age (and still am) and in any case I didn't mind it much, to tell you the truth, because running had always been made much of in our family, especially running away from the police.

The focus here is immediately thrown on the *I* of the story, and we expect that *I* to be the central character whose desires and decisions impel the action. But from the opening lines of R. Bruce Moody's *The Decline and Fall of Daphne Finn,* it is Daphne who is brought alive by attention and detail, while the narrator is established as an observer and recorder of his subject.

> "Is it really you?"
> Melodious and high, the voice descended to me from behind and above—as it seemed it was always to do—indistinct as bells in another country.
> Unable to answer in the negative, I turned from my desk, looked up, and smiled sourly.
> "Yes," I said, startling a face which had been peering over my shoulder, a face whose beauty it was apparent at the outset had made no concession to convention. It retreated as her feet staggered back.

The central narrator is always, as the term implies, at the center of the action; the peripheral narrator may be in virtually any position that is not the center. He or she may be the second most important character in the story, or may not be involved in the action at all but merely placed in a position to observe. The narrator may characterize himself or herself in detail or may remain detached and scarcely identifiable. It is even possible to make the first-person narrator plural, as William Faulkner does in "A Rose for Emily," where the story is told by a narrator identified only as one of "us," the people of the town in which the action has taken place.

That a narrator may be either central or peripheral, that a character may tell either his own story or someone else's, is both commonly assumed and obviously logical. But the author and editor Rust Hills, in his book *Writing in General and the Short Story in Particular,* takes interesting and persuasive exception to this idea. When point of view fails, Hills argues, it is always because the perception we are using for the course of the story is different from that of the character who is moved or changed by the action. Even when a narrator seems to be a peripheral observer and the story is "about" someone else, in fact it is the narrator who is changed, and must be, in order for us to be satisfied by our emotional identification with him or her.

> This, I believe, is what will always be the case in successful fiction: that either the character moved by the action will be the point-of-view character, or else the point-of-view character will *become* the character moved by the action. Call it Hills' Law.

Obviously, this view does not mean that we have to throw out the useful fictional device of the peripheral narrator. Hills uses the familiar examples of *The Great Gatsby* and *Heart of Darkness* to illustrate his meaning. In the former, Nick Carroway as a peripheral narrator observes and tells the story of Jay Gatsby, but by the end of the book it is Nick's life that has been changed by what he has observed. In the latter, Marlow purports to tell the tale of the ivory hunter Kurtz, even protesting that "I don't want to bother you much with what happened to me personally." By the end of the story, Kurtz (like Gatsby) is dead, but it is not the death that moves us so much as what, "personally," Marlow has learned *through* Kurtz and his death. The same can be said of *The Decline and Fall of Daphne Finn;* the focus of the action is on Daphne, but the pain, the passion, and the loss are those of her biographer. Even in "A Rose for Emily," where the narrator is a collective "we," it is the implied effect of Miss Emily on the town that moves us, the emotions of the townspeople that we share. Because we tend to identify with the means of perception in a story, we are moved with that perception; even when the overt action of the story is elsewhere, it is often the act of observation itself that provides the epiphany.

The thing to recognize about a first-person narrator is that because she or he is a character, she or he has all the limitations of a human being and cannot be omniscient. The narrator is confined to reporting what she or he could realistically know. More than that, although the narrator may certainly interpret actions, deliver dictums, and predict the future, these remain the fallible opinions of a human being, we are not bound to accept them as we are bound to accept the interpretations, truths, and predictions of the omniscient author. You may want us to accept the narrator's word, and then the most difficult part of your task, and the touchstone of your story's success, will be to convince us to trust and believe the narrator. On the other hand, it may be an important part of your purpose that we should reject the narrator's opinions and form our own. In the latter case, the narrator is "unreliable."

To Whom?

In choosing a point of view, the author implies an identity, not only for the teller of the tale, but for the audience as well.

The Reader

Most fiction is addressed to a literary convention, *"the reader."* When we open a book, we tacitly accept our role as a member of this unspecified audience. If the story begins, "I was born of a drunken father and an illiterate mother in the peat bogs of Galway during the Great Potato Famine," we are not, on the whole, alarmed. We do not face this clearly deceased Irishman who has crossed the Atlantic to take us into his confidence and demand, "Why are you telling me all this?"

Notice that the tradition of "the reader" assumes the universality of the audience. Most stories do not specifically address themselves to a segment or period of humanity, and they make no concessions to such difference as might exist between reader and author; they assume that anyone who reads the story can be brought around to the same understanding of it the author has. In practice most writers, though they do not acknowledge it in the text and may not admit it to themselves, are addressing someone *who can* be brought around to the same understanding as themselves. The author of a Gothic romance addresses the story to a generalized "reader" but knows that his or her likely audience is trained by repetition of the formula to expect certain features—rich lover, virtuous heroine, threatening house, colorful costume. Slightly less formulaic is the notion of "a *New Yorker* story," which is presumably what the author perceives that the editors perceive will be pleasing to the people who buy *The New Yorker.* Anyone who pens or types what he or she hopes is "literature" is assuming that his audience is literate, which leaves out better than half the world. My mother, distressed at the difficulty of my fictional style, used to urge me to write for "the masses," by which she meant subscribers to *Reader's Digest,* whom she thought to be in need of cheering and escape. I considered this a very narrow goal until I realized that my own ambition to be "universal" was more exclusive still: I envisioned my audience as made up of people who *would not* subscribe to the *Reader's Digest.*

Nevertheless, the most common assumption of the tale-teller, whether omniscient author or narrating character, is that the reader is an amenable and persuasible Everyman, and that the telling needs no justification.

But there are various exceptions to this tendency which can be used to dramatic effect and which always involve a more definite characterizing of the receiver of the story. The author may address "the reader" but assign that reader specific traits that we, the actual readers, must then accept as our own if we are to accept the fiction. Nineteenth-century novelists had a tradition of addressing "You, gentle reader," "Dear reader," and the like, and this minimal characterization was a technique for implying mutual understanding. In "The Loneliness of the Long-Distance Runner," by Alan Sillitoe, on the other hand, the narrator divides the world into "us" and "you." *We,* the narrator and his kind, are the outlaws, all those who live by their illegal wits; and *you,* the readers, are by contrast law-abiding, prosperous, educated, and rather dull. To quote again from "The Loneliness of the Long-Distance Runner":

> I suppose you'll laugh at this, me saying the governor's a stupid bastard when I know hardly how to write and he can read and write and add-up like a professor. But what I say is true right enough. He's stupid and I'm not, because I can see further into the likes of him than he can see into the likes of me.

The clear implication here is that the narrator can see further into the likes of us readers than we can see into the likes of him, and much of the effective irony of the story rests in the fact that the more we applaud and identify with the narrator, the more we must accept his condemning characterization of "us."

Another Character
More specifically still, the story may be told to *another character or characters,* in which case we as readers "overhear" it; the teller of the tale does not acknowledge us even by implication. Just as the third-person author telling "her story" is theoretically more impersonal than the first-person character telling "my story," so "the reader" is theoretically a more impersonal receiver of the tale than another character. I insert the word *theoretically* because, with regard to point of view more than any other element of fiction, any rule laid down seems to be an invitation to rule breaking by some original and inventive author.

In the *epistolary* novel or story, the narrative consists entirely of letters written from one character to another, or between characters.

> I, Mukhail Ivanokov, stone mason in the village of Ilba in the Ukrainian Soviet Socialist Republic, greet you and pity you, Charles Ashland, petroleum merchant in Titusville, Florida, in the United States of America. I grasp your hand.
>
> Kurt Vonnegut, "The Manned Missiles"

Or the convention of the story may be that of a monologue, spoken aloud by one character to another.

> May I, *monsieur,* offer my services without running the risk of intruding? I fear you may not be able to make yourself understood by the worthy ape who presides over the fate of this establishment. In fact, he speaks nothing but Dutch. Unless you authorize me to plead your case, he will not guess that you want gin.
>
> Albert Camus, *The Fall*

Again, the possible variations are infinite; the narrator may speak in intimate confessional to a friend or lover, or may present his case to a jury or a mob; she may be writing a highly technical report of the welfare situation, designed to hide her emotions; he may be pouring out his heart in a love letter he knows (and we know) he will never send.

In any of these cases, the convention employed is the opposite of that employed in a story told to "the reader." The listener as well as the teller is involved in the action; the assumption is not that we readers are there but that we are not. We are eavesdroppers, with all the ambiguous intimacy that position implies.

Gary Provost

The Secrets of Writing Powerful Dialogue

"Janet," I said to one of my seminar students, "what do you do for a living?"

"I'm a waitress," she said.

"That's nice," I said.

Thirty other people were in the room, listening to this conversation. They were bored.

"Janet," I said again, "what do you do for a living?"

"I'm a waitress," she said again.

"A waitress?" I said. "Don't you think that's a pretty moronic way to make a living?"

"Well, well no," she said. "I like it."

"You like it? You're sitting there seriously telling me that you actually like lugging hamburgers around for a bunch of idiots who don't know how to cook?"

By now all the people in the seminar were leaning in the direction of the conversation. They wondered what Janet would say next, and what I would say after that. They cared about the conversation. I had their attention.

I carry on conversations like this once at every seminar to point out one of the common mistakes writers make in using dialogue in fiction and nonfiction. It is one of six dialogue mistakes I have found over and over again during a year of reading and critiquing manuscripts, and I will tell you about it after we've discussed the other five.

1. Too Many Direct References

When was the last time you had a conversation like this?

"Hi Randy, how you doing?"

"Oh, I'm fine, Gail. I see you've got a new dog."

"Yes, Randy, a cocker spaniel."

"That's a nice looking dog, Gail."

Probably never. Occasionally when we speak to someone, we use his name. Usually it's an expression of affection. And many times parents use a name when they are angry, as in "Jamey Murphy, you get out of that trash barrel right this instant." But that's about it. In real life we rarely use the name of the person we are speaking to, and the listener's name should occur just as infrequently in your dialogue. New writers have a habit of using it constantly. It's awkward, it's artificial, and it marks the writer as an amateur.

Can you hear the awkwardness, the intrusive quality of the direct references in the exchange between Randy and Gail? The dialogue is like a stream and the *Randy*s and *Gail*s are like boulders interrupting the flow. Now read the dialogue without the *Gail*s and *Randy*s and you'll hear the dialogue flow more smoothly.

Using direct reference is just a bad habit, and you can break it easily. If you glance at a page and see that you have one character using the other's name ten times, cross out at least eight of them. Then read the dialogue without the other two. You probably don't even need them.

If you are making this mistake because you think the reader won't know who is speaking to whom, don't worry about it. The reader has a number of clues. The change in paragraphs signals a new speaker. The attribution (*he said, she said,* etc.) shows who is speaking. The style of speech often tells the reader who is speaking. And, of course, the content of the dialogue tells the reader who is speaking. If we know that Gail owns the dog, there's no doubt about who Randy is speaking to when he says, "Your miserable mutt nearly chewed my leg off and I'm going to sue you for every cent you have."

The only time you should use direct address is when you are getting something in return for it, such as characterization or story value. The word *Gail* in "Well, Gail, I see you have a new dog," doesn't do any work. But if you wrote "Well, honey, I see that you have a new dog" or "Well, jerko, I see you have a new dog," the direct address tells the reader how the speaker feels about the person he is speaking to, and it communicates the tone of the conversation.

2. Describing Dialogue

Writers often are insecure about their dialogue because they aren't sure the reader can hear the tone of voice, understand the implication. They try to solve the problem by describing the dialogue. The character says something, then the writer tells you *how* he said it. The tools the writer most often uses to make this mistake are verbs and adverbs. With verbs it looks like this.

"I'm not afraid of you," I announced.
"Oh," Joel snarled, "what are you going to do, scare me off with a song?"
"Maybe," I shot back.
"Or maybe you're going to hit me with a karate chop," he chided.

In this case the variety of verbs (*announced, snarled, chided,* etc.) is distracting, silly and unnecessary. When we know the characters and the situation, we can hear the tone of voice without the writer interrupting the dialogue to tell us.

Here is how the same mistake would look with adverbs.

"I'm not afraid of you," I said quickly.
"Oh," Joel said, sarcastically, "what are you going to do, scare me off with a song?"
"Maybe," I replied weakly.
"Or maybe you're going to hit me with a karate chop," he said derisively.

The writer in this case thinks he's improving the dialogue by writing *sarcastically, derisively,* etc. In fact, he is robbing the dialogue of its impact and its spontaneity by constantly interrupting to explain how something was said. That dialogue is from *Popcorn* (Bradbury Press), a children's novel my wife and I wrote. But when we wrote the dialogue, we didn't use any adverbs or any verbs, except *said,* a word so common and so easily understood that it sails right by without interrupting the dialogue.

Use *said* or no verb at all most of the time. Rarely use adverbs to describe dialogue, and only when necessary. Remember that 90% of your dialogue should contain its own tone of voice, and not require explaining. Your reader is no dummy. If you have given him a clear sense of who your character is and what he is experiencing, the reader will hear the tone of voice without your explaining.

Much will depend on the characterization you have done in other parts of the story, but one key to getting tone of voice into dialogue is to do what professional actors do when they work on lines. For each character, ask the questions, "What is my motivation?" and "What am I feeling as I speak these lines?" Often a writer throws lines of dialogue down on paper without really thinking about the emotions of the character. So, get inside the character's skin. Is he angry? Scared? Is he offended by what was just said? Amused? Is he trying to be clever, or is he trying to hurt someone's feelings, or make her laugh, or manipulate her? What is he trying to accomplish with these words that he is speaking? If you can feel what your character feels, your reader will probably hear what you hear.

3. Heavy-Handed Dialogue

Heavy-handed dialogue occurs when the reader can see the writer at work, loading the dialogue with a lot of information that just wouldn't come out in normal conversation. Most of the manuscripts I read were loaded with heavy-handed dialogue. Here's an example.

> "You and I stole ten thousand dollars, Sam. We embezzled it from the Valentine Corporation, and when Jervis inspects the books on June fifth he's going to know it. Your brother Warren is a lawyer and he's married to Valentine's sister. I say we tell him," Tony said.
>
> "We can't tell anybody. You're already on probation for beating up that guy at the Rainbow Lounge last summer, and how long do you think I would last as a cashier at Rockingham Race Track if they knew I stole ten thousand bucks on my last job?"

It's obvious that the dialogue is there not to inform the characters, but because the writer wants to communicate it to the reader. The reader is annoyed, just as he would be if he could see how the magician was palming the cards.

Dialogue should be lean, and to the point. It should not be weighted down with details and background information.

There are two ways to solve the heavy-handed dialogue problem. One is to be direct, not devious. For example:

> Sam's brother was a lawyer and he was married to Valentine's sister.
> "We've got to tell your brother," Tony said. "He's the only one who can help us."

This doesn't disturb the reader because it implies what Tony was thinking. We will believe Tony was thinking about the fact that Sam's brother is a lawyer married to Valentine's sister. We won't believe that Tony would tell Sam things Sam obviously knows.

The other way to repair this heavy-handed dialogue is to be devious, but not direct.

You can get information across to readers in dialogue smoothly if you make the reader believe the character would say that. A speaker can believably repeat information the listener knows if the information answers a question, or requires emphasis. For example:

> "Ten thousand bucks, Sam, that's what we stole and I don't think the Valentine Corporation is going to overlook it when they find out."
>
> "How are they going to find out?"
>
> "Jervis is checking the books on June fifth. He'll spot it. We've got to tell your brother."
>
> "What the hell has my brother got to do with this?"
>
> "He's a lawyer, isn't he? He's married to Valentine's sister. He can get us off the hook."

"No. We can't tell anybody."

"Why not?"

"You're already on probation for that fiasco at the Rainbow Lounge."

"Look, I never beat that guy up. I was framed."

"Doesn't matter. The court says you did it. And what about me? You think the Rockingham Race Track is going to be thrilled to find out one of their cashiers stole ten thousand dollars from his last employer?"

If a speaker is giving a listener information the listener doesn't *need,* then the speaker must have a *need* of his own. In my last example, Tony *needs* to convince Sam to tell Sam's brother. Sam *needs* to convince Tony to keep their secret. The important thing is that each speaker is speaking out of *his own need, not the need of his listener.* The dialogue becomes heavy-handed when the speaker starts throwing in known information that can't serve his need. For example: "Doesn't matter. The court says you did it. And what about me? Do you think Roz Bagley, my boss at the Rockingham Race Track in Salem, is going to be thrilled when she finds out that one of her cashiers, along with you, stole ten thousand dollars last June from the Valentine Corporation?"

So when you hunt for heavy-handed dialogue to cut from your manuscript, ask yourself, "Is this information known to the listener?" If the answer is yes, ask, "Is repeating this information serving some need of my speaker?" If the answer is no, get rid of it, or rewrite it so that it does serve some need of your speaker.

4. Unnecessary Dialogue

Dialogue has a number of legitimate jobs. It moves the story forward. It characterizes people in the story. It provides information. But dialogue should never be used to fill up space on the page, to create scenes that could be replaced with a simple transition, or to cover ground that could be covered more quickly or more effectively with simple narrative. That's unnecessary dialogue.

One of the most common examples is dialogue in introductions.

"Beverly, I'd like you to meet William Warner," Angie said. I reached out and shook Mr. Warner's hand.

"Hi Beverly," he said, smiling.

"And this young lady is Mr. Warner's secretary, Deanna Frost," Angie said. "Deanna, this is Beverly Conti."

We shook hands. "Hi Deanna."

"Hi," she said. "Nice to meet you."

Some writers do this every time one character is introduced to another throughout a novel. It's boring. Just write: "Angie introduced me to Mr. Warner and Deanna Frost, his secretary." Then get on with it.

Also don't have characters saying things if you can say them better yourself. To use an example from nonfiction, my book *Fatal Dosage* has Anne Caputo, defendant in a murder trial, coming to the courthouse for the first time. I could have created dialogue like this:

> "The courthouse is kind of scary, isn't it?" she said to Pat. "It looks like a big granite monster that's going to gobble me up."
> "I suppose," Pat said, "but at a time like this everything is frightening."
> "Yes," she said, "even you. You look like you're on your way to accept an award. With your three-piece suit and your brief case, you're really one of them, aren't you?"
> "What do you think is in this brief case, Anne? The secrets of the bomb?"

I could have gone on like this and created an acceptable dialogue scene. But I wanted to create a sense of Anne's aloneness, her isolation even from her own lawyer, and I knew I could do it better than my characters could. So the dialogue was unnecessary. I wrote it this way:

> As Anne followed Pat Piscitelli along the courthouse path that sunny morning she trembled inside. She felt as if the courthouse were a huge granite monster waiting to gobble her up. The building was frightening. But then, she thought, everything is frightening. Even Pat, walking ahead of her in lively steps as if he were on his way to accept an award. He wore an expensive three-piece suit, and a brief case hung from his hand. He seemed to be one of "them" and that's what frightened her. The brief case reminded Anne of the man who follows the President around, carrying a brief case handcuffed to his wrist. The secrets of the bomb are in Pat's brief case, she thought, and she wondered who would win the war.

So, dialogue is unnecessary when it's used to do work that could be done by a simple sentence like, "Marie introduced me to her parents"; when it does work you could do more effectively another way; when it doesn't reveal character or move the story forward; and when there is no tension present in the scene, which I'll explain when we get to common dialogue mistake #6.

5. Repeated Information in Dialogue

When I first became a newspaper reporter, I had a bad habit of stating something, and then repeating it in quotes. Typically, I would write something like this:

> Mayor Ferguson told the City council last night that he will not support the bond issue for a new recreation center.
> "I've decided not to support the bond issue for the new recreation center," he told the packed council chambers.

Of course, I was getting paid by the column inch so maybe my redundancy was making me richer. But that kind of redundancy in your dialogue, another common mistake, will only make you poorer. Here's an example from one of the manuscripts I read.

> Holly had quit her job as a secretary to form her own company, Colorwear. She would take common sweatshirts and T-shirts and, with an airbrush and immense talent, turn them into works of art.

And then, a few pages later.

> "I quit my secretary job to form my own company. It's called Colorwear."
> "What do you do?" Paul asked.
> "I do airbrush paintings on sweatshirts and T-shirts, that sort of thing."

One of those sections must go. Which one? It depends. If you just want to get some information across, some foundation for future story events, a few direct sentences of narrative will work best. If you're trying to show some conflict, some tension, some character, or something developing in a relationship, the dialogue will work best. The dialogue, of course, can accomplish both jobs, but it usually takes up more space. If you spend more words, you should get more work done. But remember, dialogue that only repeats information is doing no work at all.

6. Dialogue Without Tension

Do you remember my conversations with Janet the waitress that opened this article? The first was boring and the second was not, because the first had no tension. I asked Janet what she did for a living, she told me and I said, "That's nice." There were no unanswered questions, nothing more for her to say, and no resulting conflict between us.

In the second conversation, I ridiculed her job. She had to defend herself. I had to support my previous statements. Eventually she would have had to criticize me. I would have had to insult her, and maybe we would have started throwing punches at each other. That's tension. What will she say to that? What will he answer? Will they slug each other? Tension makes the reader ask questions, and it makes him continue reading for the answers.

Whenever you write dialogue, tension should be present. It doesn't have to be two people on the verge of a fight. It could be two people in love, each trying to get the other to say it. It could be two people cracking a safe. It could be two people talking about almost anything, but an element of tension must be present in the scene for the dialogue to hold the reader.

Many writers write dialogue that has information, but no tension:

"I'm glad you made it," Ellen said when her mother arrived at the door. "I was getting worried."

Marge came in and dropped her bags on the floor. "I got tied up in traffic on the Connecticut Turnpike. It's a real mess today."

"Did you stop to eat?"

"Yes. I stopped at Burger King for one of those, what do you call them?"

"Whoppers," Ellen said. "They call them Whoppers."

This dialogue is believable, but it's not exciting. It doesn't fascinate the reader because it doesn't create questions in his mind. It doesn't make him worry or wonder about what happens next. Tension could be added to this scene in a variety of ways. You could put tension directly into the spoken words. For example:

"Well, you finally made it," Ellen said when her mother arrived at the door. "I was getting worried. I wish you had at least called."

"Called? How am I going to call when I'm stuck in the middle of the Connecticut Turnpike? It's murder out there."

"Well I hope you at least had enough sense to stop and eat. You know how your blood sugar is."

"I ate, I ate."

"Where, Ma, where did you eat?"

"I stopped at Burger King, I had one of those Big Macs."

"Whoppers, Ma, Whoppers, that's what they call them. Big Macs are at McDonald's."

"OK, so I had a Whopper."

In that example, the tension is between the characters and it comes out in the words they speak, the dialogue. However, tension in a dialogue scene doesn't have to be in the dialogue. In this next example I will leave the dialogue just as it was originally, but I will increase reader interest by adding tension between the lines of dialogue. Also, I will change the source of the tension to show you that the two characters don't have to be antagonistic toward each other.

"I'm glad you made it," Ellen said when her mother arrived at the door. "I was getting worried."

Marge came in and dropped her bags on the floor. She stood by the counter as if she needed it to hold herself up and she took deep breaths. For the first time she looked old, frail. The light had gone from her eyes. Ellen's heart pounded.

"I got tied up in traffic on the Connecticut Turnpike. It's a real mess today," Marge said when she finally caught her breath.

"Did you stop to eat?"

"Yes, I stopped at Burger King for one of those, what do you call them?"

"Whoppers," Ellen said impatiently. "They call them Whoppers." Tonight she would cook, she thought, cook her mother a good healthful meal, and then everything would be all right.

So tension is that quality of "something else going on" during the dialogue. It's what makes the reader concerned enough or curious enough to keep reading even when the actual spoken words are mundane. Remember, if the reader doesn't care what happens next, the dialogue is not working.

There's no absolute rule about when you use dialogue and when you shouldn't, but here's a good generalization: If a stranger were nearby, would he try to eavesdrop on the conversation? If the answer is no, don't use the dialogue. If the answer is yes, use it. And you can quote me on that.

Robyn Carr

"Dialogue," Said the Writer, "Is a Fantastic Tool for Enriching and Enlivening Your Fiction."

When I'm reading a book so involving that I still turn pages when the print is blurring, I find myself scanning long narrative paragraphs, searching for quotation marks. I don't miss a word in quotes; I want to know what *the characters* are saying to each other. *They* are the story. And they should help tell their own stories.

In social interaction, we use verbal communication in only about one fourth of our communication. Nonverbal signals carry the rest: diverted eyes, arms crossed protectively, knees spread and arms slack in openness, reception. When you have a "feeling" about someone, chances are you subconsciously synthesized all the nonverbal information available to you.

The situation differs in fiction. You must depend more heavily on verbal communication—dialogue—because too much description, too much narrative about characters, is weighty and straining. And, as in life, the reader doesn't really know those characters until they actually speak.

The part of the book that appears in quotes determines whether the entire story is convincing, *real*. Characters must live up to their creation by the way they speak, when they speak, how they speak and what they say.

> "Ah, it's you, milord," she giggled.
> "Have you had the opportunity—"
> "Aye, 'e just left, milord. A bit sooner and you'd 'ave passed 'im on the stair. I'll 'ave me money first, milord."
> "Then you have something to tell me?"
> "I do, but I'm not 'bout t'be spillin' me guts without me coin. An' I'll not be takin' that stinkin' swine to me bed again. 'E ain't no gentleman. 'E's right mean, 'e is."
> "Did he hurt you?"
> "Aye, 'e did! I'd 'ave turned the beastie out but fer the twenty pound ye said was mine if 'e talked. Squeaked like a parrot."

The woman speaking is a tavern prostitute in 17th-century England, in my novel, *Chelynne*. She is inarticulate, opportunistic, self-centered and slovenly. Narrative description of her surroundings and physical appearance imparted one dimension of her character; another came to life with her words. How you build, reinforce and solidify characterization with dialogue determines whether the events and people you write about are at all believable.

With that in mind, consider these three rules for effective dialogue.

Rule #1: Dialogue should tell the reader something about the character's personality or emotions, or at least reinforce something already established—anger, impatience, perfectionism, timidity, cruelty, etc. Ordinary greetings, farewells and small talk about the weather seldom fulfill this first rule. But don't necessarily give up these conversational gimmicks; *use* them. In my novel *The Blue Falcon* I used one such greeting.

> Edythe stopped when she saw him and paused for a moment to behold him. "I was afraid you would not come."

She could have said "good evening," and the writer, the narrative, could have explained that she had been afraid he wouldn't come. We might believe it, but we wouldn't know her as well.

Rule #2: Dialogue must propel the plot, so that we get to know characters through the way they react to the external stimuli that direct and manipulate their lives. Their words must establish or reinforce their feelings, their relationships to each other, and the parts they specifically play in the plot—all in an effort to heighten the conflict and tension. (Remember this, even when writing comedy—characters reacting, bouncing off each other, is conflict in its technical definition.)

From *The Blue Falcon:*

> "Do not push me too far, Tedric," she warned. "If I do find a way to money, mayhaps I will use it to have you killed."

The threat and evident anger shows something about the woman speaking and elevates the tension because it adds another possibility to the plot—*will* she find a way to have him killed? Will he, in a defensive move, get rid of her? Because of the many variables, the reader keeps reading to see which way the plot will go . . . because of what one character said and how she said it.

Rule #3: Dialogue must individualize each character. We all sound different, use different words, expressions, euphemisms, dialects, speech styles and varied inflections. *What* we say, *how* we say it, *when* we choose to speak reflects who we really are. Our personal habits, value systems, emotions, motivation, and the many varied circumstances we're in define our own speech. The characters in a book can no more sound alike than the people in our various neighborhoods and families.

If you desexed and numbered your characters, would they stand apart from each other?

From *The Blue Falcon* three characters, all from similar social spheres and economic and educational levels, speak:

"You will be punished for your sinful lust!"

"When the punishments are being given out, madam, I think mine will be the lesser crime."

"Jesu, should the two of you live under the same roof I dare not guess which would survive."

Although the characters have much in common, they have some distinct differences. One is as strong as the others, but is more driven to maintain honor and dignity—she is not always aggressive, but neither is she squeamish about defending herself. Another is timid and evasive, fleeing from conflict whenever possible. In fact, if she were attacked verbally, she would more likely weep than argue. The third is aggressive, hostile and so single-minded that she appears most often as abrasive and threatening—unless she uses contrived sweetness to gain something for herself. From the dialogue above and these brief personality descriptions, you should be able to match the speaker with the quotation.

Silence Is Not Golden

Every piece of dialogue has a big job to accomplish for the story. Here are some exercises to help make that job routine rather than complex and difficult.

Create a character sheet. This is a crucial beginning to establish who the characters are. First outline the physical description of the character and basic background information (i.e., where she was raised, by whom, the basic conditions thereof, significant life experiences, etc.). Next consider more pertinent information that will affect her dialogue:

● Consider her literacy and how articulate she is in conversation. List special components like the tone of her voice, the quality (hoarse, weak, squeaky, loud, soft, etc.) of the voice, verbal ticks, ability to speak on the spot, directness, evasiveness, dialect, jargon, colloquialisms, choice of words (does he/she swear habitually? Use slang or the King's English?), abruptness, single-word answers, questions for answers, speechy and long-winded phrasings (specifically—long speeches that are meaningless, or long, articulate and well-chosen words?).

● Outline the history and motivation of the character; is she aggressive, wicked, single-minded, generous, polite, abrasive, sensitive, honor-bound, honest, irreverent, spoiled, power-seeking, insecure . . . the list goes on and on comprising virtually every personality trait.

● Add the important dimension of how the character sees herself. Is she angry because she is frightened? Because she has been wronged? Because she has never been loved? Because she is hurt? She's chronically angry and discontent? It takes little to anger her. Determine such things as whether her education gave her an edge in society so that she expresses herself with articulate conviction, or was college forced on her by a threatening parent and does she reject it, collapsing in social interraction?

Remember how combinations of traits will affect a character's personality and speech. For example:

Character traits: uneducated, contemptible.
Dialogue: incomplete, curt sentences, common use of slang and name-calling, loud voice that interrupts frequently, brief insulting quips, expresses anger rather than ideas.
Character traits: uneducated, sensitive.
Dialogue: poor grammar and usage, asks obvious questions, heavy slang, inoffensive, friendly chatter, thick dialect, relies on common polite responses.

As you determine which dialogue traits go with which character traits, your worksheet will become more involved because of the many possible combinations. And as long as your character remains true to the design, you will have created a distinct, complex and interesting person. Rethink the combinations if opposites begin to mingle. It will be hard to convince a reader that a character can be shy, uneducated, fearful and still speak with good grammar in a loud clear voice. A powerful and direct person will not stutter and blush in a new introduction.

The character worksheet gives you an intimate knowledge of your characters that you can use to determine what they are likely to say, when they are likely to speak and how they will deliver their words. For example, two characters in *The Blue Falcon* are sisters, raised in the same house. They even look very much alike. But my character work-sheet notes that one was ill as a child and indulged. Not only has illness become an escape for her, but also she has become so passive that her voice is light and soft, and she withdraws from conflict. When she speaks, her motivation is almost always to avoid conflict. The younger sister was healthier, robust and energetic. Her voice is firmer, more res-olute and (perhaps because she could play hard, challenge herself regu-larly and was praised for doing so) she does not cringe from conflict, but faces it with conviction.

> Chandra: "How do you abide that woman?"
> Edwina (laughing softly): "Though it would be a fancy sight if you were ever near to protect me from her, I doubt I could bear the strain. Je-su, should the two of you ever live under the same roof I dare not guess which would survive."
> Chandra: "Have no doubts who it would be, Edwina. You should not let her treat you so badly!"
> Edwina (shrugging): "But what is to be gained by fighting her? Bet-ter to bear what she flings at me as quietly as I can and let it affect me but little."

Use the unexpected voice. There is a difference between *out-of-character* dialogue and *unpredictable* behavior. A docile woman who has always loved and respected her father would neither speak brutally to him or curse him, but she might have a tear-filled argument with him. Letting one of your characters speak out of character robs you of all the work you've done in making her believable. But an unpredictable re-sponse now and then adds depth and intrigue to the story.

For example, Chelynne is strong-willed, but polite. She is attractive and educated, and she chooses her words carefully—indeed, her words are most often well thought and cautious—until her husband's ex-lover visits and they both taunt her maliciously. When her husband insists on her polite presence at dinner (a tremendously challenging situation), she loses her temper in a rare shouting match: "On my word! You expect me to coddle your whore?" Take note: she *is* strong-willed. She chooses her words carefully and she is articulate. That statement would be out of place if she were not involved in a passionate fight. It is unexpected, but completely within her character.

Play with the extremes. Try writing an entire scene in dialogue; then just in narrative. Unfolding an important scene through the character's words alone eliminates the temptation to explain away an important happening without involving the characters directly. Add to the dia-logue version the best of the narrative—the setting, movements of the people, actions, expressions, tone of voice, special characteristics and descriptions.

Between the two versions, you should come up with a scene that is fully described and actively moving, sustained by characters that are making it all come to life by their words.

Begin at the beginning. Whatever the scene, try writing the dialogue first. Pretend that introductory information has been given and that you're at the heart of the scene. When you go back to revise that scene, you might discover that it needs very little "setup." Maybe only a couple of sentences are required to ease the reader into where and why the actual dialogue is taking place.

One chapter in *The Bellerose Bargain* begins this way:

> "Not another day, lovey, not another minute. I've had my fill of your schemes and deals and should've known before I left the country that you toted a pack of lies from the first."
>
> "There's no place for you to go, save the streets, Charlotte," Perry said coolly. But for all his calm exterior, there was a rage burning inside of him that he found more difficult to control with every passing second.
>
> "Ah, you're wrong about that, love. I'm taking myself to the court and I'll find someone there who'll listen . . ."
>
> Perry's loud and cruel laughter rang through the small, filthy room. "You honestly think anyone will listen to *you?*"

Here I started with the dialogue at the heart of the conflict (Charlotte is running out on her companion in crime) and saw with a second look that I could easily establish the setting and circumstances without writing material that didn't get to the point. For exchanges about the weather or the draperies (unless, of course, the lightning storm will ignite the draperies and burn down the house) people don't have to buy books; they can walk down to the barber shop. There's no reason to play it safe with your character's dialogue. Let them at each other. *You* might have to worry about offending your mother-in-law, but your character might really charge up the story by offending hers.

Don't depend too heavily on dialogue. Recall the last time you heard a good piece of juicy gossip. (Two mothers of Little Leaguers who got into a blistering fight at a game? A salesperson's husband who got drunk at the office Christmas party and insulted the chairman of the board?) If you have ever wished that you could have *been* there rather than hearing about it secondhand, you have the best incentive available for working hard to give your readers the feeling of "being there."

Telling the readers about a duel by having one character "describe" it to another is as frustrating to a reader as hearing about the office Christmas party catastrophe from the receptionist. Quotation marks around narrative information are as flat as day-old beer.

As I Live and Breathe

Characters live when every piece of dialogue further develops the characters' personalities (Rule #1); when the action, tension and drama are heightened because of what they said, how they said it, when they chose to speak (#2); and when the characters' complex individualism sets them apart from each other (#3).

For example, Chelynne, impetuous and high-strung and convinced her husband Chad does not love her, slips into an intimate romantic involvement with his best friend. She is mortified both by her own unexpected passion and his determination that it means nothing, is not binding in any way.

> "Better I should not have known," she murmured.
> "Don't worry with it, love. It's not going to happen again. From now Chad would not allow us in the same room together and it is certain he will be keeping a closer eye to you."
> "He won't even know," she huffed, turning away from him.
> "He will know," John returned, gently touching her hair.
> "He wouldn't care if he did," she said dejectedly.
> "You're wrong, darling. For this he will kill me."

I'm not going to tell you what happens, because *if* Chad finds out and *if* he kills his best friend and *if* Chelynne is wrong and Chad truly does love her, you won't hear about it thirdhand. *The characters* will tell you themselves.

Rust Hills

Setting

Setting is often described as "the element of place or location in fiction"—*locale* was the old-fashioned word for it. But setting implies location in time, time of day as well as historic time, and such matters as the weather out of doors or the temperature in the room where it all happens—all of these factors are customarily included in the term "setting." It may seem of small consequence, and in stories where the setting doesn't matter, it *is* of small consequence. But in successful stories, where everything works together, it's useful to see what choice of setting contributes. With a writer like Hemingway, for instance, who seemed to have a choice of milieu for his stories—Spain, Africa, upstate Michigan, and so on—one could easily think through why each story is set wherever it is. Putting aside biographical considerations, one sees that it is the perfect setting chosen, and that it contributes to the whole successful unity of the story.

As with all other aspects of a successful story, the setting may be basic to the original conception or may be the result of conscious and deliberate choice in the course of composition. If it is a question of choice, then the first decision about setting for any author—especially the author of a short story, where economy is always at such a premium—is the selection of the place itself, for here he can make use of certain attributes of his setting that already exist either actually in the place itself, or can be presumed to exist in the reader's conception of the place, without having to create these connotations himself.

One notices this best if he has the occasion to consider a number of stories by different authors all about the same place—as, for instance, in preparing an anthology of stories about New York City. Virtually every American writer has written a New York City story—Melville, Crane, James, Fitzgerald, Wharton, Wolfe, and Malamud, Cheever, and James Baldwin, and so on—and it is fascinating to see how the single similar element, setting, functions in each in a different successful way. You could do the same with a group of stories about "the sea" or "Paris" or "farm life" or "the South" or "suburbia" or whatever. I put each of these locales in quotation marks, for it is their connotations as much as their actuality that is put to work in fiction.

In the case of New York City, for instance, it is clearly a place about which certain generalizations can be made—whether they are inaccurate clichés or even contradictory is not important—and this makes the city useful and effective as a setting for an apparently limitless variety of situations and themes. In terms of plot and character, there is so much mobility in the city, both upward and downward, that it is an appropriate setting for any character's quick rise or fall. Because the city has more people of all social classes in close-crowded conjunction, it is an appropriate setting for any odd encounter—as between an actress and a bum, between a playboy and a secretary—with corresponding opportunities for depicting the injustices of social distinction and the extremes of poverty and wealth. New York City is between America and Europe and hence is a likely scene for conflict between the two. There are, in fact, so many comings and goings of all sorts in New York that an author can make virtually any plot or characterization plausible.

Achieving an Effect

Many of the traditional themes of fiction—the corrupting powers of ambition, the nature of one's responsibility to self and to others, the tragedy of loneliness, the paradoxes and ambiguities of compromise—all seem congenial to the city's qualities—its crowded loneliness, its veneration for the new, its bustling immorality, its commercialism, its sense of busy pointlessness. The city is available as a symbol of opportunity and freedom and success, and of the empty underside of these qualities. Useful as these connotations of New York have been to many writers, however, it would be absurd to set a story there, rather than some place that is better known to the author, if that place would function as well in his story.

Conrad used the sea, Faulkner used the South, Cheever used suburbia, and in so doing, these authors managed to create, from story to story and from novel to novel, a world with connotations not just of the place itself, but from their own individual perception and creation of it. Setting can work this way: There can be a valuable reinforcement back from the depicted "world." Hardy's "Wessex" takes on connotations from book to book that the actual Dorset or West Country never suggest in themselves, and the same is, of course, true of Cheever's "Shady Hill" and Faulkner's "Yoknapatawpha." The beginning writer, however, experimenting, ought not to expect any virtue as such from what's disparagingly called "regionalism." What he should concern himself with is how the setting of each story enhances it, or can be made to do so.

This is as likely to be achieved by description of place as it is by choice of place. "Description" has been given a bad reputation by bad writers. Reading Sir Walter Scott, you'd skip the "description"—he'd imprison a heroine and then describe the castle for two pages, how and when and whyfore it was built, and what of, stone by boring stone. It was description for description's sake, or for "verisimilitude" or "historical accuracy" or something. It had no integral part, no function in the narrative, and one was right to skip it. This is not true of a passage of description in Thomas Hardy or any other good writer, where the description contributes to the whole work symbolically or emotionally—enhancing in a variety of ways that can be demonstrated.

"Passages" of description, as such, seldom appear in today's fiction, at least not long ones. But whatever description is provided can be analyzed, can be shown to be "loaded" or "slanted" or "colored" in such a way as to achieve an effect. The language can be effectively freighted (with adjectives or adverbs that are dolorous or cheerful or whatever); details of the place described can be selected or omitted depending on the sort of effect desired; or the point-of-view character can be made to view the setting with an attitude which suitably colors the description of it. There are these and all sorts of other ways in which an author can render the setting so as to create a desired effect.

In fact, it is an instructive exercise for a beginning writer to put himself to: to describe the exact same place—a room or a garden or a city street—in two ways, first as forbidding, say, then as attractive, without changing many of the actual details.

But that is, of course, simply an exercise. What matters is to render the setting of a specific story exactly so it perfectly enhances all the other aspects of that story. A passage of description should foreshadow action for the reader, whether symbolically or otherwise; the perception of the setting should help delineate character, whether of the point-of-view character or otherwise. Henry James, speaking of the artificiality of separating "parts" of fiction, said he could not "conceive a passage of description that is not in its intention narrative, nor a passage of dialogue that is not in its intention descriptive." Thus the setting must contribute to the other aspects of the story, as well as to the whole.

Roy Sorrels

How to Start Smart

Let's start with a tea cup. Imagine this: Someone is slowly pushing a valuable tea cup along the smooth surface of a table, toward the edge. As long as the tea cup is near the center of the table there is no drama, little imminent interest. But as the cup inches closer and closer to the edge of the table, and especially when it teeters on the brink, ready to crash to the floor, there is suspense, drama, a sense of wondering what will happen next.

Think of the tea cup as the central character in your story, and the moment of the cup teetering on the edge of the table as your story's opening. Your imaginary character had a childhood, grew up, had all sorts of experiences in his imaginary life. He got up this morning, showered and brushed his teeth and got dressed—that's the tea cup near the middle of the table, edging along. But now, at the moment that the story is beginning, we see your character *teetering on the edge of something*.

That's the moment when you start your story. Things will never be the same again, change is imminent, suspense is percolating, and the reader wants to know what happens next.

The first sentence of a story, any story, has one basic function. Whatever else it accomplishes, its primary purpose is simply to make readers want to read the second sentence; and the first paragraph should make them want to read the second paragraph. And so on.

Character Sketch

Think about the way most of us read short stories. When we go to a movie or a play we've made a commitment, we've bought a ticket, we're sitting there comfortably in the theatre, and we're not likely to get up and leave even if the first five minutes don't grab us in some way. But with a short story it's very easy to flip to another page of the magazine and read that article on the latest diet; in an anthology we can simply move on to the next story.

Even when watching TV we often sit there, too inert to flip the dial, and submit to something that's not all that interesting. But readers never continue to read a short story that doesn't immediately interest them enough to make them want to read on.

Think, too, about how editors read stories, because you've got to *sell* your story before you can even think about thousands of people eagerly reading it. Fiction editors are inundated with submissions, sometimes hundreds in a single week, and it's quite simple for them to slip your manuscript back into its SASE, if the opening doesn't draw them into the story right away. Why should they invest their scarce and valuable time in reading a story by a writer who can't even make the opening paragraph compelling? You can't stand there with a gun to their head saying, "Read on, you'll get to the good part soon." That's like meeting someone at a party who says, "I'm really fascinating when you get to know me, but let me bore you for a while first"; you'll head for the punch bowl.

Your readers start your story in a state of complete ignorance. They need to know some basics.

Who, for example, is the story about? Usually you want your readers to form a picture of your character immediately. They need to know the basics as soon as possible. Gender, for example, approximate age, and social status and race if it's important. In a third person story, revealing this information is relatively easy to accomplish; it's more difficult with a first person point of view.

Something else readers need to know right off is *when* the story is happening, especially if it's not right now. Most readers will, I believe, assume that a story is contemporary until they get information to the contrary. If your story is not set in the present, then you need to convey that information in the first few lines.

Alternate Reality

Where is your story happening? You need to communicate this in the opening, and usually without an elaborate description of setting. Setting, as important as it is, is usually secondary information: Stories are about people and what they do. But *where* they do what they do is crucial also, if, for example, the central character of your story is a priest. Then it makes a lot of difference if we meet him dressed in his vestments saying Mass, or dressed shabbily and wandering the Bowery.

Viewpoint should be clear in the first paragraph. Most readers will probably assume that a story is told in the third person, because that's most common—until they find out otherwise. So if you're writing in anything other than third person, make that clear as soon as you can.

And in a first person story with a male byline, most readers will assume a male narrator, and *vice versa,* so if your narrator is the other gender, make that clear. No one likes to read the first couple pages of a story assuming that Joe is telling the story, and find out later that it's really Josephine.

Your readers will also want to know *why* they should care. What's at stake? What's the *conflict?* Sometimes you can put this in the very opening lines of the story; sometimes you can delay the tension. But the longer you wait, the longer you keep this vital information from the reader, the greater the risk they'll opt for the diet article on the next page. They *already* care, after all, about losing weight.

Creating fiction is more than a little like making love. Many of the same techniques apply. There's a bit of seduction, there's a conspiracy of pleasure that you want your reader to join in, and there's the importance of being considerate to the state of mind of your co-conspirator.

When your readers sit down and open a magazine or a short story anthology, they are surrounded by a very real, very compelling world and need to be seduced into the alternate reality of your story. The readers' real world is filled with sharp images, with things and people they care about, with personal problems and real conflicts. How can we possibly compete with this real world? The advantage is that when our readers pick up that magazine and turn to the short story, they are begging to be taken away from it all.

They *want* to be involved in an alternate reality, they want to leave the kids and the sink full of dirty dishes and their jobs and their spouses and problems behind for awhile. They start out on our side. What we must do is try not to disappoint them—we must immediately create a compelling alternate reality for them.

Never the Same . . .

Here are some specific ways to do just that:

First, *don't start at the beginning.* Neophyte writers start countless terrible short stories with the sound of an alarm clock. The hero wakes up, stretches, climbs out of bed, showers, shaves, brushes his teeth, eats breakfast. We get lots of mundane details of his personal life, realistically depicted. Somewhere about page three something interesting may happen, but few readers stick with one of these "alarm clock" stories long enough to find that out.

So, the corollary to this rule is *plunge right in.* Start when the tea cup begins to teeter. Or you can *start* the story as close as reasonably possible to the *end* of the story.

Another way to seduce your readers into your story is to *give them some really fine writing in the first couple of lines*. Now it's possible there are lots of readers out there who wouldn't know fine writing if it punched them in the nose. But unconsciously at least every reader will respond to an arresting image, a fresh metaphor, a crackling line of dialogue, a flash of humor. Of course, the rest of your story should be filled with fine writing too, but don't save your really good stuff for later. Remember, the first line is to make them want to read the second line, and. . . .

You can also capture your readers' interest in the opening lines of your story by *a strong appeal to their senses*. We experience our everyday world through sight and sound and touch and taste and smell, and you can ease your readers into your short story world by a strong appeal to one or more senses.

Or show us someone *arriving* or *departing*. "Once upon a time a man without a penny in his pocket left his village to seek his fortune." "A few minutes past dawn on a quiet Tuesday a tall dark stranger with a scar across his face rode into town." Both of these opening lines push the tea-cup to the edge of the table, one with a departure, one with an arrival. They promise that something interesting is beginning and that *things will never be the same again*.

It's this sense that things will never be the same again that will glue your reader to the page.

Another excellent story start is with interesting and involving *dialogue*. But don't begin with "Good morning." "Oh, good morning." "How've you been?" "Fine, and you?" "All right." "Lovely day, eh?" "Uh huh. A little humid." Show us a scene right away, cutting into a conversation that is crackling along at a good clip. Start with conflict, with a character trying to get something he's not sure he can get, or with someone surprising someone, or somebody making somebody angry, or. . . . You get the idea.

Your opening will also set the *tone* of your story. If there's humor in your story, horror, mystery, violence, romance, or a tough, realistic look at contemporary life, let the reader taste it in the opening sentence, the opening paragraphs.

Read on . .

Actually every short story starts not with its first line, but with its *title*. In Lawrence Block's fine collection of short stories entitled *Sometimes They Bite,* we encounter these titles: "Strangers on a Handball Court," "A Bad Night for Burglars," "Like a Thief in the Night." In Simon

Brett's collection, *Tickled to Death,* we find "The Thirteenth Killer,"
and "The Haunted Actress." Wouldn't you be drawn to dip into one of
these rather than something called "The Wash Tub," or "Clouds," or
"Uncle Joe"? Your titles don't have to have the sensationalism of cheap
journalism, but why not make them intriguing: why not let them tease
and tantalize and attract?

One of the best ways to learn to write a terrific opening yourself is to
examine the openings of good stories with a critical writer's eye. Let's
take a look at a couple of beginnings that work, and see why they work.
Here, for example, are the opening few paragraphs of Simon Brett's
brilliant short story, "Tickled To Death."

> If a dead body could ever be funny, this one was. Only intimations of
> his own mortality prevented Inspector Walsh from smiling at the sight.
>
> The corpse in the greenhouse was dressed in a clown's costume.
> Bald plastic cranium with side-tufts of ropey orange hair. Red jacket, too
> long. Black and white check trousers suspended from elastic braces to a
> hooped waistband. Shoes three foot long pointing upwards in strange
> semaphore.
>
> "Boy, he's really turned his toes up," said Sergeant Trooper, who was
> prone to such witticisms even when the corpse was less obviously humor-
> ous.
>
> The clown's face could not be seen. The back of a plate supplied a
> moonlike substitute which fitted well with the overall image.
>
> "Going to look good on the report," Sergeant Trooper continued.
> "Cause of death—suffocation. Murder weapon—a custard pie."

Now, didn't that first paragraph make you want to read the second?
We're given a very arresting image, humorous and deadly. Brett sets a
tone, unmistakably light, and creates some immediate tension with a serious subject: murder. We know immediately who the characters are,
where they are, something about their relationship, their attitudes, and
status.

And here are the opening lines of Roy Sorrels' excellent story, "The
Flower Lady."

> The morning of Gladys Mann's death I pronounced her in excellent
> health and likely to live another twenty years. Well, in my half century or
> so of doctoring I've made my share of errors, but this wasn't one of them.
> Gladys Mann died of a bullet that punctured a lung and nicked an artery. I
> could give you the name of the artery but I won't.
>
> Least I can do though is give you my own name. Dr. Mattie, they call
> me in the small town where I've been practicing medicine for as long as
> most of these folks can remember. Matilda Flint, M.D., grew up here,
> went off to med school and came back in 1935 to cure when I could and
> alleviate some aches and pains when I couldn't.

And to pronounce Gladys Mann dead in the middle of the meadow behind her house a couple of miles outside of town.

Since this is a first person story with a female narrator by a male writer, we need to know right off the gender of the storyteller and we do. We also learn her approximate age, and her profession, and we get a flavor for the kind of folksy old gal she is. We know the setting is a small town. We know something out of the ordinary has happened—the murder of an old woman. And the tone of the story is set clearly through the voice of the first person narrator.

Well, I've given you some rules, and we've looked at ways some of those rules can be practiced. In your own writing you'll undoubtedly come up with some of your own. Your stories will be unique, your way won't necessarily be mine, and every rule will not apply to every story.

Now go back to the one hard and fast rule that never changes, if you want anyone to read your story. *The first sentence has got to make your reader want to read the second . . .* and so on.

Dwight V. Swain

High Middle

It's a terrific story. The beginning hooks you 100 percent. The end leaves you limp and gasping; it's that intense.

Nor is it afflicted by any of the no-no's that too often surface. That is, it isn't bogged down by the presence of too many characters. Or a plot so complicated you need a compass, an Indian guide, and a seeing eye dog to find your way through it. Or a tangle of subplots that confuse you worse than the Okefenokee Swamp on a dark night.

The only trouble lies in the middle. It sags.

And a sagging middle can be the kiss of death.

Don't despair. A sagging middle can be diagnosed and remedied.

What's the problem, then?

Probably it's four-fold.

First, odds are it's *static*.

Second, it doesn't *build*.

Third, it's loaded with *distractions*.

Fourth, essential elements aren't *planted*.

Shall we take these one at a time? Working from the analogy of something with which we're all familiar: a checker game, of all things. (It works just as well with chess, incidentally, or any number of other games. But let's keep it simple.)

You know how it is with checkers. You start with two players, you and an opponent. Or, to translate it into fictional terms, a hero and a villain.

You're the hero, of course. And as you set up the board with your twelve pieces, you plan your strategy: You want to win the game, wipe out Opponent. As a first step, you try to devise an opening move or two or three that will freeze the competition with its brilliance.

Opponent has his own ideas on that. He's already piled up a stack of (checker) monkey wrenches to throw into your plan's machinery. So with each move you make, he plots a countermove. It's designed to rock you on your heels and tilt the game in his favor.

Because each of you has a mind of his own, the game isn't static; it's dynamic. Each move changes the situation. That's what makes the game interesting.

Which brings us back to fiction, short stories, and the first point made above: Stasis is a major hazard when you're writing middle sections. *Change* is what brings the middle to life. Because change creates conflict.

Do Something

Conflict is what middles are built of. Two forces in opposition clash. The balance of power between them shifts. That precipitates a new action or situation. One word, one move, one development gives birth to another.

That's ever so important to remember. A successful story doesn't just lie there in a sodden lump once you've got it started. It grows and mutates. Or, to put it another way, story circumstance is dynamic, just as it is in our hypothetical checker game. Your central character's state of affairs and state of mind keep changing, evolving.

I can't tell you how vital this element of change is. But I can tell you *why* it is. Nothing that stays still holds a reader's attention for too long; and if you don't believe me, try focusing your undivided attention on a doorknob for a couple of minutes.

What does that mean, when it comes to writing? It means that you can't be content just to grab your readers' attention once and let it go at that. Rather, you must *capture* and *recapture* it.

How? You have to introduce new reasons for him to stay awake. You have to keep his eyes open and on the printed page. You have to compete with the TV screen.

To put it in the simplest possible terms, you must refuse to let your story stand still.

When you say that a story stands still, what you really mean is that nothing happens. Or, more specifically, *nothing happens that advances the story.*

Our checkerboard, again, offers us an excellent analogy. Often, in many games, there comes a point when a king is locked in. So locked in that it can move only back and forth from one square to another. The result is a stalemate, a deadlock in which neither player can make progress.

Similarly, the term "action" in a story means more than running in place. Endless kissing of a willing girl is no attention-gripper. Neither is spying that reveals nothing, nor rowing here and there about a lake in search of fish that don't bite. Not when the issue is to win a bride or learn a secret or defeat a villain. That's "nothing" action—action that doesn't advance the story.

Exhibit A: Hero and Girl are ever so much in love. But when they ask Girl's father's blessing on their union, he not only denies it but swears he'll see Hero fired and blacklisted if the unhappy couple even so much as pass the time of day again. Whereupon, Couple moan and groan and gnash their teeth and tear their hair. Eight pages drag by, until a convenient miracle clears the track for them to clinch and close.

Exhibit B: Person or persons unknown slay Heroine's father or brother or beloved. She sets out to bring his killer/killers to justice. But her probings bring denials of knowledge from everyone she queries.

Exhibit C: Contact with alien planet/race/virus/rock group brings devastating outbreak of disease to Earth colonists on Luna. Scientist's efforts to culture the bug that is causing it prove futile.

In each case, for all practical purposes Central Character runs in place. No progress is made. Nothing happens that will advance the story.

What is needed, clearly, is change on a different level. The story demands some sort of development that will knock the situation off dead center. Someone—preferably, Central Character—needs to do something meaningful to the tale being told. It's essential that he or she take action which will transform the opening condition into something new and different. (And again, let me emphasize, it matters not if a hydrogen bomb explodes, nor even if the lost world of Atlantis rises from the sea. Not if it doesn't advance the story. To count, the change *must* move Hero closer to his objective and the story's climax.)

Thus, in Exhibit A, Hero perhaps tells Girl not to worry, because he has a new job already lined up with Father's chief competitor. (Does Girl swoon with delight at this? Or does she view it as treason to Father? A change in state of mind can give shattering birth to an unanticipated state of affairs. After all, one thing ever so frequently leads to another. People don't always react as you expect them to.)

In Exhibit B, quite possibly some odd bit of behavior on the part of one of the people Heroine questions may rouse her suspicions. Maybe, in consequence, she attempts a breaking-and-entering bit. Or she shadows someone. Or she impersonates someone else. Or whatever. The big thing is to keep the story moving and the readers interested. Because otherwise you've lost the game.

Exhibit C? Same difference; there's more to science fiction science than inspecting petri dishes. Remember: *something happens.*

Something big? Something dramatic? Not necessarily. Could be it's only that a culture that's supposed to show red turns up green or blue. And then, after that, for appropriate good and sufficient reasons, one thing leads to another.

Next question: *Why* does a story stand still?

More often than not, *initiative* is the issue.

Specifically, the central character lacks or loses initiative. Faced with a problem, an actual or potential disaster, he sits gnawing his nails while he waits for the feathers to grow.

What he *should* do is *do something*—grab the ball and run with it; drive forward.

For him *not* to do so is a cardinal sin, believe me. Readers by and large feel frustrated and helpless enough in life. Most don't enjoy wallowing in such in stories also. So do strive for dynamic story people if at all possible.

Build

Furthermore—and now we come to point two—your story must *build*.

"To build" in fiction means to intensify interest/excitement in a story—ultimately, it's hoped, to the point that readers can't stop reading.

Back to our checker game. The opening moves are made. You and Opponent—Hero and Villain—are jockeying for position.

That can get pretty dull, upon occasion. So the old Egyptians, or Greeks, or whoever invented checkers, came up with a bright idea to help keep the players awake: the king row.

You know how the king row works. It gives you an intermediate goal—a series of them—to strive for en route to ultimate defeat of Opponent. Each time you get a piece through to it, that piece is "crowned." A crowned piece, a king, acquires added power, added value. It gains the ability to move and jump backward as well as forward.

When you get a king, it strengthens your position and influences the outcome of the game. Given three kings—or even one—to Opponent's none, for instance, the odds in favor of winning move over to your side. Strongly.

That means that each time you maneuver one of your checkers closer to the king row, the game's excitement and tension soar. Both you and Opponent breathe a little faster. Why? Because if one player gets a king, he's revealed to be stronger and harder to beat. So though this is only a game, an added element of worry has been introduced. You feel what amounts to fear vibrations. For thanks to that new king, the potential outcome of the game has been influenced pro or con.

In a word, because of that worry, that fear, the game's excitement *builds*.

Same way with a story. Once it's started, the situation established, the middle segments must see interest, excitement, tension grow. If they don't, odds are that your reader will stop reading.

How do you bring about an appropriate rise in tension?

Two steps are involved: 1) You create a character your reader wants to see succeed or fail, win or lose. (Yes, a character can be negative as well as positive. Readers can want to see an appropriately malevolent character lose. But positive sells better, and I have the rejection slips to prove it.)

How do you create such a character? You give him such appealing hopes/dreams/strivings that Reader is caught up in them. Largely, the issue is one of caring. We'll talk about that later.

2) You plunge this character into more and more threatening situations. That way, your reader experiences increasingly intense fear that some danger/disaster will befall Character.

In other words, you increase Character's peril, physical and/or emotional, a step at a time, as if she were climbing a damaged stair. It may collapse at any moment. Thus, Reader's fear that disaster will strike down Character is increased with every step Character takes.

(In practical terms, not the worst way in the world to manage this is to make a list of bad things rooted in the story situation which might possibly strike Character—and the worse, the better. Then, play jigsaw puzzle with them, muscling Character into whatever corners seem most appealing.)

In the case of our earlier Exhibit A, for instance, Hero has what he thinks is a locked-in line of credit with which to start a business of his own. But Father's power and rage are on a level with those of Fu Manchu plus Dr. No plus Elm Street Fred. Hero not only ends up jobless, but with no money to start over. He's in deeper trouble than before. In consequence, reader tension increases. Or, to put it in a word that I trust is now thoroughly familiar, excitement *builds*.

Exhibit B? Heroine pries open a window and enters Potential Informant's apartment. There she finds said informant murdered. Heroine flees. Picked up by the police later, she learns that she's left fingerprints behind her. Now, she's a prime suspect in Informant's murder.

As for Exhibit C, Scientist's efforts to uncover the secret of the alien problem render him suspect where the Earth colonists' commander is concerned. Result: He's caught between the proverbial rock and a hard place. To continue his research, he has no choice but to flee the safety of the colony camp for the perils of the alien-infested Lunar wastes.

False Plants

You see how it works? To build your story, you simply push your readers' tension ever higher by making your central character's predicament worse and worse. Recognizing that readers want to worry, you give them reasons.

On to point three: the matter of *distractions* or *false plants*.

False plants are things that throw your reader off the story track you've outlined for him. They're emotional road signs that point him the wrong way, away from the feeling-pattern you want him to follow.

The thing to remember here is that readers unconsciously take it for granted that anything included in a story is there for a reason. "Each line in a play," theatrical wisdom says, "should either advance the plot, develop character, or get a laugh." And a pulp editor used to advise writers, "If you want to describe a sunset, put it in a footnote. Don't let it get in the way of the story."

Sometimes a false plant can be obvious: You let your allegedly kindly hero kick a dog or slap a baby. Sometimes, subtle: Subliterate character says he's "narcissistic" or "self-abnegatious."

Whatever the issue, a character behaves in a manner that creates a false impression. In so doing, he disturbs what's called the reader's "suspension of disbelief," his involvement in the story world you're trying to build.

In considerable measure, this matter of false plants in stories centers on the writer who includes too much detail about inconsequentialities.

Why? What happens too often is that Writer just falls in love with his own words, instead of focusing on the effect said words are going to have on his audience.

More frequently, though, he gets the feeling that once the beginning is out of the way, his story is on the weak and flabby side. So, unconsciously or otherwise, he tries to pump it up with what might be termed "cover" information. That is, he focuses on details that seem clever but actually are distracting or meaningless and that add little if anything to the story's progress. I mean, the heroine's fondness for garlic sandwiches doesn't cut it. Not if what is needed is a new complication to strengthen the story structure. Same for Hero's preoccupation with an antique watch that won't tell time, if it has no bearing on his efforts to capture the gang that robbed the bank.

Any of these items may be entirely legitimate, you understand, if you make them truly important to your tale. But make sure they're not merely fillers, introduced because you haven't devoted the thought necessary to make them pertinent—essential. To let that happen throws both you and your story into trouble. Readers will keep expecting them to play a role and then be irritated when you don't deliver.

And yes, you can see this, too, on the checker board. By accident, one player so places his pieces that his opponent decides that Player is setting up a trap or clever ploy that will give him an advantage.

The catch is that the maneuver *is* an accident. It's the product of short-sightedness or stupidity rather than superior skill. Discovering this, Opponent concludes that Player isn't bright enough to hold his interest. Whereupon, he terminates the game as soon as possible, then finds excuses for not playing another.

Proper Plants

What about point four: the lack of proper plants?

Obviously, it's the reverse of point three. Let's sum it up by reiterating that everything in a story—and that means, particularly, in its middle area—should be there for a reason.

That reason is to bring Story to its conclusion, its final outcome. Believably.

That being the case, a plant is some bit of information you include in a story in order to prepare readers to accept something that they'll need to know later. Is someone going to be poisoned with curare somewhere along the line? It's probably wise to establish the availability of the poison earlier. Maybe you have someone call attention to the display of Jivaro arrows on the study wall. He warns that the heads are curare-dipped and hence deadly. If the lovely villainess is to choke to death on her false teeth at the climax, the fact that she wears such would best be brought in considerably before her demise. And so on.

You can plant anything, of course; not just physical objects. Knowledge of a language, for instance. A habit of thought. An attitude. A psychological twist.

Whatever the issue, do plant. Failure to do so has a distressing tendency to confuse readers. Hence, it contributes to a sagging middle.

So if you need braces on your teen-age heroine's teeth at the climax, make an issue of them earlier. Introduce the leaky samovar early enough that your readers aren't surprised when tea seeps from it to blur the love letters in the final scene. Are blue-tinted contact lenses crucial? Find an excuse to bring such to someone's attention *before* the question of Spy's identity holds the spotlight. Don't give Reader cause to do a shocked double-take when they appear, crying, "Hey, where did those things come from?"

Plants can be handled one of two ways, or by a combination.

The first is to plan your story in painstaking detail, inserting the information desired as you go.

The second is to tell your tale as it comes to you, then figure out where to put your plants later.

Whichever way works best for you is the right one.

Care

And now, perhaps the most important point of all. Though it's vital from the first word to the last of any story, it's especially pertinent in the middle segments.

Readers must care if they're to keep reading.

For readers to care, your characters—especially your central character, your hero or heroine—must care first.

What must he or she care about? In all honesty, that hardly matters. What's vital is that he/she care about *something*. It must be desperately important to Central Character to attain or retain that thing, whether it's the heart of his lovely wife or the location of his secret fishing hole. You can make it believable if you sweat enough.

But that "something" *must* make sense to your readers. Also, don't bring it up just once. Keep reminding them of how vital it is to your central character's happiness, so that they don't forget it.

You build that importance in your story's middle.

How do you do this?

You *show* that the something is significant beyond measure.

That is, you don't just *say* it's of tremendous importance to Character. You devise incidents that demonstrate it, prove it.

Consider a man whose beloved dog has fallen into a turbulent, swirling creek in flood. Are you most impressed with how much he cares for the animal if he cries out in panic—or if he dives into the water after Dog despite the obvious risk to his own life?

No, not all proofs need be as melodramatic. But as my father used to say, "Talk's cheap, and it takes money to buy whiskey." "Don't do as I say; do as I do" has its points as a maxim. And planning appropriate behavior for a character in your story's middle segments may prove more to the point than the words you put in his mouth.

Do the strong, colorful bits and incidents that you need to build solid middles come into being by magic or osmosis?

No, of course not. Most of the time they'll be the product of planning and planting and floor-pacing. But not always. Once in a blue moon they'll emerge as a seat-of-the-pants sort of thing. Or they may explode on your consciousness in a blinding flash, born of a heaven-sent moment's inspiration.

When that happens, give thanks, genuflect to your private angel— and buckle down to working harder.

Because middles are that important. Indeed, you won't go far wrong if you think of them as the heart of any story . . . the part where said story takes on strength and depth and meaning and in the process comes to life.

And that, in turn, makes it worth any time and pain and strain you take to shape such segments:

- to make them move with change and conflict

- to build in excitement, rising tension

- to trim out flab, confusion, excess verbiage

- to weave in whatever plants you need to make your story tight and believable.

Master such and you'll end up with stronger stories, believe me.

Esther M. Friesner

End Games

My college playwriting instructor once told us to write a three-act play as follows: 1) Get your hero up a tree. 2) Surround the base of the tree with hungry alligators. 3) Get your hero out of the tree, preferably un-eaten if it's a comedy.

When I applied the Hero/Tree/Alligators method to my fiction, though, I discovered one major flaw in my old professor's magic three-step to plot construction:

He never told us what to do with all those alligators.

In fiction as in life, getting into trouble is a breeze. Anyone can tie Little Nell to the tracks and aim the Superchief right at her. Getting her untied and/or stopping the train is something else again and is usually the point at which the writer panics. (I know I often have.) How to get from Point A (the tracks) to Point B (the happy ending)?

Here are some possibilities:

The deus ex machina. Literally, the "god out of the machine," a divine safety-net the ancient Greek dramatists used when they'd gotten their characters into a jam. A platform descended from on high, an actor playing the part of a god stepped out, fixed everything, and took the next platform back to Olympus.

Or, "This looks like a job for Superman!," who stops the train with his bare hands. The author calls up an unbelievably powerful or knowledgeable character to chase off the alligators. The key word here is *unbelievably.* In fantasy fiction, for instance, there's the constant temptation to bring a wizard on stage for this purpose, but you could just as easily summon up a corporate giant, a super-sleuth, or a political string-puller. Wizards and gods wear many hats.

The US 7th Cavalry. Many a western movie of my childhood was ruined by the unheralded arrival of these boys in blue when the settlers were down to their last cartridge and up to their Conestogas in Comanches.

Had anyone in the wagon train talked about the cavalry before this climactic rescue? Had anyone glimpsed so much as a smudge of blue on the horizon? Had one of the settlers casually remarked to another, "Think we should've asked directions at that US 7th Cavalry fort back aways?"? No.

This isn't the *deus ex machina*. The *deus* is a character whose existence has been mentioned previously and whose abilities are too good to be true. The US 7th is a brand-new character, conjured up by the author at the last moment, whose abilities *and timing* are too good to be true. The woodsman who just happens to be strolling by Grandma's house and hears Red Riding Hood's cries for help is a good example.

The Luck of the Irish. This is also called the Fortuitous Coincidence. It happens when Little Nell exclaims: "Thank goodness the Superchief just happened to derail a scant hundred feet before it reached me. Fortunately, I had already cut my bonds with the Swiss Army knife I found in the pocket of these pants which are my brother's and which I put on instead of my own this morning by mistake. Whew." Too many things "just happen."

What Sigmund Never Told Me. When the villain tying Nell to the tracks tries a sheepshank knot, the word *sheep* triggers memories of a childhood trauma involving his wool blanket being hidden from him by a cruel Nanny. The villain Tells All to Nell, who never had so much as an inkling of this rotter's bruised psyche. Neither has the reader. Nanny's not the only one who's been hiding things.

The villain repents, unties Nell, pays her taxi fare home, then seeks a good therapist.

None of the Above. Good choice. All of the above ways of dealing with the figurative 'gators share one basic flaw: The author produces plot resolution like a magician plucking a rabbit out of a hat. The rabbit-act is dangerous because it is easy to perform, and therefore tempting, but beware: Alligators hate rabbits. So do editors.

This still leaves us with a ring of hungry alligators and an increasingly nervous protagonist. What's the best way to resolve your character's problems and have your story end the way you'd like it *without* the resolution appearing to be contrived?

Grow a plot.

The Three Seeds

Aren't *constructing* plots and *growing* them just about the same thing? No. *Constructing* is a mechanical, artificial process. *Growing* is organic. The ending that grows naturally out of the rest of the story will satisfy the reader more than contrived endings.

Grow an ending the way you grow a garden (both involve plots): Before you even break ground, decide what you want to harvest. Begin with a clear idea of how and what you want your ending to be. This sounds as if it contradicts both the Rule of Alligators ("First get your hero up a tree!") and *Alice in Wonderland* ("Begin at the beginning!") but it works.

An organic ending—happy or otherwise—can't grow out of nothing. It requires the proper seeds: *characters, predicament* and *place.*

Characters are an author's best friends. Too many writers subordinate characters to action. The result is often two-dimensional, cardboard characters who get blown away on the first stiff breeze when the action gets rough. They really need the help of their local *deus ex machina* to get them out of trouble.

Interesting action will come more readily if you're dealing with interesting people. Give your characters plenty of depth and know *when* to show it. Don't rely on the last-minute revelation or its close kin, the convenient flashback. The time to show the villain's childhood trauma is not when he has Nell on the tracks, but earlier on. He could have a brief aside with one of his cronies, who asks, "Whatever became of your old Nanny?" Better yet, have Nanny herself appear and remind the villain of what she once did to him as a child "for your own good, dear."

Let your characters find the solutions to their problems from within themselves, from their personalities, their wits, their inborn talents, and the abilities they've picked up in the course of the story. In one of my fantasies, *Harlot's Ruse*, the heroine is magicless in a world of all-powerful wizards, dragons, demons, heroes and gods, yet the factors that save her from peril time and again are her own charm, quick thinking and kindly nature.

This last often gets her *into* trouble, too. Interesting weaknesses add humanity and credibility to a character, and often provide the way out of plot problems. In *Androcles and the Lion*, Androcles's wife rails at him for being too much the soft-hearted animal lover, yet this weakness gives the timid soul courage to pull a thorn from a suffering lion's paw. It also saves his life in the end.

When relying on your characters to provide the means to the ending you will be tempted to over-endow them. You have some pretty nifty perils in store, and you don't want them to be unprepared, so you pile on the physical and mental gifts. Instead of having your protagonist saved by the *deus ex machina,* he becomes the *deus.*

Play it safe: *Divide* those strengths of mind and body among several different characters. They can pool their complementary abilities and help each other out of danger.

Predicament should be interesting enough to place your characters in jeopardy and rich enough to provide them with ways to get out again, without benefit of the cavalry. Too many writers feel they've done their job by satisfying the first condition alone. There's the wagon train in the middle of the desert, no water, ammo running low, Indians from half a dozen tribes all around . . .

Suppose that while setting up the Indian raid you sketched in a scene showing that the warchiefs had a habit of bickering among themselves; that factions within the Council wanted to see one chief fall more than they wanted to kill the palefaces?

Remember Nell and the lucky derailment/knife set-up? You can get away with it if, early on, you mention the bad condition of the tracks, the poor safety record of the Superchief, your heroine's absent-minded habit of grabbing her brother's clothes frequently (her brother the wood-carver, Boy Scout, or Swiss army officer, of course).

Place is generally a part of predicament. The hero's predicament may consist of where he is: the scene of the crime, the edge of a cliff, the middle of the ocean. Here the same rule applies: Make the environment dangerous enough to put the hero at risk, yet complex enough to give him a way out. The waterless desert where we left our wagon train can grow acres of water-storing barrel cacti.

Dire Straits

Seeds alone do not a garden make. Proper cultivation is required, and part of that is knowing when to plant. Authors capable of using rich characters, predicaments and places still can drop the ball when it comes to timing. They wait until the hero is in dire straits before revealing the secret passage out of the dungeon or the curiously short shelf-life of the poison he's just swallowed. This is not much better than calling in the cavalry. *"Suddenly . . ."* is a weed.

Foreshadowing roots out such weeds. Foreshadowing plants the seeds of your ending while the reader watches. No one feels cheated because nothing is hidden. However, nothing is shoved right in the reader's face, either.

Red herrings make wonderful fertilizer for what you're growing here. The mad aunt from Maine who will be instrumental in revealing the murderer's identity at story's end is casually named in the midst of a slew of other eccentric relative stories. The bookish Eastern boy notices the barrel cacti as the wagon train enters the desert and mentions their water-storing quality while trying to impress his girlfriend with a lot of other chitchat about wilderness flora and fauna.

Another application of this method—popular in mysteries but usable in all fiction—is to scatter the elements of the solution, showing each one plainly to the reader but leaving it to him, and your hero, to piece them into a coherent whole.

However you decide to foreshadow your ending, remember to be forthright and brief. Don't hide things, yet don't harp on them either. Mention the barrel cactus, the villain's cruel Nanny, Nell's brother the knife freak *once or twice*, then let it go. If you don't, you'll have the reader getting to the ending before you do.

If you find foreshadowing difficult, remember that you don't have to do it on the first draft. You might have begun your story with the intention of having Nell saved by some aspect of her predicament, yet in the course of writing you discover yourself more interested in the villain's personality and what turned him villainous in the first place. If you find this alternative means to the ending more interesting, chances are it will show in your writing and the reader will find it more interesting, too. You can go back and insert foreshadowing as needed in the rewrite.

Now, What Do We Do with the Alligators?

All this still leaves us up a tree. How to get down? Put our three seeds to work:

Characters: In his pre-tree travels, the protagonist has befriended a guide who knows this is 'gator country, and therefore always carries a big shotgun; a professional alligator wrestler; and a talent scout for the handbag business. Sufficiently foreshadowed as being in the neighborhood, they now show up on the scene. A good thing our protagonist has shown his wonderful lung power in previous scenes, or they never would have heard his cries for help!

Predicament: Our protagonist wouldn't be in this predicament if he hadn't ventured into 'gator country in the first place. After foreshadowing the fact that our hero's no fool, it stands to reason that he'd pack proper equipment, such as a knife, some sturdy line and fire-starting materials. If he's not the handy sort who can improvise a way out using these, he could just wait until the sun goes down. Alligators are cold-blooded and get sluggish in the cool of the night.

Place: Remember that alligators are not commonly found in one-tree neighborhoods. Early on, our protagonist notices the thickly growing swamp flora, especially the webwork of sturdy vines between trees. *I wonder if they'd bear the weight of a man?* he wonders. Have him find out first-hand.

James B. Hall

Making the Scene

Immediately pen is seriously placed to word processor, at the moment of fictional composition—yes, and even before—all writers face the immensely important issue of scene.

Important because scene is the common denominator of plot-structure, characterization, thematic considerations, and the exploration (as against concept) of character and action.

Hence HALL'S FIRST LAW: *He who cannot write a scene cannot write prose fiction.*

I

A lot depends on scene, the scenic method. For example, strong openings and well-remembered closures may very well be functions of either an opening or a closing scene. Dialogue and scene are so closely linked as to be axiomatic; without adequate scenic context, dialogue wilts into mere talk. Moreover, the scene is multivalent in function: It forwards the action, explores character, motive; clarifies locale, engenders atmosphere, verifies author-sensitivity to nuances of speech. Scenes which do less than all these things are not working hard enough.

In summary, the scene is one of fiction's chief building blocks. As such, they are minor art forms by nature pictorial and by intent narrative.

Visual Elements

Nor is scenic exploitation limited only to fiction. Stage productions from plays to opera rely almost entirely on the scene, often augmented by music; film and television are purely scenic. Radio drama is a special use of the scenic concept for being virtually all dialogue, speech must also set the scene ("Pass me that catsup bottle, from the table with the red table cloth, please.").

The scenic conventions are the stuff of dramatic poetry, and increasingly inform works of nonfiction. Here is the scenic impulse in an imagined interview-article: "We were comfortable in her loft-apartment. Below, the waterfront and Manhattan were fog. After she poured Black Label, *Esquire* asked, 'When did you first sleep with him?' "

Although not generally credited, the scenic method serves the short story writer (and novelist) in the non-compositional phases of his or her work. In the pre-writing process, an author may rely on a *scenic* outline. Here scenic outline is distinguished from a prose summary or a so-called plot-outline.

Likewise, in revisions a reconsideration of scenic deployment may be the place to begin.

For example, if a story is flat, repetitious, sprawls; or is too long or too short, has weak structure or an unsatisfactory close, then almost always the underlying problems are with scene. No matter: In original composition or revision, to the author the scenic elements are visual elements. We allow ourselves to *see*—and to feel—it happening.

Hence, HALL'S SECOND LAW: *He who does not see a scene cannot write it.*

II

Before how-to guidelines (below), a glance at what may be called the "scenic tradition" is useful.

The poet's, the fiction writer's exploitation of scene is very clear in primitive literary works such as legends, myths, parables, and the tall-tale.

Literary Virtues

The *Beowulf* epic (circa 900 A.D.) was a pagan, narrative poem with Christian overtones and was recited by scopes to an audience. This epic presents strong elements of scenic management to include combat (man against monster); scenes of pitched battle; the elegiac death of the hero, Beowulf.

Some 700 years later, with words not on a printed page, Henry Fielding in *Tom Jones* wrote "big" scenes which are today still models of their kind. His scenic strengths no doubt are a continuation of his dramatic interests, for Fielding was first a London playwright.

By contrast, the scenic awareness of Defoe (a contemporary) was minimal. Even at a high moment of English fiction, Crusoe's discovery of Friday's footprint in the sand, the passage succeeds almost in spite of itself.

One measure of Charles Dickens' growth as a writer is his increasing mastery of the scenic presentation of materials. Dickens very much liked the stage; often he read in public from his own works and imitated all the voices, took all the parts.

As a generalization, fiction writers strongly committed to scene often have past experience with the other dramatic or visual arts: drama, opera, painting; film, photography, the writing of movie scripts professionally.

In American prose fiction, Hawthorne is uncommonly sensitive to scenic elements and without scenic virtues, *The Scarlet Letter* could never have become his masterpiece. Hawthorne's neighbor, Herman Melville, on the other hand, is a more irregular writer, but is strong with scenes, even when he handles improbable, fanciful, or thin materials. The handling of scene is surely one index of literary talent.

Above all other American writers, Henry James is both our prime practitioner *and* theorist of the fictional scene—to the point of obsession. His novel, *The Ambassadors,* is an admirable example of his theory and practice, especially in the ways he handles large, mass-effects, such as garden parties and receptions. At the level of scene, these mass-effects are difficult to sustain, so James repays study.

Common Denominators

Among modern American literary and/or popular writers, Hemingway's short fiction is notable for scenic values. In fact, many of his stories are but one scene, with minimal foreshortening. Possibly because he was sophisticated about painting and art history, Hemingway's scenes show strong elements of visual composition.

Although Faulkner's prose style is highly rhetorical, his concept, his realization, his range with fictional scene is astounding. His story, "Spotted Horses" is a scenic masterpiece of humor, of regional fidelity, and telling, visual, detail.

Among writers of the same era of popular intention, Jack London, Max Brand, and Ernest Haycox, offer good scenic models. Their concept of scene, however, emphasizes action, conflict, and clear resolutions. They wrote a great deal, often quickly; they do not always deal with the finer points of the scenic method.

Nor do all authors repay study for their reliance on scene. They have other, necessary strengths.

One of America's greatest novelists, Theodore Dreiser (*American Tragedy*), handles scenic opportunities almost indifferently; in his work there is a high percentage of expository materials, and this contributes to a generally acknowledged turgid quality in much of his later work.

As another example, Sinclair Lewis is an irregular writer. When he is good in a scene, he is very, very good, but on balance he has an indifferent scenic awareness. Much the same thing may be said of diverse literary artists as Mark Twain and Thomas Wolfe.

Of current short fiction writers (and novelists) the late Irwin Shaw's work shows strong scenic practice and consistency; the same may be said of Brian Moore, McDonald Harris, and the short stories of J. F. Powers and Flannery O'Connor.

In any event for the maker of the scene, the irregular writer's practice is valuable: the near-miss, the artistic failure by a strong talent offers the enlightenment of negative capability.

In conclusion, resourcefulness with scene may or may not track with overall literary quality, scope, profundity, or humor. A sow's ear made into a scene becomes no purse.

Nevertheless, scenic commitment is a common denominator of the successful short story and is to be ignored at peril.

HALL'S THIRD LAW: *He who reads for scene encounters the future strength of his own work.*

III

Scenic or Narrative

And now to the doing: to make the scene, the short story's interior castle.

First, however, we understand there are two main ways to present fictional materials: by "foreshortening" and by scene.

Foreshortened (condensed, told about, summarized) materials work artfully with scenic elements and together form the gross anatomy of narrative fiction.

Some work is largely scenic, with little foreshortening; other work is predominantly foreshortened (i.e., not dramatized). Theme, materials, and author's intention are all factors in this mix of narrative methods.

Here are two brief passages, the first foreshortened, the second fully scenic:

> The next day he walked into town and returned with parts he needed, and a can of gasoline. Late in the afternoon, terrible noises issued from the shed and the old woman rushed out of the house, thinking Lucynell was somewhere having a fit.

> . . . they pushed about ten new prisoners into the court. I recognized Garcia, the baker. He said, "What damned luck you have! Didn't think I would see you alive."

"They sentenced me to death," I said. "Then changed their minds, I don't
know why."
"They arrested me at two o'clock," Garcia said.
"Why?" Garcia had nothing to do with politics. . . .
"They arrest everybody who doesn't think the way they do." He lowered
his voice, "They got Gris."

Each method has its weakness, its strength (thrust and drag).

The scenic method takes more space, more words, is "thin," finds
"ideas" difficult to convey and reads quickly. A foreshortened version
of identical material requires less space, fewer words, and is more general, dense, accommodates "ideas," and reads more slowly.

Whether to use the dramatic or the summary resources for a given
passage is an artistic decision of importance; fluidity of judgment in this
matter comes with practice.

There is much to be said about the conventions of foreshortening in
fiction, but our business is with the scene.

Even so, what follows is neither formula, nor construction-job
forms to be filled with literary concrete. Instead, these guidelines are
much like an architect's elevation or section-plans on a blueprint; they
resemble the circuit layouts for audio equipment. As suggested practice,
these guidelines are probably sound in theory, but not risk-free—and I
nearly said foolproof. As always, in imaginative writing, so much depends on the doing.

So let us say our story opens with this foreshortened passage:

Because the snowdrifts away from the Interstate beyond Submerged Terrace finally stalled the car, the boy leads the girl to the nearest house.

Reader Orientation

On the chart that follows, the RO (reader orientation) is low on the tension scale (left column). If the door opened suddenly and the young man
faced a gun, tension (conflict, or simply brute literary interest) would be
considerably higher.

The reader may be oriented directly: "When the airplane banked
she saw the lights of Manhattan—all of New York—through a neon hole
in the overcast."

Or a writer of Westerns, for reader orientation, might evoke sagebrush, a camp fire, coyotes, cattle, the timeless West. No matter, reader
orientation may be done in a thousand ways but it must be done effectively.

Elementary as this may seem, a predictable weakness in the work of
new writers is in tentative or misleading reader orientation at the scene's
onset. "Any street," "any bar" in "Any City, U. S. A." is not enough.

A journeyman rule for reader orientation has some truth in it: To be remembered by a reader a place must be mentioned three times, perhaps as with, "Baltimore, oysters, the tides of the Bay—Oh, my Maryland."

Named, yes; and also evoked. Crude stuff, of course, but the job gets done.

With the reader oriented, the scene "set," the protagonists, the characters arrive, are "discovered," come into play.

Note that with the introduction of "people" the tension, the reader-interest in the scene, rises. Obviously well-conceived protagonists engender a higher quality of tension, of anticipation; ill-conceived protagonists put a scene immediately at risk.

Possibly because Shakespeare lacked the advantage of stage scenery as we know it, and was also obliged to keep a play fast-paced, his expertise in getting protagonist into a scene, and developing the scene quickly, demand close study by any writer of fiction.

Dialogue

The next major issue in making a scene involves dialogue.

Dialogue is the representation by words on paper of protagonists speaking. If dialogue inevitably characterizes (especially the speaker), confirms tone, mood, and atmosphere, this selectively captured speech has an even more important function.

This rock drill of dialogue bores into the face-rock of the material: reveals, exposes, finds new resources. The artistic result is rising tension. Properly exploited, the dialogue, itself, is an exploration.

Stripped to illustrate only revelation/penetration, here is a swatch of two-person dialogue at work:

"But David. you *look* well."
"I've just told you. Their second opinion."
"Lymph glands heal. I know they do."
"No. Four weeks. I'll just not be here."
"It's awful—and it's her birthday."
"She's four. Christy is old enough . . ."
"Yes. Yes. Old enough to know."
"Lou, she's outside playing. We'll call her in."

When no further germane, dramatic points remain, the scene—classically—comes to its highest point of tension, its climax.

Climax

Look now at the chart's bottom line. The vertical marks suggest the changing lengths of paragraphs as the scene unfolds; as tension rises the paragraphs become shorter, and are shortest in the dialogue phase. This somewhat mechanical observation suggests that as a scene grows it tends to read faster.

The "No!" represents our generic scene's climax, a point where nothing more is to be revealed at this juncture.

Let's say our scene concerns a man who is asking a woman to marry him—possibly in an old-fashioned way. His dialogue has revealed his motives, his feelings—and his miscalculations. Therefore her response is stark, definitive: NO! Or, perhaps an AIDS victim is asking his righteous, twin brother to donate a kidney. Finally the answer is "NO." Both parties may in future passages reconsider, but their reaction marks the turning point of this time and this place, and that scene.

These examples are intentionally melodramatic. In actual stories the management of scenic climax varies widely with the occasion.

Soon after the ultimate revelations of climax, the scene comes almost immediately to closure, and tension accordingly falls away, much the same situation when a theatre curtain closes.

Typically, some one or something suggests departure: an umbrella is opened (that wet one); the rejected suitor pauses, his hand on the door; the police handcuff a suspect; outside, a car door slams. The story may go on, but the scene is over.

Narrative Hook

There remains but one additional guideline of considerable importance, a scene's final gesture, the narrative-hook (N/H), to use a colorful, journeyman term.

The N/H represents the author's promise to the reader, and signals that the writer has executive control of the material. Especially in opening scenes, and mid-story expository scenes, this convention aids unity, assures continued reader interest, and has been used over the centuries by widely diverse authors including the Beowulf poet and Graham Greene.

As with all conventions, a N/H may be painfully evident, or subtle and beautifully effective. In a Saturday afternoon serial film, the hero is hanging by his hands over a cliff; the close-up shot is of a pair of boots, stomping the fingers. That visual N/H will bring them back next Saturday.

The same convention may be only at the level of feeling, "As she watched Harry put the money in the supermarket safe, very much she wanted to meet him later. At her place."

Especially in long works which are marginal artistic successes, such as *Moby Dick* or *Nostromo,* it is interesting to note an author's almost desperate use of the N/H convention. One understands: The material is vast, sprawling, or the themes unresolved in the writer's mind. The author needs all the help he or she can get to sustain tension, unity.

As to modern masters of this technique, Faulkner is resourceful, cunning, imaginative; Herman Wouk and Arthur Hailey are only as good as they need to be at the moment.

In any event, the scene having ended on this note of narrative promise, the next passages are foreshortened transportation to the next scene.

Effective Scene, in Summary

In summary, an effective scene which serves author, reader, and above all the story itself, requires both art and craft. Now that narrative conventions of the fictional scene are more clear, the new writer does well to "read for scene," in a variety of both literary and popular works.

Interestingly, the alert observer of scenic practices will note that work of a literary artist of complex intention may not—just mechanically—do scenes as well as an experienced journeyman such as Max Brand, who writes scenes very well indeed.

Likewise, some fiction is extraordinarily effective despite indifferent management of scene: The materials, the actions, the characters sweep all before them, and again *Robinson Crusoe* comes to mind.

In a like manner some authors write exquisite scenes—all glittering, smart, hard-edged; but, alas, the author has little or nothing of fictional value to say. Thus to make a scene brilliantly is seldom an end in itself, though it may appear to be so in the work of a superior stylist such as Truman Capote.

In any event, the new writer may early-on do very well with scenes, for his or her material is often biographical, preshaped, so to speak, into scene by memory. In a later phase, however, the writer usually enters a fully dramatic phase of development for there comes an end to usable memories, exotic or no.

HALL'S FOURTH LAW: *The new writer unbundles great scenes from his past; the experienced writer makes great scenes from the wide world—for nothing else is at hand.*

IV

Our "generic," exemplary scene on the chart is only suggestive. With experience the imaginative writer comes to have his or her own concept of the scene, much as a pianist comes to have (I nearly said, earns) a concept of the keyboard.

In practice the writer may compose from a scenic "cue-sheet," or from the unwritten, minimal clues of literary convention, especially in genre work. In any event, the prose writer who knows scene probably has an easier time in other art forms: the theatre, film, television.

The dedicated short story writer's further pursuit of scenic adventures will include the following terrains.

Opening and Closing Scenes

The "opening scene," a term virtually self-explanatory.

Here the scene shows more than usual emphasis on reader orientation, the specifics of landscape, weather, mood, atmosphere; moreover, because the protagonists may be important minor or more probably major figures, the reader must see the introduction of the protagonist (I/P on chart) phase of such a scene with clarity and in some depth. In fiction the full-scene opening is not extreme practice, but was not common with 19th century writers. Poe's practice in this matter—generally irregular—is instructive.

If there are opening scenes there are also "closure scenes" and they also have typical configurations.

Now emphasis is on the resolution of plot-structure, character development, change, fate. The N/H (narrative/hook) will extend the narrative in the reader's mind after the text, itself, ends; the passages after the scene's climax will claim more attention.

In the 19th century, closure scenes often focused on the distribution of rewards and punishments for all concerned. Current practice shows a more complex analysis of human affairs; closure is more subtle, and a tone of detached irony is common.

Half Scene

A less well-known, exceedingly useful practice in the dramatic presentation of materials is the "Half Scene."

As the term implies, this scene is in the miniaturist tradition. These short scenic examples are neither compromises nor carelessness on the part of the author. Rather, they "show" the reader vividly an aspect of the story which is necessary to know, but not necessary to develop or to explore.

For example, Ambrose Bierce opens, "One Kind of Officer" with a half-scene, the first line being, "Captain Ransome, it is not permitted to you to know *anything*. It is sufficient that you obey my order . . ." The half-scene is ten lines long; it functions to demonstrate beyond any reader-doubt, the tone of the order which the officer received. As a result, in a later, full-scene, Ransome fires on his own troops.

More commonly, half-scenes are transitional in nature, offer ironical comment on the action, forward the action economically, and are more vivid than the same materials merely told about, foreshortened. In addition, there is a useful distinction between a small, full scene and a calculated half-scene; naturally, in practice, there will be gray, overlapping areas of scenic presentation.

As to artistic effect, a story with many half-scenes tends to sprawl, to "run rough" (as we say about engines); moreover, the author who relies excessively on the half-scene may not know, ultimately, what the story is about. Otherwise, would there not be more fully developed, functional full scenes which focus on the main dramatic points of the material?

Set Scenes

Finally, and not surprisingly, author-intention and structure influence or even dictate some scenic values. A reference to film practice is helpful. In silent film, the chase across the roofs was a set scene; this was done many times, was even obligatory with the Director; likewise, in Westerns, the bar-room fight scene has predictable content and devices, such as the chair-as-weapon which always "shatters," the break-away chair.

In fiction, there are set-scenes by virtue of their materials, their contents: the love scene, the fight scene, the scene of pursuit, and many others. These are broadly descriptive terms, and are less a concern of the writer than of those persons who talk about film, fiction, drama and thus see the scene from the outside, so to speak.

The resourceful author finds additional uses for the scenic method in the pre-writing process, during composition, and as a guide to correct weak areas of structure if revisions or re-writes are necessary. And everywhere, there are decisions to be made, not the least being to determine which scenes are obligatory *on the writer,* imposed by the nature of the material itself. For example, if the main character of a story is a preacher, an obligatory scene may well be to show the man preaching.

The subject of scene is complex, but good fortune is everywhere for the masters of fiction lay before us the secrets of their craft, for the reading. So a main point beyond writing the scene is the necessity of reading for scene. For there lies our literary treasure.

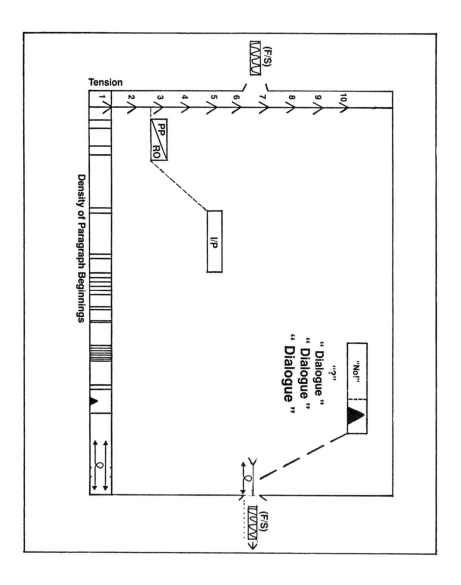

Scene Development

Key to Chart:

Sidescale (left)—1-10 suggest rising tension as scene moves ahead.

Basescale (bottom)—irregular marks suggest paragraph lengths; as the scene moves into dialogue, paragraphs become shorter.

F/S—foreshortening:

In F/S, material is "told about," summarized, recounted, contracted.

PP/RO—Picture Peg/Reader Orientation:

This technique (usually visual) makes clear to reader the time, place, location of the scene. Typically the new writer fails to orient the reader sufficiently.

I/P—Introduction of Protagonist(s):

A protagonist appears, or is discovered, or if two protagonists are present the roles become clear as dialogue begins.

Dialogue—" Dialogue "
Scenic dialogue is information-giving, revealing, rises in tension, penetrates issues, complexities and dramatic aspects of the material.

Climax (of scene):

At this point nothing more can artfully be revealed; tension is at its highest; ex., when someone refuses, says, "No!"

Narrative Hook:

Rhetorical or visual cause for reader to remain interested, or turn page.

Paul Darcy Boles

Sensing Extra Perceptions

Eye

Bringing a story into the light calls for the interplay of sight, hearing, smell, touch, and taste. All the writer's sensory gifts are working at once, and they are alert to the creation of images that use every one.

Your eye works like that of a camera, moving in for a close-up and back for a long shot, inspecting minutiae as well as overall composition. It lingers on the color of a strand of hair, passes quickly over a landscape or the cement canyons of a city.

The power of visualization is a gift you either have or haven't, but in the storywriter it can be improved with steady practice. "The train went past" may be a serviceable statement, but if the train is important to your story, you can evoke it in strength with, "Then it was there alongside, the locomotive sudden as a tornado, black, huge, screaming, the whistle sounding again in two heavy blasts, cinders and smoke streaming, and the car roofs like the backbone of a dragon." The *roofs like the backbone of a dragon* is going to fix that image in the reader's eye.

A jaunty little fox terrier becomes memorable as soon as you have told us that it "tacked along like a sailboat against the wind."

Simile and metaphor are your fast friends when it comes to passing along to the reader what your eye wants the readers to see. There have been storywriters who worked without them—John O'Hara is a notable example—but it is a little like a painter who is color-blind.

Don't overuse them. If you're good at the striking, apt, and not overdrawn metaphor, the simile that sums up much in a splash of color, save them for moments in your story when you want the reader to see very clearly what you also want to stand out. A string of similes wearies the reader because it makes the eye work too hard. A bunch of metaphors in a line is—to speak metaphorically—a bunch of boxcars passing while the reader waits. They stop the motion of the story dead as the train does traffic. Both metaphor and simile are points of color, illuminations that give the rest of the story special life by their reflections; they are not objectives by themselves, to be flaunted for their own sake.

If you don't easily see vivid correspondences in the life around you,

you can teach yourself to begin looking at mundane objects for the first time—actually *seeing* their likeness to others. A bowling pin, for instance, has a marvelous shape, like a diminuitive monk with a spherical stomach. A fountain pen is a spear with its point split. A small child's hand spread in the air is a wriggling starfish. On a clear soft night the full moon is a nailhead holding up the sky. If you stare into a garbage can— holding your nose meantime—the orange rinds and the wilted lettuce and the eggshells form islands of matchless color and gradations of tints which would intrigue Paul Gauguin in their Tahitian brilliance.

Nothing is actually "like" anything else. A pebble on a beach has its own integrity of being. But in the story your eye's ability to compare can bring to the reader a close approximation of what you want him to see, and since every story is, in part, a quick series of flowing impressions, it's important to use your eyes, and the reader's, to the limit of what both can take in.

Remember, always, that too much eye imagery can get arty and offputting. The stories of Katherine Mansfield that deal with her remembered childhood in New Zealand—"At the Bay" is one—are steeped in her homesickness, which is all that keeps the eye from blinking and turning away from the heaped-up images, wonderful as they are.

Yet used carefully and with judicial impact, the eye image can lift a reader with the sort of inner approval that exclaims, "Yes! That's how it is!" This touch with the reader is the real strength of the storywriter's eye.

Ear

Acute hearing is more to the storyteller than the ability to write good dialogue. It's the ability to hear what people really say between the lines.

If you take a page of Hemingway dialogue and read it aloud, you'll find that it's flat and doesn't play well. It has a tension that needs to bounce off the reader internally for its full effect. It says more inside the context of the story than it can ever say outside it. It's highly stylized, played close to the chest like a top poker hand.

What people mean and what they say is the difference between the reef under the ocean and its bland blue smile. "Yes, Charlie was always such a big spender" may mean that Charlie was the skinflint of the world. "Myra, your hair looks wonderful today" may be a compliment, but the operative word might also be "today" and the implication that Myra's hair is usually unsightly. Dialogue is never mere talk, but a way of characterization, of advancing the story and deepening it without narrative.

The way in which your ear hears is the way you'll write the story. Overtones and undertones are all-important. This applies to much more than an accurate ear for human speech.

The whistle of a train in the early morning has a distinctively different sound from its sound at noon and at dusk. The effect of music can be communicated by close approximates, by putting the reader into the mood for its genuine sound and feeling.

A good many of this writer's stories are about musicians. The job of soaking the reader in the sound is accomplished by images aimed like little solos at both the reader's eye and ear, but concentrating on the ear. Here are the opening and the first few lines of a story about the loneliness of the profession, the personal half-bitter, half-moody exploration of the self concentrated in a young man who has played all night and needs to find something to approximate his love for what he does on the stand.

> Down the street in this edge of spring every leaf seemed its greenest, and the sky held the moon like a white dime on fire, looking through the sharp edges of the poplar boughs. It was the time before dawn, milky and serene, and a little used up as though all the music that had been played along the street—Rush Street, Chicago—still echoed far back in the inner ear, making an undertone for the thought and the spirit. The loud music and the soft, the bad music and the good—all of it pulsed softly now in some dim background, worked its way between the weary bones.

And a little later:

> Rennie walked on, listening to the hollow but wonderfully alive sounds of his own heels on the paving—this time of morning the sound was like it was at no other time, it seemed to hold the feeling of the city in its beat. There was an afterbeat to each step, too, echoing down the surfaces of the buildings, charming the ear with its lost, dark and rhythmic bounce.

And still later, when in the first flush of morning Rennie is playing horn while a girl sings:

> She said, "I know the words now," and he set the mouthpiece to his lips again. As he did so, he felt everything he was—his inmost being, the quiet center—pour itself through the trumpet. And she began to sing; her voice like a bird's, artless, and singing for the joy in the act. And as clear as a stream coming down through pines on a warm morning, with everything bright-polished and steady and also everlasting.

But a story needn't be about music or the people who make it to use the full range of sound in order to get over its complete message. Fitzgerald's "the Tap, K'Tap of ping-pong balls" sums up a lot better than "He could hear them playing ping pong" might do, and "the ruffling of a hen with iron wing-feathers'' applied to another story of mine, plays on the reader's imagination more sufficiently than a great deal of automotive-engine-sound description could do.

Dialogue, too, is always a form of description. The use of qualifying adverbs such as "He said sternly" is necessary once in a while, but too many adverbs create a curly effect like poodles running around the page. There is a quality of delivery that can be picked up quickly and given the reader, which will tell the reader how anything is being said— if you're introducing a person whose voice is low and clipped, the reader will know from this that "I'm terribly sorry" came out that way, and you don't have to add that it was clipped and low. Voices tell an enormous amount about the people who have them, so that a voice full of sandpaper is going to speak in an entirely different manner from one that's as rich as old Burgundy. Skip the qualifiers whenever possible— lay down the manner of speaking and let the spoken words be delivered from then on with that in mind.

In straight first-person narrative—"Call me Ishmael"—the voice is going to be implicit all through the story, even though it's never described. This is where your ear comes in on all frequencies. Following are the first two paragraphs of a recent story written specifically for a particular magazine, *Rod Serling's Twilight Zone*. It's a fantasy, but I wanted my narrator, Jeb Malifee, to be a down-to-earth but imaginative man, both self-sufficient and a little ingrown, like so many of the natives I admire in Maine, and the task was to make him sound like what he is without saying what he looked like or going out of character.

> She was a quiet woman, the best kind. Up around the rocks nobody much goes in after Labor Day. But there she was, here into October, stroking in as if the water wasn't fit to chill a lobster. Naked, far as I could see, but for what looked like a shell necklace. Clean arms, with the shine of silver along them in the twilight and her legs scissoring nice and smooth, and no strain to it at all. A wonderful swimmer. Quiet, as I said.
>
> Sun was just going out of sight out at Bradford Point, hanging behind the old lighthouse and making it look like a black candle in the middle of the afterglow. It's a time when I always like to be by myself on shore. The summer people—the "straphangers" we call them, and you can figure out why—are gone and the pines and the rocks just sort of turn into themselves again. The boards of the docks look bleaker and quieter. The ring of green weed around the dock pilings gets a gentle, lost light in the evening. Molly's Fish House down the line gets its slabby contented look back again. It seems to be about to fall into the sea but it never does. The smell of the water is stronger and like iodine around a scratch. Some places on the island you can stand still and hear a moose drinking from one of the creeks. It's a near-to-wintering time when the sun feels better than it will again all year.

Eye, ear, *and* nose are working with the reader there, but the ear is most concerned because the reader is listening to Jeb and judging him while he tells the story, accepting his laconic but pointed style of reminiscence. And receiving from him a series of impresssions which are more believable and effective than they'd be if the story were told outside him in the third person.

Sound penetrates every good story and gives it resonance and extra echoes. The "kreef kreden kreden" of crickets—a phrase used by Robert Nathan—is straight onomatopoeia, which is the Greek word for the formation of words in imitation of natural sounds, such as *crack, splash,* and *bow-wow* and the "brek-a-kek-kek, co-ax, co-ax" of Aristophanes' froggy friends.

The First Experiment

Before you go on reading, step into a room where people are talking and, trying to take as little part in the conversation as you can, listen. Listen to the murmuration and hesitation that precede a sentence. Hear how sentences themselves are rarely complete and how a surge of silence between words says as much as the words do. Filter out all the extraneous sounds—television and similar clatter—and try to pick out which words you'd use to sum up the gist of what is being said.

Now stand outdoors and listen to the sounds of a city, trying to separate the far-off noises from those near at hand—describing them to yourself either in onomatopoeia or approximates. "The prowling cat wail of a siren," "the wind's fingers fumbling poplar leaves," "the yoo-hoo of a mother calling children," "the slish-slish of slow traffic."

Go to the place where you write and while everything is fresh, put down in metaphor and simile, without pausing and straining for effect, everything you can of sight impressions and sound remembrance. How the talkers looked as they spoke and what stands out in your mind about them. Don't do complete descriptions. Try to catch them on the wing in impressions. Do the same with the sounds. [If you don't live in a city, use the country sounds you just heard.] Then sum up the talkers' dialogue in five or six pertinent sentences.

Let all that cool and look at it from time to time.

Thinking how you could say it better.

Nose

While we're talking about sensory stimulation in the story, let's consider the nose.

Television and movies haven't as yet, in this sense at any rate, really begun to smell on a wide and fully accepted scale. Back in the '60s, Mike Todd, trifling with the olfactory organs of potential millions, introduced a device called Smell-o-Vision; how it worked this writer has no idea, but his reference sources are unimpeachable and he can only say that he is glad it died. And in *Brave New World* Aldous Huxley projects a nauseating device which rejoices in the name of "The Feelies" and gives the benighted but delighted slaves of tomorrow substitutes for intimate human touch. Also, a good many science fiction storytellers and novelists—see Ray Bradbury's "The Veldt"—have taken for granted the future use of a complete sensual wraparound environment.

Meantime the marvelous gift of the human nose is there for you to play upon in short stories.

Three samples:

There was a fragrance of honeysuckle along the fence and of early apples fallen in the small and unattended orchard just behind the brick Colonial house that had been built between 1825 and 1830.

The store in which the Justice of the Peace's court was sitting smelled of cheese.

Cautiously, as one might test the edge of a cliff before crawling outward to an eagle's nest, I smelled the air. And again the feeling of wonder and strangeness filled me, for the air was different.

Those are very different uses of the sense of smell to evoke reader response. The first is from John Bell Clayton's story "Sunday Ice Cream," the next is the opening line of Faulkner's "Barn Burning," and the last is from my "Night Watch." Each is fitted to its special time and place and is meant to place the reader directly inside the scene, so that he or she not only sees and hears with the protagonists but exercises still a third sense to inhale the essence of the scene and enrich understanding. The reader's nostrils work as the writer's do, and when the reader's memory is touched by familiar odors—or unfamiliar ones carefully described—the reader becomes a physical participant in the story.

Clayton wanted that honeysuckle—a particularly southern scene, perfect for the mood of his story—and those early fallen apples with their slight tinge of rottenness to summon up a slow-moving Sunday in a specific section of Virginia. Faulkner wanted that general-store cheese to fill your nostrils as it fills those of the always hungry boy, Sarty Snopes, whose father is on trial for malicious arson. I wanted the beckoning, olive-laden smell of the shore to drift through the sweep port of a Roman galley and to quicken the nostrils of a rower who was resting on his oar after a storm.

There are, of course, a thousand ways to use smells in your story, and along with them goes, once more, the cautionary reminder that as in the case of simile, metaphor, and sound evocation, enough is far better than a feast—a story is not a guided tour through a fragrance factory, and the fragrances are not there to dominate but to help create the feeling of a true and whole experience.

But they are there for you to *use*. To use with an appeal to primitive alertness: "the smoky tang of flint." To use with more sophisticated nostrils: "the warm delicate hothouse puff of Chanel Number Five." To use as a reaction to raw nature: "For three seconds after the lightning, the world was pure ozone." And to use as ideal evocation of a full experience in seven words, as when Huckleberry Finn tells us: "It felt late. It even *smelt* late."

Reading a story about a grocery, a barbershop, or a tree in summer without a few illuminating words about the smell of fresh produce, the heady sharpness of bay rum, or the living smell of leaf sap is like having an important sense arbitrarily blocked off by the author.

Try never to write as though both you and the reader shared a bad cold. Think of your story as appealing to the hunting dog in everybody.

Taste

The sense of taste is connected to those of sight, sound, and smell by tiny invisible conduits which work together to create a single immediate effect—of enjoyment or revulsion or mere neutral acceptance.

"It was good" is one plain manner of describing a meal your story character has just eaten. "It was bad" is another.

And these may be serviceable and adequate methods of telling the reader what went on in somebody's mouth. If your natural storytelling style is flat and direct, there's no need to labor to describe the effects of grits and gravy on a Yankee or Midwest pot roast on a Southerner used to Brunswick stew.

But if you believe in and are able to think of the kind of color that lights up the demanding framework of a story, you may want a few analogies to strengthen "good" and "bad." Sinclair Lewis, in *Main Street* and numerous other books, seldom fails to produce a bright little series of snapshots underlining either the awfulness or the splendor of the cuisine. Hemingway is often as rhapsodic over varied Spanish dishes as his style will allow. Rex Stout's Archie, with his favorite reports on the preparation and intake of the food from Nero Wolfe's kitchen, lends firm authenticity to Wolfe's reputation as a gourmet. Certain stories revolve around food—Paul Gallico's "The Secret Ingredient" is one—

and when they do, the reader usually salivates.

M.F.K. Fisher, as well as being a masterly storyteller, is a great writer about food, and her work is worth relishing not only for its excellence in other respects but for its dazzling insight into gastronomic mysteries. Writers who love food, respect it, and believe it to be a primary mover and shaker of civilization are likely to vivify the human palate in their fiction.

You are not, of course, composing a cookbook when you write a short story. A dash of salt and Tabasco—the communicated realization that what your story people eat and their reactions to what is served sometimes have direct bearing on who they are and what they are—is often enough. When Joe Christmas, the running, haunted, angry, displaced no-man of Faulkner's *Light in August,* eats cold corn bread, we know how it tastes to him. We can taste it with him. The delectable goose in "A Christmas Carol" is an elevated piece of goosehood that takes central position and soaks the revelry of the Cratchits in its juices. Your story may skip the acts of eating, tasting, entirely—it may have completely other aims—but if these happen in it, particularize; let the reader know how they sat on the tongue.

Touch

The sense of touch is another glorious gift to humanity and a constant companion of the alert writer of stories. Textures animate our lives much more than we have the ability to notice and constantly record. They consist of much more than mere harshness and softness—all gradations of tactile experience are encountered in the course of a day and night, and nerve endings are steadily caressed or assaulted by both simple and extremely complex forces. A little of this entering a story by suggestion can be splendid; too much of it can spill over into a mere sensory list of pleasure or displeasure. Like the other sensory attributes of men and women and children and animals and all of nature, when touch is kept in balance in a story, the reader recognizes it and nods in recognition; when it's insisted upon to the detriment of spirit, the story slips into self-indulgence—which is one reason why pornography for its own sake is so boring.

Waking with rough blankets around your chin and touching the floor with your bare feet while you feel an autumn sun warm them and walking over to put your hands on a cool oak windowsill constitutes a series of light enjoyable shocks which can be transferred to a short story with wholeness and great reader pleasure. Relaying the feeling of salt wind as it fills your pores, the elegant substance of new-cut wood, the almost murmurous life of human hair, the yielding toughness of the dirt in a freshly plowed field, and a hundred other experiences of the receptive and appreciating body can be done without neglect of any other story element—in balance, so that it feels right to you and to the reader and so that, by the use of artifice, you have passed along more "naturalness" than so-called naturalism would ever achieve.

As for sex, in the short story the sense of touch if kept in balance is an essential part of it—as long as it doesn't slop over into silly excess. Used sparingly, it underlines the warmth between people, between people and animals, people and seemingly inanimate objects. Instead of running on with heated descriptions of lovemaking—which are impossible to convey without honest passion running beneath them—simple suggestions are always more effective.

In Willa Cather's *A Lady Lost* there's no word that could offend a Puritan of the stripe of Cotton Mather. But there is one of the most effectively done scenes of adultery in literature, which tells us forever that Marian Forrester is an intensely desirable woman in the physical sense, as well as helping us to sympathize with her and dislike her despoilers. As in all writing, in the short story when sex is clinically handled—even in a time when anything can be said—the act of love becomes dispassionate and cold. But if it's expressed in an electric touch, shared laughter, the impress of a head on a pillow, it turns into story magic.

The Second Experiment

Make a list of smells that start your thoughts going backward to moving or outstanding times in your life. Hay, horses, new-cut clover. Pencil shavings and black ink in a schoolroom. Blackboard eraser dust. Sweeping compound. Milky and soupy smells in a cafeteria. Grain and feed smells. Smoke of leaf fires. Crisply ironed handkerchiefs. Old leather and faintly musty paper. Anything that reels in from the past your good or bad experiences. Brassy cartridges on a firing range. Raw pink puppy smells. The swarming sharpness of ether.

Linger on these until each brings up a living image. See if any of the images fit into the story you've been thinking toward. If they don't, keep on smelling backward and try to find a few that do.

Remember how something you really liked tasted the first time. Rhubarb pie, chocolate, a tomato off the vine, an egg cream at Schrafft's, cider sharp from a barrel, a girl's astonishingly peppermint-flavored lipstick, a man's earlobe. And how something you hated actually tasted. Castor oil, green quince, creamed carrots [if you like creamed carrots, shift this to the good side], and whatever else is tastebud anathema to you. Work at remembering what happened around you while you were reveling in the good and recoiling from the bad. Find images for this—faces of people, backgrounds of places, shapes of a room or a landscape. Again, try to fit these, without forcing, into the story you're leaning toward.

Put your hand, palm flat, on a concrete surface. An automobile fender. A human cheek. A chair, a carpet, the bricks of a fireplace. An egg. A rough, scarred board, a smooth-planed one, a stone in a wall, the trunk of a tree. Whatever you touch, keep your eyes shut and let words form describing it quickly and rightly to anyone. Then go write them while they're new and clean, without thinking in "literary" terms at all but just trying for your own sort of accuracy.

After you've let your lists simmer awhile, think how you could improve them without borrowing from any other source or getting the least shade fancy.

Jean Z. Owen

Trouble-Free Transitions

In virtually every piece of fiction, the author encounters the problem of moving his characters from one locale, time, or mood to a different locale, time, or mood. In stories told from the multiple viewpoint, there is the additional task of shifting the focus of interest from one character to another. These moves or shifts, called *transitions,* must be written in such a way that story action is not decelerated or the continuity diminished.

Let us examine a rough paragraph obviously in need of condensing by means of a transition:

> That evening, when Jeff finished going over his books, he realized he would be ruined if he couldn't get his hands on some money, fast. Tomorrow, he would go to the bank and ask for a loan. There was no other way. Having made up his mind, he closed his checkbook firmly, snapped off the light, went upstairs, undressed, and showered. He put on his pajamas, brushed his teeth, and went to bed. When he began to get sleepy, he turned off the light and went to sleep. As soon as it was daylight, he got out of bed, shaved, brushed his teeth. He dressed and went downstairs. He put on his overcoat, locked the front door, and went out to the garage to get his car. He backed the car down the driveway, turned left on Maple Street, and drove to the Freeway. He took the Briarwood turnoff to Ninth Avenue, drove eight blocks east, and turned in at the bank parking lot.

Dull, isn't it? While an occasional background detail is needed for color and verisimilitude, this kind of writing is the mark of an amateur; professional writers know it would never get past the first reader.

The easiest transition, of course, is accomplished merely by leaving an extra space and a wider indentation. This is sometimes the *best* transition one can select, but a writer should not rely exclusively on this type, for too many of these space-jumps in a story cause the reader to feel he is playing a game of literary hopscotch.

If a space type of transition were used in a revision of the foregoing sample paragraph, it would very likely appear like this:

> That evening, when Jeff finished going over his books, he realized he would be ruined if he couldn't get his hands on some money, fast. To-

row he would go to the bank and ask for a loan. There was no other way. When he walked into the bank the following morning, etc.

Transition hooks

Various authorities have used a wide assortment of similes to describe a transition, and you may have one you prefer. My own favorite is one a perceptive teacher gave me years ago, when I was struggling with transitions in my first multiple-viewpoint story. He advised me to think of a transition as a hook attached to the rope a mountain climber wears around his waist. During an ascent, the climber throws the hook up to the next ledge, then uses the attached rope to climb to it. In fiction, a writer can deliberately mention an activity that will take place later or in a different locale. (This is throwing the hook up to the ledge.) Then when you want to move to a different time or place, a single phrase (the rope) is all you need to make the climb.

For example, in the illustration above, the hook is: *Tomorrow he would go to the bank.* Then when you read, *When Jeff walked into the bank the following morning,* you've climbed the rope, bypassed all irrelevant activity, and are ready to go on with the story.

Weather has always served as an effective transition hook:

> The sky was clear and blue when Sue went to work, but when she left the office at five o'clock, the sky was slate-colored and rain drummed on the streets.

Seasons are frequently used to denote longer time spans:

> The trees were gaudy with autumn color when Frieda went to work for the Hildreths, but by the time the first spring crocus bloomed, she was such a part of the family it seemed she had always lived there.

Name transitions provide an effective way of hooking into the viewpoint of a different character:

> When Lola heard of Tom's marriage her first thought was of Margaret, who had always secretly loved him. Concern for her sister blocked out all other emotion. What would Margaret *do?*
> Margaret was at the theater when the news reached her. Just before the last curtain, Hazel Montgomery leaned forward, tapped her on the shoulder and said, "Isn't it exciting? Imagine Tom's eloping with that girl from Houston! You *have* heard about it, of course?"
> Numb with shock, Margaret managed to nod and smile.

Telephones often provide convenient transition-hooks:

> Julia stared out the window, trying to decide what would be best for her to do. *Ken,* she thought. Ken could advise her. Impulsively, she reached for the telephone.

In an apartment across town, Ken Littleton's wife, Irene, put down her drink and answered the telephone in a voice so slightly slurred she felt certain no one would notice.

Objects of almost any type can be used as transitions. If the object is one that undergoes a change with time (a snowbank, a rosebud, a lighted cigarette), this quality can be utilized to show a time lapse:

Elizabeth filled a glass with ice cubes and poured tea over them. She would come to grips with her problem *now*. She told herself, by the time she finished her tea, she would have made her decision, once and for all. But she drank the tea, the ice cubes melted and became tepid water, and Elizabeth continued to sit at the table, her mind vacillating.

If objects themselves do not undergo a change, they can still be used to show the passing of time:

Charles would surely return in a few minutes, Mr. Thorndyke assured himself. He picked up the book, intending to read only a few pages, but he became so engrossed he was halfway through the volume when he became aware of the chiming hall clock. Midnight, and Charles still hadn't come back.

Appearance can be used to denote either a long or short period of time:

Long term

Jeremy remembered his father as he looked the day he waved good-bye to them from the train platform—a tall, slim, dark-haired man, the light of adventure in his eyes. Surely it could not be his father coming toward him now. Even twenty years could not have changed him into this white-haired, stooped old man with faded eyes. Jeremy felt a little sick as he walked toward him and said, "Hello, father."

Short term

Anita was more meticulous than usual when she put on her make-up that evening. She must look perfect for Hal. But by the time Hal finally rang the doorbell, her lipstick had worn off on the stubs of the cigarettes Anita had nervously chain-smoked, and hot, angry tears had ruined her mascara.

Activities sometimes provide transitions, adding color and background to the story:

Swinging his tennis racket in anticipation, Frank loped down to the court where Ruth waited for him, her brief white dress gleaming in the sun. Three sets later, they were warm and pleasantly exhausted, ready for a shower and a leisurely dinner.

Emotionally Involved

These are only a few of the more frequently used types of transition hooks. Your own discernment will help you choose the one that blends most perfectly into the forward movement of the story. You will find that there are times when one of the types of transitions we have illustrated is the best to use, usually when you are linking two highly charged emotional scenes together. But now we come to the *most* important rule in your selection of a transition: *Never settle for any other type of transition without first trying to use one in which an emotion is involved.*

Occasionally, you will want to use one in which emotion provides the *only* outright transition hook, although passing of time is usually implied. Here is an example:

> Gradually, his sadness dissipated; new hope and a growing sense of purpose stirred within him.

More often, it is helpful to use a time or place transition *plus* an emotional factor:

> *Time only.*

> She started job-hunting that morning but by evening she had not yet found a position.

> *Time plus emotion*

> She felt brave and full of hope when she left the house that morning to go job-hunting; by evening she was weary and discouraged.

You will notice, in the above examples, that when we added the characters' *feelings* to the time-transition, we increased the number of words required to make the transition smooth and complete. This almost always happens, and the words used to achieve this are well spent. If you are struggling to keep your wordage down, *don't* attempt to economize by deleting the emotion. Find some other place in the story to do your whittling.

Sequence transitions

Although use of emotion is important in simple transitions, it can be more vital in writing effective *sequence transitions*—those in which the change occurs in progressive steps. Note the following examples:

> *Time-emotion sequence*

> They quarreled all during breakfast, and for awhile, after Tim slammed out of the apartment, Barbie seethed with anger and resentment.

But by lunchtime, her anger had begun to wear thin; by four o'clock she was willing to assume all the blame for their disagreement. Two hours later, when she heard Tim's key in the lock, she ran to greet him, her eyes shining with love.

Place-emotion sequence

When he boarded the plane at La Guardia, Fred was certain he had made a mistake in accepting the new position. An uneasy premonition of failure was still with him when they touched down at Chicago's O'Hare Airport, but as they left Denver the air turbulence seemed somehow to jolt him out of the downbeat, portentous mood that had clung to him. When he walked down the ramp at San Francisco International, he was buoyant and confident, and he knew his decision to come West had been a wise one.

Sequence transitions are especially helpful when a long span of time or a large area of space is to be covered rapidly. I once read a memorable story in which the author covered 20 years in a single, brief transition paragraph by describing the different refrigerators a couple had purchased during that time. Another story used a woman's changing hair styles to depict the passing of 30 years. In these two stories, as in many I have read, the transitions were so expertly written that they did far more than take pleats in time and place; because the emotional factor was woven into each one, the transitions served to deepen and enrich the stories.

To most beginners, transitions are difficult and frightening, but with the many examples given here, plus the ones an alert writer can spot as he reads, the technique should be relatively easy to master. And few skills a writer develops give him a greater sense of accomplishment than the knowledge that, if he needs to, he can whisk characters deftly across the country, around the world, or through half a century of time with a few expertly written words.

Darrell Schweitzer

How to Make Your Fiction Three Dimensional

Imagine a tent without its poles or stakes, lying flat on the ground. We can see its outline. We know it is a tent, but we can't go inside. It's not much good for anything. The first stories I ever wrote were like that— flat and useless. Even then, at the age of 14 or so, I knew what the problem was. The solution, however, was less obvious.

The problem was *synopsis*. Like a vast number of beginning writers, I did not know how to create a true narrative, so I was summarizing the events in my stories. I had a flat tent.

Here's an example from a horror story I wrote sometime in my teens. The strongest evidence of literary promise I showed when composing this particular opus was in my failure to finish it. But six pages of hideous first draft still exist, single-spaced, in red ink, no less terrifying for prose like this, concerning a maladjusted young man with developing lycanthropic tendencies and assorted superpowers he will use to anti-social ends:

> I awoke to the sounds of growling and snarling. The cave was full of wolves! And they were my wolves too! My friends had come to find me!
>
> And having found me, they started feasting on those who would harm me. Most of the corpses had already been torn apart and eaten. . . . Then I joined them in their meal. That was the first time I had ever tasted human flesh. It was a turning point for me . . .
>
> . . . I drove from city to city, searching, following up rumors of were-creatures and monstrosities of various kinds, leaving the entire country looking fearfully over its shoulder for the Phantom Murderer (as the papers had dubbed me). I found barbarous practices among the humans in my travels. Often they caged up live animals (including wolves!) in places called zoos where they would come and stare at them. Always I would go along and melt the locks on all the cages and set the animals free. They would immediately set upon their tormentors and devour them. . . . For years I went on like this . . .

Those six pages seem to go on for years too. Obviously something is grievously wrong with the way the story is written: It isn't in *scenes*. All the briefly mumbled-over atrocities are not *events* that the reader may witness. Even the shocking goings-on in the nation's zoos are no more than briefly listed. The whole story is a veritable heap of flat tents. Nobody is going to feel the slightest touch of excitement or fear from such a story, no matter how many victims are messily devoured.

A true narrative raises the tent. We can go inside. When we read a really gripping story, we say that it draws us into the action. We experience the events and respond emotionally. We pay the author the supreme compliment of saying that the story really "comes alive."

Let us engage in a little tent-raising, by taking a synoptic (and considerably more promising) passage from a famous historian and turning it into a fictional narrative.

History vs. Story

Edward Gibbon's *The Decline and Fall of the Roman Empire* tells a magnificent, 1,500-year tale in resounding (if by today's standards, a bit florid) prose. Generations of historical novelists, and even some science fiction writers (such as Isaac Asimov, whose *Foundation Trilogy* owes a large debt to him), have turned to Gibbon's work for inspiration, and rightly so, because it contains the germ of a good novel or short story on virtually every page.

Here's a novel plot for the taking (on pages 102-105 of the Heritage Press edition). It's exciting, horrific stuff: Emperor Septimius Severus dies (A.D. 211), leaving the empire to his two sons, Caracalla and Geta. Both young men are degenerate scoundrels, Caracalla the worse, and they hate each other intensely. As they progress from Britain across Europe to Rome, tensions reach an explosive level. Each tries to murder the other. The imperial palace is split in halves guarded by the soldiers of the two brothers, as if under seige. All attempts at reconciliation fail. The Empress Mother, Julia Domna, thwarts a plan to divide the empire between the brothers, exclaiming that they might as well carve her in half as well. The world trembles on the brink of civil war, until:

> . . . Caracalla obtained an easier though more guilty victory. He artfully listened to his mother's entreaties, and consented to meet his brother in her apartment, on terms of peace and reconciliation. In the midst of their conversation, some centurions, who had contrived to conceal themselves, rushed with drawn swords on the unfortunate Geta. His distracted mother strove to protect him in her arms; but in the unavailing struggle, she was wounded in the hand, and covered with the blood of her younger son, while she saw the elder animating and assisting the fury of the assassins.

Synopsis is the natural language of the historian, who must deal with the broad scope of events, rather than the immediate experiences of individuals. Thus Gibbon relates the entire tragic rivalry between the imperial brothers in two and a half pages, and the bloody climax in less than a paragraph.

Now, let's retell that climax in the technique of the storyteller:

They sat for what seemed like hours, Geta mostly sullen and staring into his wine cup, Julia occasionally trying to engage him in conversation about some household event, or some nostalgic memory from the happier days when Severus was alive. But Geta merely brooded.

After a while, Julia's maid brought them a light repast. The Empress toyed nervously with her food. Geta never touched his. Shadows lengthened in the broad, marble room. Slaves came and lit the lamps, then hurried away. The tapestry of Alexander the Great over the door billowed in a sudden draft.

Then there were footsteps in the corridor outside. Julia sat up suddenly on her couch. Geta put down his cup and rose from his seat.

The door opened and Caracalla stood there. The two brothers eyed one another in silence, Geta's face an expressionless mask, Caracalla's split with that sinisterly ingratiating smile of his. Caracalla stepped forward to embrace Geta.

The younger brother froze, then backed away.

"Go *on*," Julia Domna said.

Reluctantly Geta took Caracalla's hand, then the two of them embraced like old friends. Geta smiled weakly. The Empress sighed with relief.

"Brother," Geta said, his words obviously forced, "I hope this will be a new beginning."

Caracalla walked with his arm over Geta's shoulder, leading him in a slow circle back toward the open door.

"I hope it will be the end."

"The end?" said Geta. He paused, but Caracalla urged him on.

"Of our childish quarrels. I hope to make an end to that, once and for all."

"Yes, that would be a good thing," said Geta.

"Quite."

They stood at the doorway. Suddenly a fully armored soldier burst into the room, sword drawn.

Geta broke away and turned to his mother in stupid astonishment, then screamed as the soldier gave him a broad slash across the back.

Four more armed men appeared. Screaming, too, the Empress leapt up and put her arms around her younger son, trying to wrestle him away from his assassins.

The swordsmen stabbed him again and again.

Caracalla shrieked, trembling with fear and lust and triumph. "Kill him, you fools! Kill him quickly!"

Then it was over. Geta fell limp in Julia's arms, sliding to the floor, clinging for an instant to her knees. Their eyes met. He looked at her imploringly, but when he tried to speak, blood poured from his mouth.

Caracalla put his foot to Geta's shoulder and shoved.

The younger emperor was dead. The sole ruler of the world stood unsteadily, leaning on a centurion's shoulder, while Julia knelt and cradled her younger son's head in her lap. She began to sob gently. She put her hand to her face, then took it away when she realized for the first time that her hand was cut badly and bleeding profusely.

"Mother," said Caracalla. "Remember that it is treason to mourn a traitor."

"Monster," she said. "I would rather have died than given birth to you."

Caracalla raised his hand as if to strike, but then seemed to lose all his strength and nerve. He pushed one of the soldiers toward the door.

"Take me away! Quickly!

Facts vs. Experience

Now consider the differences between the two passages. The historian gives us the facts, that Caracalla killed Geta by a ruse, and the younger brother died in his mother's arms. But the storyteller must take the reader into that room and recreate the murder as it happened, supplying from his own imagination the details no historian could know.

I turned the historical summary into a story by means of the following devices:

Viewpoint. Ask yourself, as writer/editor William Sloane once put it, *Who is the reader supposed to be?* That is, what viewpoint will make this scene work most effectively. I chose a limited omniscient viewpoint. The reader perceives the scene as a disembodied set of eyes and ears in the room with Geta and his mother. Therefore, we do not see Caracalla until they do, when he arrives, and we do not know that the assassins are lurking just outside the door. We are just as surprised as Geta and Julia are. Other viewpoints are possible. I might have done it from the viewpoint of Julia, so that the reader is inside her head, sees and hears only what she does, and shares her thoughts. Or I might have asked the reader to be Geta, though that would have required that the scene terminate before the final exchange between Caracalla and his mother.

Time. There is no time in a synopsis. Events are merely catalogued. But in a story, the writer must give a sense of hours or minutes. But don't write the equivalent of "And then the next ant came in and got a piece of grain." Notice how I speeded things up, reducing the long period of waiting to "They sat for what seemed like hours." When Caracalla arrives, we return to direct story-time, the events told precisely as they happen. Then we speed up again, instead of recounting every last spurt of blood ("Then it was over"), and drop back into direct story-time again for the final exchange of dialogue.

Pacing. Pacing refers to the number of things happening in a given length of narrative. This scene begins slowly, with very little happening, but by the end, the pace was frantic. The slow start is deliberate, to offset the frenzied conclusion. Synopsis generally recounts happenings at an even, unvaried pace, with no pauses, no elaboration.

Description. No historian needs to, or plausibly *can,* describe marble rooms or billowing tapestries, let alone such details as the servants lighting the lamps and hurrying away to avoid the obviously dreaded confrontation. The storyteller must fabricate such descriptions to make the experience more complete. Notice that I did not describe walls or tapestries or lamps once the murder was in progress. Again, the storyteller tries to relate the incident as someone there would have perceived it. No one is going to pay attention to the decor when an emperor is being butchered at stage center.

Action. Every action in the scene, from Geta fidgeting with his cup, to Julia sitting up suddenly, to the centurion slashing the doomed emperor across the back with the sword, is my invention. This is more tent-raising. If the scene is to come alive, the characters in it must move and act like real people.

Dialogue and characterization. We know, from history, what sort of people the principals were, but both the historian and the storyteller must create their personalities from a mixture of analysis and imagination. The historian then summarizes his conclusion. But the storyteller must *show* his characters in action. I decided, for purposes of this scene, that Caracalla has a vicious wit, and that Geta is sullen and dull. So Caracalla's dialogue drips with irony and he feigns friendship by embracing his brother, who remains reluctant and suspicious. Of course everything Caracalla does is part of his plan to maneuver his brother to the doorway, where the assassins can get him. He kicks over the corpse in a final gesture of contempt, but then (as the real Caracalla often did on these occasions), loses his nerve.

Starting from Scratch

A story must be made up of such scenes. You may vary the pacing, dropping out of real story-time to speed things up ("Three nights passed before the messenger arrived with the news . . .") but most of the story must consist of events told as the characters experience them. Keep exposition, actual lecturing in the author's voice, to a minimum. It is an interruption, as if, in the middle of the play, someone comes out onto the stage and starts explaining things to the audience.

It's all right to start with an outline or synopsis of what is to take place in the story. Just don't confuse that for the finished product.

Turn your synopsis into a full-blooded story by going down the list: Have you gotten into some consistent viewpoint? Fine, now imagine the event as if you can see it before you. Describe what you might conceivably see, hear, feel, smell. Science fiction writer Poul Anderson has often explained how he likes to involve as many senses as possible in the first paragraph, so the reader will be immediately pulled into the scene.

Now imagine what sort of people your characters are. *Don't* just tell the reader that so-and-so was brave, noble, and generous, or conversely treacherous and cowardly. Show him being those things in the course of the scene. If your characters say anything as they act out their roles, write down only the interesting parts. Notice that I did not include the desultory chatter between the Empress and her son. It mattered only, to underscore Geta's mood, that she spoke and he wouldn't answer.

Now choreograph the scene. The characters should be *doing* something. The key to my scene here was Caracalla embracing his brother and steering him toward the door. It is a completely fictional detail, but it emphasizes the whole point of the encounter, that the older brother is delivering the younger to his executioner.

In the end, if you do it well enough, the reader will come away saying, "That story was really good! It made me feel like I was *there*!"

Rega Kramer McCarty

Using Symbols as a Shortcut to Meaning

Our culture is full of symbols: The barber pole, the turkey at Thanksgiving, the wedding ring, the wedding veil, the christening . . . in each, the object or the ceremony takes the place of hundreds, thousands, of descriptive words.

If you would like to give added dimension to your story, consider using a symbol as a shortcut to meaning.

A symbol may be an image standing for a small moment in the story, or it may be a substitute for action—a literary figure used throughout the work, pervading it, carrying the deeper meaning.

I once wrote a play titled *The White Fences of China,* based on a story told me by a missionary. The mission orphanage built a white fence around its grounds, not to keep the orphans in but to keep others out, because the mission was already over-crowded and was without funds. Day after day, Chinese children, homeless and hungry, came to stand outside the fence, peering longingly in. One small girl wouldn't leave. Every day she came and remained far into the night . . . until at last the missionary could stand it no longer and invited her inside.

The fence became symbolic of the limits put upon missionary help by the lack of funds, and the little orphan symbolized all the orphans of China who looked longingly for help. Thus, the symbol also helped to carry the story's theme, or meaning.

Fences have been used as symbols in fiction many times, but in different ways. I recall a story of a "spite fence" built to shut out a neighbor's view of the ocean. Other objects frequently used are bridges, vases, birds, the seasons, to name a few. The writer must strive to find fresh uses for familiar symbols. Or to find new symbols.

Resolving Device

A symbol must be carefully selected as the one best able to bring subtle inference to the meaning to be drawn from it. *The symbol should come naturally from the environment and the characters, and should fit easily into the action and movement of the story.* One of my students wrote a story of people in a coal-mining community. The main character, a young woman, longs to escape the environment. As the story opens, she is planning her escape. In the background she hears the train whistle, a symbol of her means of escape. One feels an urgency in her actions, but it is not until the end of the story that one discovers a part of the urgency is due to a murder she has committed in order to have the money for escape. At the end of the story the town marshal comes for her. The train whistle she hears then, growing fainter and fainter, symbolizes her receding hope of escape. Other images used in the story were in keeping with the grime and hopelessness of the girl's environment.

A symbol must have universality—be an object familiar to all. It must have an emotional quality. The train whistle spoke for the emotions of all miners, perhaps of all people who feel trapped in the hopelessless of their environment.

The symbol must have purpose. The writer must know when and how to bring it into the story. It might, for instance, have a parallel in nature. I recall the story of a mother whose son wants to go to camp. His father feels he should be allowed to go, but the mother fears for him. One day she goes outside to feed the cat and sees the mother cat push her nursing kitten from her toward the saucer. The kitten cries and clings to the mother, but she pushes him forward and walks away. Thus the mother realizes that she, too, must push her child toward maturity. This symbol has been used many times in various ways. A fresher way to use it might be to have a mother and son loading a truck when they are moving, and as they lift a heavy carton over the tail-gate, the mother realizes that, for the first time, the son is lifting more than half the load. Thus she realizes that he can shoulder his share of responsibility.

In these stories, the symbol is used as the resolving device. It causes the main character to achieve new insight which changes her attitude and thus resolves her problem by bringing her to a decision. *When the symbol is used as a resolving device, it must be planted early in the story,* so that it is present when the time comes to use it. It should be planted in such a way that its purpose is not obvious. For instance, when the cat and kitten appear early in the story, they seem to be only part of the background. The boy is playing with them; this serves to underscore his immaturity and to support the mother's feeling that he is too young to go to camp. It isn't until later that their real purpose becomes evident. In the story of the mining camp, the reader is led to think of the train as a means of escape rather than, as he later discovers, of typifying her abandonment.

The idea is to lead away from the real purpose of the symbol, actually to divert the reader from seeing its real purpose until the time comes to use it in resolving the problem.

Parallel Story Action

A symbol must never be too abstract to be understood. If too abstract, its inference is lost upon the reader. The purpose of a symbol is to emblematise, to imply, rather than to obtrude.

In some stories a symbol parallels the story action. For instance, suppose a man has withdrawn to his cabin on the Bay to struggle with a depression which threatens to bring him to a suicidal act. His wife has died, his business is failing, life seems to be falling apart. About to take his life, he sees a boat fighting the rising storm on the Bay, and he identifies with its struggle for life, seeing it as akin to his own struggle. As he watches, sometimes thinking back to his past which throws light upon the present condition, the reader knows that the boat's success in riding out the storm will determine the man's decision as well. The story could take one of several different turns. The man could get caught up in the boat's struggle and liken it to his own (with the help of the flashbacks of his own struggle). When he sees that the boat can come through what seems like insurmountable odds, he feels that he, too, can overcome if he continues to fight.

Perhaps if a writer wished to shape the story differently—the boat could be battered and sink but the man could come to the conclusion that while the boat is defeated because it can't win out over the storm, *he* can call upon his strength of will and determine to win his struggle. If the story were shaped in this way, the boat and the storm would still serve as a symbol, acting as a resolving factor. Thus the man's conflict is paralleled and made more dramatic by the struggle of the boat. Such a parallel is often used when otherwise the conflict would take place only in the mind of the main character, offering little drama or suspense.

Worsening Plight, Personal Fight

Symbolism was at its best in the movie *The Defiant Ones,* in which Tony Curtis played the role of the white prisoner, and Sidney Poitier the role of the black prisoner. The surface, or visible story, was of the two convicts chained together, returning in the prison truck from a day's labor. They escape, but cannot escape each other because of their chains. During the days following they come to despise each other, hurling at each other all their buried resentments and hatreds. The surface story is filled with action and suspense, but it is at its deeper level of meaning that it becomes great. The entire story stands as a comment upon the relationship of the two races. The theme is that neither white nor black race can save itself alone, for the two are irrevocably chained together, the fate of the one hanging on the fate of the other. The chains are the symbol of their bondage. Even when they are finally able to sever them and the black man goes on, while the white man remains in the lonely cabin to rape the woman living there, he is not free, for he sees the captors heading toward the cabin and knows he must return to warn the white man. If he is captured he realizes, he, too, will be overtaken.

Sometimes a symbol is used to create mood, such as a bleak moor to create somberness, or a raging storm to create violence. The symbol both implies and intensifies action. The recurring wail of a wolf in a wilderness background can symbolize loneliness, or can foreshadow and intensify danger.

Sometimes writers have more than one symbol at work in the same story. Take, for example, a story by Esther Wagner titled "The Slip" which appeared several years ago in *Atlantic Monthly.*

The main character has an alcoholic problem and has gone to the oceanside to visit her sister-in-law, who is away from home as the story takes place. One knows early in the story that she has gone with the secret purpose of "slipping." She sees a car on the beach, mired in the sand, and three young men trying frantically to free the wheels as the tide comes in. As she imbibes quite freely from her sister-in-law's liquor supply, she watches the frantic effort of the boys, and though she knows that the tide will overwhelm the car, she goes down the long flight of steps from the cottage to the beach, to offer them at one time the suggestion that there is a gas station where they might seek help (well knowing the man couldn't leave his station to come); at another time, when that has failed, she goes down to offer them a drink from her bottle. Each time the trip up and down the long flight of steps grows increasingly difficult, and the plight of the boys worsens.

Here you have two symbols—the steps and the worsening plight of the car, though the parallelism is stronger with the car's plight and therefore the frantic plight of the boys, since the father of one of them owns the car. The steps are directly related to her own physical condition. Throughout her watching of the car and her trips down to the beach, there are flashbacks giving clues as to what may have caused her problem (mother, husband, particularly the older husband's role) as well as incidents showing how her condition has worsened through the years, until she has been told that one more time will be the final time for her. As the story ends, she manages the uphill climb of the long steps, but falls as she reaches the top. The boys have had to abandon the car to the tide.

I am often amazed to find an object in a story that would make a perfect symbol, yet the writer has failed to make use of it. Perhaps instinctively we reach for symbols, yet do not always recognize them or find their use.

Symbols are everywhere. They will enhance your writing. It will take practice to use them effectively, but the enrichment they bring to your work is well worth the effort.

Hal Blythe and Charlie Sweet

Naming Names: How to Make Your Story Real and Accessible

When Steven Spielberg made *E.T.,* the company that makes Reese's Pieces *paid* to have the cute extraterrestrial go bonkers over that brand of candy. We suspect that Spielberg would have used a specific brand of candy in the film even without getting paid for it, because when E.T. munched something that everyone in the audience had also munched at one time or another, the creature—and the entire story—became more accessible, and more real.

Making specific mention of places, products and other items in your story gives you the same results: accessibility and reality. This technique has been called brand-name realism and trademark detail, and writers from Stephen King to Bobbie Ann Mason employ it. For example, Mason's prize-winning "Shiloh" is filled with Popsicle sticks, Rexall drugstores, Lincoln Logs and Diet Pepsi. These details capture the essence of her characters and their values.

To be exact, the precision of "brand-name realism" offers these advantages:

Specific names reduce the potential for confusion. When your names are specific, readers can't assume your "Southern region" is Hazzard County when you mean Yoknapatawpha, your restaurant is McDonald's when you mean Tavern on the Green, your wine is Ripple when you mean Dom Perignon.

Specific names sharpen the picture you are creating in readers' minds. To use the examples above, the readers aren't forced to imagine vague, generic Southern regions, restaurants or wines (and the stereotypes that such imaginings might be based on) when you name them specifically. Such names present clear images, and dispel fuzzy ones.

Specific names make the fictional world seem real by tapping the readers' "reality." Eight-year-olds eat Cap'n Crunch and forty-year-olds eat Wheaties, and when they spot these precise references in fiction, they more willingly cross the threshold into the fictional world made less distant and foreboding because it is now as familiar as their own kitchens. Stephen King uses this technique well. He sets his horror tales in worlds people know exist—because they live in them, too. King lines his fictional cupboards with Lestoil, Top Job, Diamond Blue-Tip matches and Scotch tape. When King introduces the abnormal, it shocks because it seems all the more possible in the readers' world.

Naming the Devices

Specific names also allow you to control reader understanding and perception of the world you are creating, in these ways:

Specific names help define character. We're not talking about character names here, though the name you give to each character *is* important to how readers perceive that character. Instead, we're referring to the names of the elements of the character's world.

Let's say you're writing about a teenager. To convince readers that they've stepped into a 15-year-old's world, you don't just put a pair of sneakers in the scene. Toss a pair of loose-laced Air Jordans on the bed. Don't describe the room as covered with pictures of rock bands; paper the walls with posters of REM or David Bowie. That portable radio with earphones on the dresser? It's a Walkman. And those crumbs on the pillow aren't from just any junk food—they're the remains of a Twinkie.

Suppose you replace the posters with a picture of Amy Grant. Now you're suggesting a completely different character: someone who's more outwardly religious. Or suppose a "Be All You Can Be" recruiting poster hangs on the wall. And what happens if you substitute shreds of Skoal for the Twinkie crumbs, or if the Walkman becomes a refinished Victrola? Even changing the Air Jordans to Reeboks implies differences in character.

Specific names communicate atmosphere. Atmosphere is the emotional aura of a story, which establishes the audience's expectations and attitudes. Names help you control atmosphere and, therefore, how your readers feel about the fictional world they have entered. Their use can be more subtle than the verbal foreshadowing of an intrusive narrator.

Suppose you want to telegraph to your audience that something is amiss in our teenager's room. A couple of changes will create a foreboding atmosphere. Those posters now are of Janis Joplin, Jim Morrison and Jimi Hendrix—all dead rock singers. Instead of Air Jordans on the bed, we see books—and not just nameless books: *Papa Hemingway: A*

Personal Memoir and *Hedda Gabler*—both about people who committed suicide. These details contribute to the audience's sense of impending death.

Specific names can establish the time frame of your story. Surface details can quickly communicate approximately when your story takes place. Instead of Twinkie crumbs and a copy of *Self* in our teenager's room, we find Moxie and an issue of *Liberty,* and we know immediately that the story is not set in the present.

A few years ago, we sold a story called "Evidence in an Elegy," set in 1649. We convinced the audience of the time frame by referring to historical figures, events and actual locations of that period. Our fictional protagonist knows poet Anne Bradstreet, is minister at King's Chapel Church, and finds the forest site of a black mass outside Boston.

Specific names establish place. Our teen's room, if scattered with Jack-in-the-Box wrappers, is likely to be somewhere on the West Coast, where that fast-food chain is located. If cluttered with Frisch's Big Boy wrappers, it is likely in the Ohio-Kentucky area, where that chain operates.

To establish place, however, you will concentrate more on geographical features than regional products and such. In our example, a quick reference to Sunset Boulevard or to the Ohio River would more quickly establish the Coast or the Ohio Valley.

False Reality

What's ironic about this business of naming names is that the names you use don't have to be real. They need only be specific. For example, mystery writer Lawrence Block has mentioned the Rabson lock he often refers to in his novels. The Rabson is the most secure lock made today. Except no one makes it. Block made it up—yet, buyers probably ask for the Rabson almost as often as a Yale or a Master.

Readers believe that such a lock exists because it is mentioned with confidence. It is part of the fiction, yet it is clearly real to the characters. Readers, therefore, also believe that it's real, and the fiction itself becomes that much more tangible.

Making up names gives you greater control over the story by increasing your control over the advantages of using specific names: namely, the control over establishing atmosphere, creating character, and so on. Block's burglar character Bernie Rhodenbarr can pick not just any lock, but a *Rabson,* the best lock in the world. Block has told you more about Rhodenbarr by creating a fictional superlock than he would have had he used a real brand.

As another example, to suggest that a character comes from an environmentally determined background, for instance, we'd probably list his hometown not as the existing Fitzgerald, Georgia, but as Kudzu, Georgia. By using the name of the creeping vines that strangle all vegetation, we imply more than we could had we used a real name.

The Name of the Beast

Despite the advantages of this specificity, you must be careful when using this tool. Just as there are proper names, there are proper ways to use those names. Keep these tips in mind:

Don't overdo it. The first time we introduce the concept of brand-name detail to our creative writing students, they roadblock their manuscripts with ultra-detailed descriptions. If you list every item your heroine wears, from her Nike headband to her L.L. Bean deck-shoed toes, you'll bore rather than engage the reader. An avalanche of detail buries people and places rather than illuminating them, and it slows your readers' progress. Remember, you're writing fiction, not a Spiegel catalog.

Detail alone is no substitute for insight. Another danger of a supermarket list of detail is you mistakenly come to think that that's all you need to reveal characters and events. In our story of the teenager, precise and full descriptions of the room and its inhabitant will not allow you to overlook the *story,* and descriptions of the teen's dialogue, thoughts and physical interactions.

Avoid playing "pin the detail on the story." Effective detail is not an afterthought—it grows out of the story. Choose a precise name because it helps you and your audience understand what you mean. Include nothing that doesn't do some "work" in the story.

Be consistent with details. If your teen's room is strewn with Twinkies and Dunkin' Donuts, don't stick a Diet Pepsi on the nightstand. A junk-food addict isn't apt to worry about the 104 additional calories in a non-diet soda. Of course, you could use the out-of-place item as contrast, or to elucidate a character quirk.

If you're setting your story in Miami, don't have your characters eat at Frisch's Big Boy. To avoid doing that, we went to the library and read a copy of *The Miami Herald* for names we could use.

If your story takes place in 1965, don't have anyone enjoying a can of Slice. Go back to magazines and papers published in '65 for the details you need.

Make up names that sound real. A Rabson lock sounds real. An Acme lock doesn't. Kudzu, Georgia, sounds real. Centerville, Georgia, doesn't. Beware of generic sorts of names, cute names (unless that's the effect you want) and outlandish names. Search for names that fit what you are describing, and that sound plausible. For our latest novel, we created a genetic engineering corporation named Virginia BioTech—a name we felt fit in with the types of names being given such corporations these days.

Make sure made-up names aren't real. We claimed that our Virginia BioTech was listed on the Big Board as VBT. We then checked the listings in the NYSE, AMEX, NASDAQ and *Standard and Poor's.* Ask your librarian for directories such as *Trade Names Directory* to make sure that someone hasn't created your "mythical" name already. And, of course, atlases and phone books are useful in this regard.

Use brand names correctly. The point of all of this is to be precise in your descriptions; continue that quest for precision when using established names. For example, if you say your character uses an osterizer for blending drinks, you risk lack of clarity by incorrectly using *Osterizer* as a generic term for blender. If it is indeed an Osterizer, say so. If it is something else—perhaps he uses a Cuisinart to blend his drinks, which could give clues to his character—say that. Leave no room for confusion. If it really doesn't matter *how* he blends his drinks, just say he uses a blender.

Finally, don't daydream too long about the manufacturer of Reese's Pieces paying you to slip a mention of its product into your latest manuscript. When we were writing the Mike Shayne detective series, we had the big redhead smoke not just any cigarette, but Camel unfiltereds. Do you think we were foolish enough to sit in our Levis and La-Z-Boy recliners waiting for the R.J. Reynolds check to come?

Will C. Knott

Using Flashback Effectively; or Is This Trip Necessary?

In many stories or novels, those crucial events that have helped to make your characters what they are may already have taken place. The trouble is that these events are back where you can't get your hands on them easily—and now you need your reader's awareness of them in order to make clear to him what is happening or about to happen in your story.

One solution is to go back:

> His thoughts returned to that incredible afternoon ten years before when first he met her. He could almost hear her again—calling to him across that field. It was a Sunday. He'd been up all that previous night . . .

And so on. You stop the story and take the reader back along with you. The trouble is that sometimes your reader would rather not make that trip; he'd rather go on with the story. As a result, you lose him. For this reason, you should think twice before writing the flashback.

Look at it this way. If what happened long ago is so important and exciting that it will add vital interest and meaning to your story, why not start back there in the first place? Tell it vividly. Then jump ahead to the time of your story and proceed from there. You could write the segment as a short, introductory paragraph to your story, or as an italicized opening portion of your first chapter. However you do it, you will be including the needed material, but your forward momentum will not be sacrificed.

What you'll probably find, actually, is that you don't need to use a full-scale flashback, that the information can be fed in gradually during the course of the narrative.

To illustrate this point, let us go first to the full-scale flashback, then show how this same material can be fed into the narrative without the use of the flashback:

> Martin flipped off the intercom, got up and went to the window. Paul Scranton—his wife Elaine's cousin—was on his way up. And Scranton had no idea that Janet had been his kid sister.

As he stood there at the window, he found himself back in the doorway of that small furnished room, straining to see in the dim light.

"Janet," he had called softly. "Janet. Is that you?"

"Yes." Her voice was ragged, hopeless.

He closed the door behind him. Janet was lying face down across the bed, the phone in her hand. She turned to look at him, her face swollen from crying.

He moved to her side, took the phone from her hand and lifted it to his ear. "You still there, Janet?" came a cold voice. "Now listen. You know you got yourself into this. You had your fun too, don't forget. We both got our kicks. But the game's over now. I'll swear the kid's not mine. So get an abortion. Don't be a sap. So long. It was real nice knowing you." He hung up.

"Who was that?" Martin asked tightly, surprised at the control in his voice.

"Paul," Janet said dully. "Paul Scranton."

He put the phone down and sat beside her on the bed and placed his hand on the small of her back. "Look sis. If you want the kid, keep it. If not, see me. Together we can handle this thing. Forget that crumb."

"I already have," she said. He didn't like the sound of her voice.

"Come on, sis. We're getting out of here. This is no place for you."

She rolled away from him. "Leave me alone, Marty. I'm all right. I'm over 21. Just let me handle this, will you?"

He got up and looked down at her. "I want to help. Let me."

"I don't *want* you to help. This is my life, Marty. Thanks. But no thanks."

He felt drained; looking down at her, he suddenly realized how little control he had over those forces that touched the people he loved. Always he'd tried to save Janet from . . . this sort of thing . . . from guys like Paul Scranton. But now he saw how helpless he was—had always been.

"All right," he said, his voice tight. "But give me a call if you need anything—anything at all. Please." He opened his wallet and dropped some bills onto the bed. "Here. Get yourself a nicer place than this. Do that much for me anyway."

She smiled wanly. "Sure, Marty. I promise. Now get out of here. I'm a mess."

So he had left her in that room. Perhaps he should have insisted that she come with him, but he hadn't. And later Janet went to some butcher for the abortion. The operation had been botched cruelly, and Janet had died in a cheap, evil-smelling room across town.

And now he was about to meet this same Paul Scranton face to face. He turned from the window just as the door opened. Scranton entered swiftly, a cocky smile on his face, his hand extended. Martin shook it and indicated a leather chair next to his desk.

Scranton sat down. "Thanks for seeing me."

"Elaine had some fine things to say about you, Paul. She wanted me to help—to see if I couldn't place you somewhere."

"That's awfully decent of her."

"Been in New York long?"

"Just got in."

"What made you ring Elaine?"

He smiled. "When a guy needs a friend, that's Elaine."

"Of course."

"And I knew her pretty well in college."

Martin caught the hint of something in that statement and tightened. All right. He would help this fellow. He would help him good. He leaned forward in his seat.

"I do have a job," he began. "It's not exactly the easiest. . . ."

Feeding in Antecedent Material

Now let's feed this bit of antecedent material in with the narrative:

Martin flipped the intercom. Scranton was on his way up. He had promised Elaine he would help him, but since the moment he realized who Paul Scranton was, he had known he would be unable to keep that promise. How could he forget what Scranton had done to his kid sister? The odd thing was that Scranton apparently had no idea he knew.

He got up as Scranton entered swiftly, confidently, a cocky smile on his face, his hand extended. Martin shook the offered hand and indicated the leather chair next to his desk.

Scranton sat down. "Thanks for seeing me."

"Elaine had some fine things to say about you, Paul. She wanted me to help—to see if I couldn't place you somewhere."

"That's awfully decent of her."

Yes. Martin remembered that voice—so hard and smooth. He had heard it three years before when he had taken a phone from his sister's hand as she lay face down on an unmade bed in a dingy furnished room. Lifting the phone to his ear he heard that cold voice—heard its chill, rasping brutality:

You got yourself into this, kid. You had your fun and games, and I had mine. I'll swear it's not my kid. Get an abortion. Don't be a sap. So long. It was real nice knowing you.

And then had come the harsh click of the dead phone.

Janet got the abortion; but it was botched cruelly. She had died in a cheap, evil-smelling room somewhere across town.

"Been in New York long?" Martin asked.

"Just got in."

"What made you ring Elaine?"

He smiled. "When a guy needs a friend—that's Elaine."

"Of course."

"And I knew her pretty well in college."

Martin caught the hint of something·in that statement and tightened. All right. He would help this fellow. He would help him good. He leaned forward in his seat.

"I do have a job," he began. "It's not exactly the easiest. . . ."

In this second version the reader gets the information he needs, and he is certainly made aware of the anguish the hero feels; but it is all part of the present scene, integrated into the narrative so smoothly that the action is hardly slowed at all.

In fact isn't this how the past acts on us all—as occasional shards invading the fabric of our present—giving sudden poignancy to an otherwise casual encounter? As we move down the streets of our lives, we have with us as constant companions the ghosts of those people and events that once were a part of our present. We get them back in fugitive bits and pieces, never as full-blown episodes. If our aim, then, is to capture in fiction the illusion of life, handling material in the manner shown in the second example seems to be the wisest course.

All Right Then: Go Back

Nevertheless, there will be times when you simply have to devote a small passage or a chapter or two to the past. You can recall novels or short stories, I am sure, in which flashbacks were used quite effectively.

Well then, how do you know when you should use the full flashback? When, no matter how skillful you are at feeding in antecedent material, you find you have not been able to impart to the reader enough of what he must know. Perhaps the material of the flashback is so dramatic, so filled with the conflict your story needs at this point that you simply can't throw away this material. And then again the information contained in the flashback may be absolutely crucial to an understanding of the lead character's motivation.

All right, then. Go back.

> Ben was asleep in the cabin loft and Will was sitting atop the corral fence, having a solitary smoke. The sight of Josh for the second time that day had sent his thoughts back.
>
> He had told Josh he was in this high country because of a promise he had made to someone. Yes, but not a promise he had made to Pike Johnson—as Josh undoubtedly thought. No, Will's promise had been to Kathy Blackmann, to Josh's mother.
>
> *With a quick sweep of her pale hand, Kathy caught the luxuriant fullness of her auburn hair and sent it cascading back down over her bare shoulders. "I want to see him, Will! I want to go back just once and see him on a horse. I want to watch him ride—see him smile. Will, he's got the finest, most honest smile. Honest to God, he has!"*
>
> *"I believe you," he said, laughing and pulling her to him, cradling her naked shoulders and breasts in his own naked arms. He kissed her lightly on the tip of her nose—a strong handsome nose, nothing cute about it.*
>
> *He pulled back and looked at her. Her dark powerful eyes burned like coals in her flushed cheeks. With a sudden ache Will realized how sick she*

was—what a terrible lie those flushed cheeks were. Kathy Blackmann was dying. She knew it. Josie knew it. They all knew it, but said nothing. He kissed her suddenly on the lips and drank deep, her warmth filling him, renewing him.

"You're not listening," she said, a hint of despair in her voice as her lips left his.

"Yes, I am, Kathy."

She sighed, "I wrote Josh's father. I asked if I could come back for just a visit. He wouldn't allow it. He wants me to stay dead. I know what he must have told Josh—that I ran off with that poor slip of a cow hand."

"Maybe you should write Josh—tell him the truth. Tell him what really happened."

She frowned and turned away. "No. It would turn Josh against his father. And right now that's all he's got. He loves his father, admires him—and someday that empire John's building will belong to Josh. I want that for him. If I did anything now to upset that it would leave him with nothing."

Will took her in his arms again, astonished as always by the tenacity and depth of a mother's love for her own. "All right," he said. "Don't write him, then. Just get better, that's all."

She nodded solemnly at that, then pulled away and looked up into his face. "Will, promise me one thing?"

"Name it."

"If . . . well, if anything were to happen to me, would you go back . . . I mean to see how Josh is getting on . . . to see that he doesn't . . . well, let his father's brutality take all the gentleness—all the kindness out of him?"

"That's a tall order, Kathy."

"I trust you, Will."

"It's a promise. But nothing's going to happen to you, Kathy. You're going to be back helping Josie run this place before long. You'll see. Now, come here—before Josie comes back in with some more of that damn medicine of hers."

Willingly, her dark eyes smoldering, Kathy raised her face to his. . . .

Will flicked his cigarette away into the gathering twilight, recalling with a dull ache the pitiless, relentless speed with which Kathy's dread illness consumed her—leaving him with only his memory of her and of his promise.

If the material in this flashback had been fed bit by bit into the ongoing narrative as suggested earlier, it would have been very difficult for the writer to capture the essence of that scene, which was this man's love for the woman and her love for her son. Meanwhile, of course, much additional antecedent material pertaining to this woman's story will still need to be fed into the narrative both before and after this flashback.

Notice the use of italics. This enabled the writer to dispense with the use of *had* in the opening of the flashback and plunge the reader instantly backward in time so that the immediacy of the scene is enhanced, thus taking the curse off the fact that all this happened in the past.

This is an important factor, since once you decide to go back you must exploit to the hilt the flashback's full dramatic potential and write the episode as vividly as you would write about an event taking place in the present. Think of it as present, in fact. This will help.

If you choose not to use italics throughout the flashback—and it would not be a good idea if the flashback were any longer than the one I quoted—simply skip four spaces and proceed as in the first example given in this chapter. Start off, using *had* with your verbs for a while to indicate to the reader that this has all happened before. But since the objectionable feature of the flashback is that the reader knows it has all happened in the past, dispense with *had* as soon as possible. Keep *had* for the first sentence of the flashback only. When you return to the present, you may indicate this by using *had* again, but remember, use this helping verb sparingly:

> When Tom at last tried his arm under the beneficent heat of the Florida sun, he found that his arm had not been convinced by his catcher's trusting diagnosis. His shoulder had bothered him with the first pitch. Yet, at that point, the pain had not been something he couldn't grit through, so he said nothing more about it and had begun to pitch regularly.
>
> Now, as Tom waited in the empty little office, his aching shoulder a constant reminder of the game he had just lost, he felt that he was slipping into a nightmare from which there was no chance of waking. . . .

In summary, try not to rely on the flashback for antecedent material that you might feed into your ongoing narrative. If, however, you feel that you will gain more than you will lose by stopping the narrative and going back, then do so.

But always ask yourself: Is this trip necessary?

Kit Reed

What to Leave Out and What to Put In

It's easier to talk about what to leave out of a short story than what to put in.

You leave out everything that doesn't belong.

The inner logic of a given story will determine this to a large extent. Each choice you make will focus and channel your work. Everything: The words you choose, ideas, characters, belong in a particular story *only as they function in that story* and you as writer are going to have to be ruthless about getting rid of anything that doesn't belong.

Short fiction is particularly demanding. Novelists are permitted occasional indulgences because the stage they occupy may be as intimate as a theater-in-the-round or large enough to accommodate a cast of thousands including elephants, but a writer of short stories has a relative space the approximate size of a puppet stage, and if he lets things get out of control he will end up knocking over scenery and threatening the entire arrangement with collapse.

The business of a short story of three to ten thousand words must be accomplished in such a limited compass that any misstep can throw the entire story out of proportion. At every point the writer needs to resist the temptations to digression: falling in love with the sound of his own voice, or following a lesser character for too long because he happens to be interesting. If he is that interesting, either the story is focused in the wrong place or else the writer is backing into something larger, a novella or a novel. If the landscape takes over then maybe the story is about the landscape and not the people in the foreground; in either case the story is out of control and you are going to have to make sacrifices to bring it into focus.

If you are working with some concern for inner logic, you'll discover before long that most of the major problems solve themselves. Given a specific set of choices, or givens, you have already excluded a great many things, beginning with anything that disrupts the mood. A comic story may be a number of things besides funny, and almost anything can happen, but it had better be told in a way that maintains the reader's sense of comedy, and a story which is essentially serious in tone will go haywire if you try to tack on a funny ending unless you have prepared for it. If you're going to throw a custard pie at the end, you'd better have it behind your back the whole time.

Given a certain point of view and a specific place to stand, you've already excluded other kinds of points of view and places to stand. Given a set of characters, you know by their nature which kinds of things they will do and which they won't, and which of these actions belong in the story. Each defining choice will strengthen your sense of what belongs and what doesn't.

The simple rule of thumb is: *Everything you put in a story had better function in the story.* If it doesn't function it doesn't belong.

Beyond the built-in understanding supplied by inner logic, you may find some use for a simple set of rules.

What to Cut

Here are some things to leave out of short stories.

1. *What characters do between scenes.* If two people have a fight at the office and then they go to their respective homes and have supper and pay the bills or make some phone calls and go to the movies and go back home to their respective beds and get ready for bed and get in bed and go to sleep and wake up and have breakfast and go to the office and meet again and have another fight, it is quite likely that we don't need to know about it. All that extraneous information can be implied by dropping them at the end of the fight:

"All right, dammit. I don't care if I never see you again," and picking them up in the next scene:

> Naturally the next morning they saw each other again, as they had every morning; after all, their desks were side by side in the same corner of the office.

If, on the other hand, one of them has gone home and constructed a pistol out of some cotton wadding and gunpowder and a length of pipe, we had probably better hear about it.

This is a gross example of an extremely complicated matter: All that eating and sleeping didn't belong in the story, but anything that grew out of the fight, anything that would affect the outcome, did belong. Anything that serves character or development belongs, but the things characters do *between* things can simply be skipped. We as readers are familiar enough with quick cuts and dissolves in the movies to be able to fill in the blanks for ourselves, and, furthermore, to assume with very little prompting that a scene has shifted.

2. *Unnecessary dialogue must go.* Only the important business stays, and although you can hint that people are having a boring discussion about the weather, don't give it in full. Another gross example:

> "Good morning Mr. Ransom," Higgins said.
> "Good morning, Higgins."
> "Nice day we're having."
> "Yes it is, isn't it, Higgins?"
> "Yes I think so, as a matter of fact it was so lovely out that I walked."
> "Did you really?"
> "Yes, it only took another ten minutes, and the sun felt so good on my back. Everything is in bloom."
> "I know, my dahlias are out already, and Mrs. Ransom is very excited about the marigolds, we're going to have thousands of them this year, but by the way, Higgins."
> "Yes, Mr Ransom."
> "You're late."
> "I know I'm late sir, but I thought you would understand, you know, how beautiful it was out and all, how lovely the flowers were . . ."
> "I love flowers just as much as you do, Higgins, but if it hadn't been the flowers it would have been your car stalled, or you found an injured pussycat, you're late today because you're always late and I'm getting damn sick and tired of you being late."

OK. The business of the scene is that Higgins takes his sweet time getting to the office and for Ransom today is the last straw. Unless their fight is going to culminate in Higgins going over and poisoning Ransom's garden, or something that happened on Higgin's walk to the office is going to function in the story later on, all you really need is:

> "Good morning, Mr. Ransom," Higgins said. "It was so beautiful out that I decided to walk."
> "Late again, Higgins."
> "The sun was so warm on my back, all the flowers are out . . ."
> "Forget the flowers, Higgins, you are late."

We have arrived at the confrontation without any detours.

3. *You can leave out anything you had to write to get from one point to another.* Sometimes this is a scene which you, as writer, had to work through in order to know what was going to happen next. Sometimes, as in the weather dialogue above, it's what you had to make your characters say in order to discover for yourself what the true business of the scene was. If the business is the one man being late and the other man being angry, we as readers might like to know that the one is late because of the weather, but that's all we need to know, and it can be done in a single line. Character descriptions written to help the author discover character, or extensive physical descriptions written to help the author

discover setting or action, should be combed relentlessly. Anything that does not enhance the finished story, anything that distracts or bores the reader has to go.

4. *You can leave out elapsed time*. This is so logical and obvious, the process is so simple that many beginning writers don't see it at first. Faced with a gap of days or weeks or years between one crucial event and another, they will find themselves writing in summers and snow-falls from a compulsion to *fill the space between events*. Movies and television have educated this generation of readers and writers to the quick cut, the flashback and flash forward, the shock cut and any number of other techniques; we have absorbed them by osmosis and whether we realize it or not, they are a natural part of our equipment. You already know these things; you can put them to use in fiction. IF NOTHING GOES ON BETWEEN ONE SCENE AND ANOTHER, CUT DIRECTLY. Most of us as readers have become so sophisticated about filmmakers' cuts from one scene to another, from one location to another, that we are more than ready to make any leap an author asks. We can be moved from one scene to another, from one location to another so swiftly that we walk into the next moment without stopping to ask how we got there.

5. *You can leave out most explanations*. You can assume that your reader knows almost as much as you do about your setting, or the occupation of your central character. Naturally he doesn't, but for complicated reasons which I'll attempt to get at here, he'll think it's his fault. There is a mysterious authority to the printed word. One of the most important things you as writer will learn is how to exercise that authority. The reader who does not know everything about offices, or newspaper city rooms or steamfitting or long-distance running seldom blames the writer for not filling him in. Instead he will feel faintly guilty in the face of your assumption that he does know, because in assuming that he knows, you are also implying that it is his business to know. What's more he will resent you if you assume he is ignorant and slow down a story in order to explain.

If it is important to the story he'll find some way to supply the missing details as best he can, and if you, as writer, choose to give him a few clues or crumbs of information to head him in the right direction, he will fall on them with gratitude. Depending on who he is, the reader will fill in the details in one of three ways:

a. He will put in what you have left out, using his own store of knowledge to create the setting. The newsroom you see may not necessarily be the one he furnishes in his own mind, but it will function for him. He'll use everything he's read or heard or seen on film or TV to put together a functioning background for your story. He will do the same whether it takes place in an insane asylum or Alaska or the army.

b. Or he will read carefully for context, and figure out the details from what you have given him, combining what you give with what he already knows to fill in the picture. In *A Clockwork Orange* Anthony Burgess imposes an entire vocabulary on his readers by the relentless use of new words in familiar contexts. After a few pages readers know that tolchoks are blows and peeting is drinking and they accept an alien vocabulary for the same reason. Burgess doesn't explain; reader doesn't refer to his glossary. Reading swiftly and for context, reader figures it out. The same goes for Ernest Hemingway and his *cojones*.

c. Or, if the reader feels guilty enough about his ignorance, he'll find some way to find out what he doesn't know. He'll look it up or ask somebody. He'll do this because he knows you are assuming he is just as smart as you are, and he is moved to live up to your expectations. He will, furthermore, be pathetically grateful for whatever he learns from context and he'll absorb whatever details you have given him into his memory banks for use the next time he's faced with a similar problem. Thanks to you, he gets wise; the next time he is faced with a newspaper city room or a steamfitting shop or a long distance race he'll nod sagely. Yup, yup, I know about this one; uh-huh, uh-huh, yeah.

Here's an example. It would be possible to begin a story about a reporter as follows:

> The city room of an evening newspaper is organized according to function. There is a U-shaped arrangement of desks with the city editor sitting at the center of the U and the rewrite person sitting next to him. On the paper in this story he is responsible for everything that goes into the paper that day; he will decide which stories to send reporters out on and which stories already written are important. He may also make the dummy (showing the composing room which headlines belong on which stories in which size type face) and mark this on top of the copy before passing it on to the people who sit around him in the U. They are called desk men and they read the copy for errors and write the headlines. The reporters all sit at desks ranged around this central U. They have certain regular assignments, but if anything important happens the city editor will make them drop everything to go out and cover the story. They will telephone the reporter or rewrite person with the details and he will put on his headphones and type out the information as fast as it comes in because the deadline is coming and they have to get the story set up in type as quickly as they can so it will be on the front page of the first edition. On an evening paper, the first edition goes to press around noon. Ralph Carlson was a reporter on an evening paper, and he was having his lunch one day when the phone rang and Henderson, the city editor, answered it . . .

Although all that information is background, there is no real reason to give it. All the writer needs to give is what functions:

> Henderson was in the slot that day and when the first call came he listened for a minute and then turned it over to Casey, who was on rewrite. Then he bellowed, "Carson, Williams, there's a hell of a fire at Wooster Square. Get on over there."
>
> "Right." Carson dropped his sandwich onto his story about the Fresh Air Fund and left the newsroom on the run.
>
> Henderson was already on the phone to the composing room. "Tell Ray to hold Page One."

If gentle reader doesn't already know he's in a newspaper office, he'll find out quickly. He will, furthermore, feel stupid for not catching on sooner. "In the slot" implies a position of responsibility and the reader will figure out that Henderson is an editor and in passing that he's learned a new phrase. By the end of the story he will know what the rewrite man does, as the embattled Casey takes in bits of information on the phone and gets the story in shape for Henderson. There is a sense of urgency about ripping up Page One to accommodate this new disaster, and if the sandwich doesn't indicate it's lunchtime, it doesn't much matter. Any real insider will know it's accurate. Meanwhile we as readers are being treated like insiders. By the time the story is over we'll have a pretty good idea what newspaper work is like without ever being instructed. We are involved because the writer assumes we are on the inside of what's going on; even though we may not know exactly where the writer has put us, we're grateful for being considered smart enough to be along on the trip. What's more, we're learning all the time.

Remember that readers hate being condescended to. We all like to think we've been around, and if you insist on explaining at length we will resent that, and, strangely, we will begin to question your authority. Who is this writer trying to convince? Is it really us, or is it himself? Look for the right details to put your reader in the picture and do it with authority. Never apologize for knowing more than he does, and never stop to explain.

6. *Leave out loving descriptions unless they function.* You can give the reader a room, a landscape, any kind of a setting, using as wide a sweep of prose as the subject commands, but you can do so only if this room, or landscape, or setting, or object is going to function in the story. That ormolu clock on the mantel in the old man's sitting room may be a marvel of workmanship, but unless you are going to use it to signify time passing or as an emblem of the grandeur of the old man's past or his regrets, or unless somebody is going to come in and brain him with it,

there is no need to describe it in detail. That autumn landscape that so takes your imagination is suspect too. No matter how beautifully you describe it, it must assert its function in the story in order to belong. You may use it as background, or as the first frame in a sequence that will narrow down to a certain piece of property, the house on the property, a given room in the house, the people in the room. You may set it against the moods of the people in the story or use it in any number of other ways, but if it is there simply because you liked the way you wrote about it, you are going to need to be ruthless. Beautiful as it is, it is going to have to go. Otherwise it is going to stand between the reader and the story like a misplaced flat in an amateur theatrical.

Deciding what to leave out, you will test everything you put in, discarding everything that does not belong. Once you have finished a story you will need to go back and look again, paring, amputating if necessary, until everything that is in the story serves the story.

Once you have developed a relatively sure sense of what to leave out of a short story, you have yet another responsibility: deciding how much to put in. Short stories written by beginners are often sketchy at best, and a new writer dealing in subtleties may assume that because he knows what is going on, the reader is going to know too. He may respond with surprise or resentment when the story fails to come across, saying huffily that it's the reader's fault if he doesn't get it.

This is not necessarily the case.

Writing, you need to put in enough to make a functioning story. You may be as sensitive and subtle as you like, but, working, you must be clear in your own mind about what you are attempting. You need to know what is the center of your story, and you have to be able to focus, to give the reader enough information so that he will know it too.

This is subtle and complex territory. Attempting to write short fiction, you have to supply the indefinable and elusive element which distinguishes story from non-story, and if there is any way to learn about it from the outside it is by reading short stories by the hundreds with some attempt to understand what the writer is doing to you as reader, and how. Having done so you will still have to write stories by the dozens, perhaps even by the hundreds until you as insider feel the movement, the extraordinary number of possibilities for different kinds of movements, and understand at least one of them well enough to convey it to the reader.

I have suggested that as writer, you are already rich in resources, that every word, object, name, action or reaction or speech or stylistic device you choose shapes what you are doing, and that in addition to its more or less universal associations and meanings, each of these has accumulated accretions in the alluvial sludge at the back of your mind, so that every element takes on added value as you use it *according to what it means to you.* If you are good at what you are doing the reader will take all these enriched elements, perhaps enriching them further with his own emotional baggage but at the same time receiving what you intended to give him.

It is here that you must take the most care.

You have to put in enough for the reader to go on.

Using your intensely personal store of references, you can be as subtle or experimental or ambiguous as you like, but there had better be something there to reward close scrutiny and it had better be precisely what you intended. If your meaning is private you can't take it for granted that a good reader is necessarily going to get it, and you'd better not be angry with him if he doesn't. It's probably your fault.

Within the framework of what you are doing, there has to be that focus, that consistency of intention or meaning that a close reading will reveal to the reader who is scrupulous enough to track it down. If the careful reader doesn't get it, don't be too quick to blame him; look at the work again and be at least as quick to question your own judgment as you are to question his. If he couldn't figure out what you meant, could it be in part because you weren't precisely sure? Or were you sure, but careless or imprecise in the way you gave it? Obscurity coming out of authorial uncertainty and imprecision is just as damaging to short stories as a monkey wrench thrown into the electric fan.

There is no easy way to talk about this.

Re-read Like an Outsider

Our friend the electrical engineer introduced me to the information theory, which was developed during a study of military cables transmitted during World War II. Since he used to talk about analog computers with a condescending aside ("giant electronic brains to you"), I have to assume that his explanation was simplistic, and there is also the possibility that I got it wrong. What I extracted has been useful to me and so I offer it here.

As I understand it, the good folks with the computers were engaged in discovering just exactly what percent of a given message had to be transmitted for the intent of the message to get through. If wartime cables were too garbled in transmission, if too many parts were left out, the whole intent was lost. Either the message was misconstrued or it didn't get through. If a certain crucial percentage of the message was presented, the mind would supply whatever was missing and the message would go through.

The writer needs to supply enough to give the reader the meaning he, the writer, intends. This can be done with great subtlety; the reader is capable of supplying enormous amounts for himself, doing a large part of the work, and so sharing in the excitement of discovery. On the other hand, as writer, you want him to make the discovery you intended him to make. You don't want him to invent some wild story loosely based on the sparse elements you have given him. The delicate balance, then, is to give the reader enough to carry him through to your intended meaning, or moment of discovery, without having to spell it out word for word.

This means that although his mind is going to supply whatever is missing, he is going to supply a wrong meaning unless you give him enough details or information to point him in the right direction. If you write a story without a center, the reader is going to try and find one; after all, he has trusted you this far, and because he trusted you enough to come this far with you, he has to assume you brought him here to some purpose. If he emerges from your story without discovering the center, he still assumes you are telling him all this for some reason and unless he has given up in disgust, he will supply one. Nine times out of ten, you as writer aren't going to like the construction he puts on your story, and whether or not he gives up on the meaning or supplies a wrong meaning, your work is wasted.

This means that it is extremely important for you, as writer, to know what you are trying to do in a story; where you pick the reader up and where you want to leave him. Then it is your business to put in *enough* detail, or action, or information or a combination of all those to reward the close reader and prevent gross misinterpretation.

You must write like an insider, because you have to be an insider to write. Having done so, you need to re-read like an outsider, and adjust accordingly.

Hallie and Whit Burnett

Style: The Manner of the Telling

Writing, to be effective, must follow closely the thoughts of the writer, but not necessarily in the order in which these thoughts occur.
—E. B. White, *The Elements of Style*

"Mrs. Hatton believed that thought came first and one developed a writing style through much practice putting his thoughts on paper," wrote Jesse Stuart about his teacher in the Greenup (Kentucky) High School, who first stimulated his desire to write. "When I stop long enough to look back over the past, I think she was one of the greatest English teachers that ever lived." And he added conclusively that above all she warned, "One shouldn't try to do a style for style's sake."

He could never explain, Jesse said, how "gray-haired Mrs. Hatton, who never wrote a short story, essay, poem, or novel, who never made a speech in public, who just taught school all her life and kept a home for her husband and son, knew all these things about creative writing." But with all of Jesse's achievements, his style, which Samuel Butler might have been describing when he advocated just "common, simple straightforwardness," has remained purely and singularly his own.

Many writers have had their say on style, and most of these statements have some value. There is a truism that the best style is the least noticeable, "the manner of which least stands in the way of the matter presented." No one denies the strong influence that Hemingway's simple, direct style has had on American writers living today.

Faulkner, on the other hand, whose Sartoris and Compson families of Jefferson, Mississippi, are known equally well in the literature of the world, seemed to favor a more complex, evocative prose. Faulkner was of the old South; Hemingway was of the North and the Middle West. Faulkner wrote in the tradition of Joyce, erecting Gothic cathedrals beside the simplicity of Hemingway's identifiable modern structures, in the manner of Anderson and Flaubert. Each went through a war, and while it was to some extent the same war, each wrote foremost in his fictional authority and perceptions, and each finally was appreciated by the great world beyond our shores, considered equally representative of the American culture. And yet consider their styles.

Individually Authoritative and Representative

Consider William Faulkner in "A Rose for Emily," which has, as Ray B. West described it, "a general tone of mystery, foreboding, and decay."

Miss Emily Grierson, who has been a concern of the town for many years, living alone with only a black manservant and discouraging all others from entering her house, has died. During her lifetime these things have happened (told almost in conversational flashbacks):

Her father died and she refused to have him buried for three days, saying he was not dead. "Just as they were about to resort to law and force, she broke down, and they buried her father quickly."

> That was when people had begun to feel really sorry for her. People in our town, remembering how old Lady Wyatt, her great-aunt, had gone completely crazy at last, believed that the Griersons held themselves a little too high for what they really were. None of the young men were quite good enough for Miss Emily and such. We had long thought of them as a tableau: Miss Emily a slender figure in white in the background, her father a spraddled silhouette in the foreground, his back to her and clutching a horsewhip, the two of them framed by the back-flung front door. So when she got to be 30 and was still single, we were not pleased exactly, but vindicated; even with insanity in the family she wouldn't have turned down all of her chances if they had really materialized.

But then, after she was ill for a time, she took in a man to live with her, Homer Barron, a Yankee— "a big, dark, ready man, with a big voice and eyes lighter than his face."

Eventually he disappeared, and the people thought he had left her. But when she died, and the townspeople pounded down a door that seemed never to have been opened, they found the body of Homer Barron "apparently once lain in an embrace" on the bed.

Ernest Hemingway in giving Whit [Burnett] permission to reprint "The Short Happy Life of Francis Macomber" in *This Is My Best,* told him to say that "Mr. Hemingway thought that was as reprintable as any other of his stories." There is the Hemingway style, even in a routine permission.

This story is so well known that it is only necessary to remind a reader that it is about Francis Macomber and his wife, Margaret, on safari with Robert Wilson, a white hunter and guide. As the story opens Macomber has been carried into his tent in triumph, having killed his first lion. But it soon develops from the scornful attitude of his wife, and Macomber's own embarrassment, that he has actually bolted and that even the native gunbearers are aware of it, that it is Wilson who has shot the lion.

There seems only one way for Macomber to redeem his cowardice, and that is to kill an animal for himself. He knows his wife will probably leave him anyway, and that the night of his cowardice she has gone to Wilson's bed; but he makes a decision to hunt the buffalo.

They set out on the hunt and suddenly come across three old bull elephants, "three huge, black animals looking almost cylindrical in their long heaviness, like big black tank cars, moving at a gallop across the far edge of the open prairie. They moved at a stiff-necked, stiff-bodied gallop and he could see the up-swept wide black horns on their heads as they galloped heads out; the heads not moving."

Both men shoot; all three buffalo fall. Macomber has a great feeling of elation. "I feel absolutely different," he says.

But the first buffalo gets up again and goes into the bush. They enter the bush in pursuit of it when suddenly they see him "coming out of the bush sideways, fast as a crab, and the bull coming, nose out, mouth tightly closed, blood dripping, massive head straight out, coming in a charge, his little pig eyes bloodshot as he looked at them."

Wilson shot for the nose, "shooting too high each time and hitting the heavy horns, splintering and chipping them like hitting a slate roof," and then Mrs. Macomber in the car shot at the buffalo "with the 6.5 Mannlicher as it seemed about to gore Macomber and had hit her husband about two inches up and a little to one side of the base of his skull."

The dialogue at the end is in a style characteristically Hemingway's.

"That was a pretty thing to do," he [Wilson] said in a toneless voice. "He *would* have left you, too."

"Stop it," she said.

"Of course it's an accident," he said. "I know that."

"Stop it," she said.

"Don't worry," he said. "There will be a certain amount of unpleasantness but I will have some photographs taken that will be very useful at the inquest. There's the testimony of the gunbearers and the driver too. You're perfectly all right."

"Stop it," she said.

"There's a hell of a lot to be done," he said. "And I'll have to send a truck off to the lake to wireless for a plane to take the three of us into Nairobi. Why didn't you poison him? That's the way they do in England."

"Stop it. Stop it. Stop it," the woman cried.

Wilson looked at her with his flat blue eyes.

"I'm through now," he said. "I was a little angry. I'd begun to like your husband."

"Oh, please stop it," she said. "Please, please stop it."

"That's better," Wilson said. "Please is much better. Now I'll stop."

Serving the Narrative

When fiction stresses less what is happening than to whom, or why, more subtleties may be brought into play. Samuel Butler was a straightforward fellow; Marcel Proust was not. Young Pontifex walks as straight a line as Butler's time and explanatory style allowed. Hemingway and Faulkner try to use it all, the facts, the characters, the subtleties, in a style peculiarly of their generation.

Sherwood Anderson's style was described by Waldo Frank. In spite of "occasional superficial carelessnesses of language," he wrote, "on the whole the prose is perfect in its selective economy and in its melodious flow; the choice of details is stripped, strong, sure; the movement is an unswerving musical fulfillment of the already stated theme. Like Schubert, and like the Old Testament storytellers, the author of *Winesburg* comes at the end of a psychological process; is a man with an inherited culture and a deeply assimilated skill."

In "I Want to Know Why" Anderson writes about a boy at the Saratoga races, a boy who loves horses and idealizes the trainer, Jerry Tilford.

> "I liked him that afternoon even more than I ever liked my own father. I almost forgot the horses, thinking that way about him. It was because of what I had seen in his eyes as he stood in the paddocks beside Sunstreak before the race started. . . ."
>
> The race is won, and the boy follows Jerry with some other men who are celebrating the race in a farmhouse "for bad women to stay in." He watches Jerry through the window, hears him bragging "like a fool. I never heard such silly talk." And then he sees him kiss a woman, "the one that was lean and hardmouthed and looked a little like the gelding Middlestride, but not clean like him, and his eyes began to shine just as they did when he looked at me and at Sunstreak in the paddocks at the track in the afternoon."
>
> The boy runs home and doesn't tell anyone what he's seen. But "I been thinking about it ever since. I can't make it out. Spring has come again and I'm nearly 16 and go to the tracks mornings same as always, and I see Sunstreak and Middlestride and a new colt named Strident I'll bet will lay them all out, but no one thinks so but me and two or three niggers.
>
> "But things are different. . . . What did he do it for? I want to know why."

Philip Roth, one of today's best writers but an erratically challenging stylist not only in his prose but also in his subject matter, writes appreciatively of his friend Saul Bellow's style. It "combines a literary complexity with a conversational ease, a language that joins the idiom of the academy with the idiom of the streets (not all streets—certain streets); the style is special, private, and energetic, and though occasionally unwieldy and indulgent, it generally, I believe, serves the narrative and serves it brilliantly."

Take this passage from *Herzog,* with Herzog remembering his second wife, who has left him. One day, in a Catholic church:

> She pushed the swinging door open with her shoulder. She put her hands in the front and crossed herself, as if she'd been doing it all her life. She'd learned that in the movies, probably. But the look of terrible eagerness and twisted perplexity and appeal on her face—where did that come from? Madeleine in her gray suit with the squirrel collar, her large hat, hurried forward on high heels. He followed slowly, holding his salt-and-pepper topcoat at the neck as he took off his hat. Madeleine's body seemed gathered upward in the breast and shoulders, and her face was red with excitement. Her hair was pulled back severely under the hat but escaped in wisps to form sidelocks. The church was a new building—small, cold, dark, the varnish shining hard on the oak pews, and balots of flame standing motionless near the altar. Madeleine genuflected in the aisle. Only it was more than genuflection. She sank, she cast herself down, she wanted to spread herself on the floor and press her heart to the boards—he recognized that. Shading his face on both sides, like a horse in blinkers, he sat in the pew. What was he doing here? He was a husband, a father. He was married, he was a Jew. Why was he in a church?

Unique Combinations

The London *Times* once stated that Hemingway's style succeeded because of his artful way of using American vernacular, which they believed most characteristic of our writing. Robert Frost has written that there are really two kinds of language: "The spoken language and the written language—our everyday speech which we call the vernacular, and a more literary, sophisticated, artificial, elegant language that belongs to books. I myself could get along very well without the bookish language altogether."

"Writing, to be effective, must follow closely the thoughts of the writer, but not necessarily in the order in which these thoughts occur," wrote E. B. White in *The Elements of Style.* In other words, the arrangement of thoughts becomes the writer's vernacular.

A note by Whit Burnett: "Style has always been in my mind the author's Self, the creative expression of that Self." But, "If a writer becomes too vague, even though one enjoys the style of writing and manages to grasp the meaning somehow, intellectually I usually am left empty. Yet if you kill style for the sake of the story, on the other hand, you kill the 'I' of the author. Do we read the author or the story? I, for one, demand that each enhance the other. To be successful, the author's intentions must be both clear and implicit."

There are other styles in which greater subtlety prevails. Eudora Welty wrote of Willa Cather that the uniqueness of her style resulted from her skill in not giving us "the landscape but her vision of it; we are looking at a work of art." It is the angle of that vision which distinguishes one writer's style from another's, that angle which is the writer's exclusive property. For the developing writer who is not yet certain how his own style may develop, such examples may not explain much. For all writers, however, there is one starting point which cannot be passed over: the use of language and its suitability. To be a master of language is to be a master chef: In the preparation of gourmet dishes no ingredient is rare in itself. The seasonings and flavor may come from many sources, but the results are dependent on the skill and imagination of the chef, if he is to produce a unique dish. Caviar and corned beef would never be combined to make a pudding.

A writer like Erskine Caldwell did not use the elegant language of a Proust to write his *Tobacco Road;* nor would Proust have written in the ribald manner of Balzac's *Droll Tales.* And it is hard to imagine J. D. Salinger creating *Franny and Zooey* in the style of Thomas Mann's *Mario the Magician.* Style is the product of a writer's culture, the imprint of his temperament, and his feeling for the requirements of the subject matter.

We also include here an example of a style which is having an influence on writers today. Donald Barthelme is described on the jacket of his book *City Life* as a "master of the languages used to conceal truth." Years after Eugene Jolas's *transition* magazine in Paris, far beyond Joyce or Kafka or Gertrude Stein, we read:

> Laughing aristocrats moved up and down the corridors of the city.
> Else, Jacques, Romona and Charles drove out to the combined race track and art gallery. Ramona had a Heineken and everyone else had one too. The tables were crowded with laughing aristocrats. More laughing aristocrats arrived in their carriages drawn by dancing matched pairs. Some drifted in from Flushing and São Paulo. Management of the funded indebtedness was discussed; the Queen's behavior was discussed. All of the horses ran very well, and the pictures ran well too. The laughing aristocrats sucked on the heads of their gold-headed canes some more.

Style is, someone has wisely said, a matter of knowing when one has said enough.

We have metaphor and simile which may be used for visual and imaginative effect. These, however, must also be un-self-conscious, acting as instinctive amplification of our thought or imagery, and not used as an end in themselves. A writer of the stature of Elizabeth Bowen sometimes created metaphors that illuminated whole passages; at other times she seemed to manufacture them as embellishments she felt obliged to insert.

A metaphor, to Virginia Woolf, was a means of "digging caves behind" her characters.

Use punctuation as it comes naturally, as an aid to breathing, or for emphasis in style, or rhythm, or emotion.

Paragraph also by instinct: One introduces a thought; one develops it; and one concludes its meaning. That's all there is to it.

Use shorter sentences for action; longer sentences for reflection or, sometimes, the development of an emotion with sensuous undertones. Anger is usually in staccato style.

Avoid colorless, tame, hesitant speech, and use active verbs when possible without strain.

Barbara Wernecke Durkin

Cut, Carve and Polish Your Story

A little boy sat on a stump, contemplating the chunk of wood in his hand. "What're you going to do with that?" his father asked. "Going to carve an elephant," the boy said, confident. "And how do you know how to go about carving an elephant?" "Easy," the boy replied. "All I have to do is cut away everything that doesn't look like an elephant."

Wise words, especially for today's writer of fiction.

That's what I call myself, and whenever I have the nerve to hang that sign around my neck, I am filled with feelings simultaneously elated and panicky. Anyone studying current markets realizes that the fiction writer has a hard time of it. With less space than ever before for prose other than "practical nonfiction," editors now demand more care and polish from storytellers. Less space, less publisher's dollar, less publicity money are given to fiction today than in the long-gone past, so what we produce these days must be extraordinary if it is to appear in print, where we want it.

It is vital, therefore, that the writer of modern fiction pay close attention to some old-fashioned guidelines in order to survive. Gone are the days of rambling, loosely-woven tales of whimsy and manner. The new fiction is succinct, crisp, lean, and neatly packaged. This would not have surprised Edgar Allan Poe, however, who attempted to haul last century's short story writers into line. Poe insisted that the short story be *brief enough to be read at one sitting,* and that *anything not contributing to the total effect of the story be omitted.*

Vacuum and Polish

The dilemma is exquisite: Although the magazine listing clearly tells us that an editor wants manuscripts of no more than 2,400 words, the story we've built runs some 3,200 words, each one a gem. *Submit it anyway,* the little voice inside us says. We comply, then feel a soggy defeat when the thing comes back looking pristine. *Darn it, it's just a few hundred words,* that voice whines. *Can't they bend a little for the sake of art?*

Oh, maybe they could, sure, for that one manuscript in a million or two that is so perfectly, so brilliantly written that to move one word would render it weak and ineffectual. The chilly truth is, however, that precious few manuscripts would suffer even one scintilla from some tough-as-nails editing. And although it is technically the editor's prerogative to excise and delete to her heart's content, it is also a fact of life that she does not derive the gleeful satisfaction from that aspect of the job that we writers imagine. How much easier and jollier her day when the manuscripts she selects are clear, pithy, and compact—pre-edited, if you will. Gaining a reputation for the consistent submission of such straight-on stories can only enhance the writer's career. Showing editors that you care enough to carve, sand, vacuum, and polish your work like a true craftsperson earns their admiration and respect.

While enrolled as a student in a fiction writing course, I was surprised at first that the teacher expected me to write such formidable assignments in so brief a word count. There began my first glimmerings of insight as to the importance of getting straight to the core of any story, impression, description, or plot. Hemming and hawing had to be snipped away; there was simply no room for it on the page.

Later, during the time I spent as coach and guide for nonpublished authors at a private workshop, I found that the most difficult point to drive home was the need for brevity, and the importance of being selective while editing.

Get On with It

I've selected myself as victim, just to prove I know whereof I blush. This was a story meant for young teenagers, submitted to Scholastic Press as "I Used to Call Him My Old Man."

After a lengthy introduction, this followed:

> It's about my father. I used to call him "my old man," but that was before. That was a long time ago, before all the trouble.
>
> We were just regular people. You know the type. Church on Sundays, watching TV and sitting around in the evenings, out to the park to hit a few when the weather was nice, family birthday parties with the relatives—typical, normal, regular people. That's what we all thought, anyhow. Then one day my mother came to pick me up at school. She hadn't done that since Tony, my little brother, fell out of the tree after kindergarten and broke his arm, and we had to take him to the hospital. So I knew something was wrong. It had to be, to see the look on Mom's face. It looked as if she'd put stiff glue on it to hold it together, and her eyes were swimming in tears she wouldn't let fall. I got scared right away. I knew something really rotten had happened.

Whew. Retyping all that, even several years later, has made me impatient with myself. Why couldn't I just *get on with it,* and stop interrupting my important story with so much extra information? Extra, that's the key word. Look now at how an astute editor trims away the excess and makes this hefty stuff readable for restless eighth graders:

> It's about my father. I used to call him Pop. But that was before the day all the trouble started.
> I knew something was wrong that day. My mother came to pick me up at school. She hadn't done that since Tony, my little brother, broke his arm in kindergarten.
> So I knew something really rotten had happened. But I wasn't really scared until I saw my mom's eyes. They were filled with tears.

It seems so simple now, of course. It makes me wonder why I couldn't see right from the start how all that mishmash about being normal and about how the mom's face was stiff was more like self-indulgence on the part of the writer than concern for my intended readers (in this case, 13-year-old kids). Ahem. My face pinkens now, but I have to give thanks to the editors at *Scholastic Scope* for being willing to let people like me earn-as-we-learn.

Editing the Elephant

But what does this mean to the writer who likes and needs to use a more sophisticated vocabulary and style? Does it have to be Dick and Jane in order to qualify for the Clean and Clear Awards? Hardly. But again, the trick is to leave on the paper only those words that *contribute to the total effect.* Anything that misdirects the reader, anything that wanders, rambles, misleads, intrudes, or otherwise detracts from the total effect is harmful to the finished product. For example, I eliminated *five pages* of extra information from a short story I sold to *Seventeen,* "When at Night I Go to Sleep," after receiving directives from the editor.

My first five pages introduced charming young twin sisters and most of their life's history. The remarkable thing about this whole phenomenon (the publishing of this story, so unwieldy when first submitted) is that the fiction editor and others of her kind are willing to read past the first page of such burdensome material in order to find the essence of a good story that both touches and moves them. But when would it *begin?* Aha! On page five, finally. She called and asked if I felt like rewriting, eliminating the first four pages and beginning the story where it truly started, at the point where the two girls find themselves untwining at puberty.

The actual printed story, the finished product, was lovely—the story I'd truly meant to write, but now the big, dense hedge around it had been properly trimmed.

There is neither time nor space in the modern short story for long, intricate descriptions, or even for the thick padded background of truth that makes an airtight story with no possible element overlooked. On the contrary, short stories should be able to evoke with spare strokes all the fire and magic inside a reader, all the brooding and blues, all the verve and tenderness—without the attendant fullness and majesty the full-length novel can bring to such perceptions. That's why the writing of short fiction is a craftsperson's dream. It is there that you get at last the chance to pare away all the froufrou and flounce. You drive straight to the heart of a situation, and let the reader bring to it his own ability to fill in the chinks and make it complete.

Several patient editors were kind enough to show me the way and I am heartily grateful. Now I find myself exercising more discipline even on my first drafts (after the initial free-for-all of the brainstorming process I use to get started on a project). All along, I ask myself one basic question: Does this contribute something to my theme and purpose? If it doesn't, no matter how clever, or how lyrical, or how interesting, out it goes, and quickly, too—before it starts to seem like a legitimate part of the whole. You see, these little words and phrases can disguise themselves to look like the Real Thing if you let them slip by you too often. If you're tired, quit and look at it later. Your circumlocutions will hit you in the eye like boomerangs.

And don't let yourself get away with less than careful construction of *any* manuscript, fiction or nonfiction, short or book-length. The same basic rule applies: It's an elephant you're trying to make, right? Anything that detracts from its elephantness has to go, right? So get tough.

Think Thin

But writers, being testy and peculiar, will seize on a suggestion like this and protest most hotly. "You're telling me to remove all my delicious little details," one wails. "That's the fun of the writing, adding all these nifty fillips and dollops that just exactly describe a character to a T."

Well, good grief, if that's the case, leave them in! Look, suppose you introduce a main character this way:

> When first I saw Doug he was looking intently out over the green fields, wiping his weathered face with a faded blue bandanna, squeezing the perspiration from his hair. Suddenly, he burst out laughing, then quickly covered his mouth with his right hand and looked sideways, and finally ducked his head and spat.

Interesting? It is to me, and I don't even know this guy. Why is he ducking his head and covering his mouth? What makes him laugh so suddenly out in the middle of his fields? Why is the narrator seeing him for the first time? If the answers are significant, relevant to this man's character, it would be criminal to strip it down to a wimpy sentence like this:

> When I first saw Doug he was looking over the fields. He wiped perspiration from his face and hair and then laughed. He covered his mouth and looked around. Then he ducked his head and spat.

We've lost something here that we needed—the fire, the electricity, the essence of this character at first glimpse. Our curiosity about him is gone. The writer of the edited paragraph took away some pieces of the elephant. Perhaps the tusks. Tight writing need not be dry and lustreless. And here's the bonus—tight writing makes room for the *necessary* details and elements of style.

Still feeling a little overstuffed with pearls of literary wonderment that simply *must* see the light of day? Do it, then. Sometimes it's good to go ahead and get certain overblown, pompous stuff out of your system by actually writing it down in the body of a story. That way you're forced to see it in black and white once and for all, and you can no longer coddle it in your secret mind and heart. There it is, now. Look at it hard. Is it all you thought it'd be and more? No? Too bad. Give it a decent burial and move on. Muddle through.

A year ago I got an assignment from a local women's magazine—a little travel feature of no more than 800 words covering five to eight weekend getaways. Quite a challenge for the woman who had to cut more than 60 pages from her published novel. But I began the piece with its limitations in mind and was able to "think thin" from the start. Today I read my article in the magazine, and was delighted to see that they used it *verbatim*, all except for the first sentence. What a feeling!

More and more of what I write now looks like the elephant when it is first sent out. And now more of it sells the *first* time out. That, I believe, speaks for the art of wordsmithing. Selling, after all, is the name of the game for writers who believe that what they have to say is valuable, and ought to be read.

Judith Ross Enderle and Stephanie Gordon Tessler

The Fiction-Writer's Polish Kit

Before you send your manuscript to an editor, take out this fiction-writer's polish kit and go over the pages one more time. You want your final draft to be clean and tight. You want to make it shine.

Clean comes from the 20-pound bond, the careful typing or computing, the sharp imprint of a fresh black ribbon. *Tight* should come from the final polish.

First comes one more read-through. This is best done if the manuscript has been sitting for a couple of weeks and you've gone on to something else. That way you come to the story fresh, as a reader does, rather than as a writer surrounded by your own words and characters and impressions. Time provides an objective eye.

Ask yourself these questions:

● *Are action and dialogue balanced?* Characters should be somewhere doing something while they speak; actions alone will keep the reader at a distance—outside looking in. Pages of description can make your reader lose contact with your characters.

Static dialogue is no better than empty space. Speech that neither defines character nor moves plot can be deleted. In general, no more than four lines of dialogue should be written without a break: some action, even a gesture.

You need the right blend of action and dialogue to keep the reader inside your story.

● *Do you detect author intrusion?* Let dialogue and action carry your story. Don't narrate. Let the readers draw their own conclusions.

● *Do you show instead of tell?* Have you told the reader what could have been shown? Compare

> The giant looked around the room. When he saw the English boy, he got angry and bellowed a threat to eat him.

with

> "Fee, fi, fo fum. I smell the blood of an Englishman. Be he alive, or be he dead, I'll grind his bones to make my bread."

• *Is your story too internal?* Have you spent too much time inside your character's head? Excessive internalization slows the story. When your character thinks or wonders about every action, you foreshadow the plot and eliminate the reader's desire to continue. It's better if the reader discovers your character's feelings through the action and dialogue.

• *Have you avoided the "mundane so-whats"?* Do your characters trudge through your story? It's not necessary to record each step a character takes. Include only those details your reader can't infer from the text. For example:

> John went to the refrigerator, opened the door, and took out the milk carton. Closing the door, he went to the cupboard, where he opened the cabinet to search for a clean glass. Finally finding one, he carried the carton and the clean glass to the table where he pulled out a chair and sat down. It had been a long, hot, tiring day, and, eager to quench his thirst, John poured and drank the milk.

By this time your reader will be shouting, "For Pete's sake, John, get on with it." Unless the glass of milk is poisoned and will play an important part in your story, your reader will be just as satisfied, and just as aware of all that went before, if you write:

> After finishing a glass of milk, John . . .

Double-Check

• *Are you in viewpoint?* Is your story seen through the eyes of the main character? If so, your reader can only *know, hear* and *see* what the main character can. Or, if you've chosen multiple point of view, have you presented it clearly?

• *Are your scenes fully developed?* Each new scene indicates change: a different time, a different character, a different setting. Each scene must move the story forward by employing conflict and solution. It should be complete, telling everything the reader needs to know, yet compact so as not to mire the reader in minutiae irrelevant to the story.

• *Are your transitions smooth?* A good transition will move the reader quickly through time and space without loss of continuity. Brevity is best; such as: "That morning"; "The following week"; "May and June were lost to me"; "The bus arrived at Fifth and Main." Use the four-space technique (four blank lines to indicate transition) sparingly.

• *Did you tie up loose ends?* Are questions answered? Are problems solved? Have the main character's goals been achieved? If not, have you shown why?

• *Does the story end when it should?* When the main character's goal has been reached, the problems solved, the loose ends tied up, stop writing.

After you've caught any of these errors and written in the corrections, read your story through again. This time look for technical and mechanical errors. Check for typos, misspellings and punctuation mistakes. And for problems such as these:

● *Be careful of eyes.* Can your eyes dance around the room or fall to the floor? Do you mean *gaze*?

● *Beware of pet words and phrases.* Here are a few to watch for: *began to; sort of; kind of; very; just; a little; some; it; thing; I guess; I think; I began; I started; only.* Most of these are qualifying or nondescriptive words. Be sure they're necessary where you've used them.

Does your character overuse a favorite phrase? Such a tag can be useful for characterization, but, overdone, it becomes an annoying affectation. Beware of repetitive actions, such as *sighing, nodding, smiling*. Be cautious of repetitive dialogue in which all your characters are saying the same thing using different words. Avoid redundancies. For example: *The blonde girl with the yellow hair.* Blonde and yellow mean just about the same thing.

● *Beware of awkward sentence structure.* Modifiers should come close (in the sentence) to the word they modify. However, an effective noun or verb is always better than an adjective or adverb. "He sloshed ahead . . ." is much more vivid than: "He slowly walked forward through the water." Try creative substitution.

● *Eliminate some of the "he saids—she saids."* Precede or follow your dialogue with an action line that mentions the character. For example:

"Like my mother before me, I inherited my magic." Gwen picked up the tattered parchment and held it before the flickering candlelight.

● *Remember that people say words.* They do not *smile, shrug, cough,* or *laugh* their words. They do *say, mutter, mumble* and *whisper* them. They can *hiss*—but only when they say a word that contains the letter *s*.

● *Beware of those special problem words—and the spelling demons.* Did you mean *like* or *as*? *Eager* or *anxious*? *Its* or *it's*? *There, their* or *they're*?

● *Double-check your vocabulary.* If you aren't sure of the meaning of that big word you used, check the definition, as well as the spelling. Use a good dictionary, a thesaurus, and *The Elements of Style. The Chicago Manual of Style* is a good guide, one used by many publishers.

● *Double-check your punctuation.* Have you used too many commas and exclamation points? Become familiar with the uses of the ellipsis, the hyphen, the dash, the semicolon, the colon, etc.

Now your manuscript shines and properly reflects the fine quality of your writing. Next:

● *Mail it.*

Sharon Rudd

The Break-in: An Inside Look at a First Fiction Sale

While working as assistant editor in the fiction department at *McCall's*, I once dreamed I was surrounded by unsolicited manuscripts. Stacks of stories, all waiting to be read. They grew taller and taller, threatening to topple and bury me beneath a blizzard of SASEs and unread prose. Trying to keep them at bay, I woke up, relieved to find myself pushing the bedclothes away instead.

I never fell as far behind in my manuscript reading as that dream suggested. Yet, keeping up with all the submissions *McCall's* received was a constant challenge. And sometimes I had the sensation I was reading the same four or five stories again and again. Birth stories, mother-daughter stories, disgruntled housewife stories, divorce stories—after a while I could almost predict what would happen in them. What made all the time spent reading worthwhile was finding a story that offered something fresh and compelling in its handling of familiar themes. If a story showed some spark that set it apart from other submissions—even if it didn't fully succeed in accomplishing what it set out to do or in meeting our editorial requirements—I might be able to work with the writer to improve it. Each time I sat down to read, I hoped to discover some seed of promise that could be nurtured into a story for *McCall's*.

Energy and Charm

What did I look for in a story? And how might I help the writer improve its chances for publication? I can answer these questions, in part, by telling what happened with an over-the-transom story about a single mother and her son. Titled "Nobody's Womanfolk," it opened like this:

> "David told me a great joke today, Mom. Wanna hear it? . . . David says I can go fishing with him someday. Fly-fishing. In the mountains . . . David thinks Jane Fonda's prettier than Kathleen Turner . . . David says . . ."
> David . . . David . . . David . . . David . . . Now this. Diana frowned,

shaking her long, dark hair loose from its confining bun. David was coming to supper. Never mind that Logan had invented him from the whole cloth of his mind. David was coming, and no amount of arguing could convince Logan that he wasn't.

She had spent a month steeped in the lore of David. "David went to Woodstock," Logan had told her. "Only, he got the date wrong so he was there a week late." Diana had stared at Logan then, trying to decipher the limits of her son's fertile imagination. He had invented the perfect hero to replace his father—a man complete with motorcycle and a past that would charm any six-year-old.

In just three paragraphs, I could see this story had energy and a certain charm. The story's premise, the imaginary friend, was intriguing, if not especially unusual. And I could see the writer was going to do something special with it. This David fellow wasn't your typical talking teddy bear. He rode a motorcycle, was opinionated about movie stars—he was even prey to human foibles. I was immediately drawn to the precocious little boy who would invent such an outlandish hero, and I wanted to find out what he'd come up with next.

The more I read, the more I liked Logan's mother, too. She's not quite sure what to make of Logan's chatter about David and his Harley, but she was willing to humor her son nonetheless. The writer had done a nice job of catching Diana's skeptical amusement toward Logan in this scene, for instance, where he pesters her about getting supper ready for his "friend"·

"What are we having?" [Logan asked.]

"TV dinners." [Diana said.]

"TV dinners?" Logan was appalled. "We can't have TV dinners. Besides, there's only two of them." So David was still coming, Diana thought, glancing at Logan's painfully disapproving face. She had expected an imaginative cancellation—a secret mission for the President, perhaps—but if that was how Logan was planning to save face, he certainly was playing his timing very close.

"OK. There's one frozen pizza. Do macho, he-men like pizza?" There was also a crabmeat casserole put aside for an emergency—that rare, impromptu situation demanding elegance—but she wasn't about to waste her emergency casserole on a man who didn't exist . . .

"Yeah. He'd probably like the pizza OK," Logan agreed, though his tightly puckered forehead warned that she wasn't coming up to David's standards.

Diana stripped the cellophane wrapper off the pizza and dropped it with a clunk onto a metal cookie sheet. "I'll pop it in and go wash up," she offered "Why don't you turn on the tube or read your bulldozer book?"

"Naw, I think I'll pick up the living room." He slid off the chair and headed for the living room, but he turned back before he reached the door.

"Do you think we could have a vegetable?"

"Sure." Diana stared after him. Something green, and he had asked for it himself. Maybe David could be useful.

"Hey, monster child," she called out, "Do you think David would like spinach?"

"Naw. Nobody likes spinach."

Spinach was too much to expect, Diana thought pragmatically . . . Green beans were a start.

This story was really fun to read. I enjoyed those apt bits of detail, and the breezy whimsical dialogue rang true. I could hear the rise and fall of Logan's indignation and disappointment in those lines as clearly as I could hear the frozen pizza drop with a thud onto the cookie sheet. And when I read that by the end of the week Diana was down to her last two TV dinners, one "emergency" casserole and a pizza, I knew she was someone I—and many *McCall's* readers—could relate to.

Win Her Over

For characters to really involve a reader in a story, they must be believable as well as likable. With touches like the ones I've just mentioned, the writer had etched a wryly sympathetic picture of this working mother stretched thin by her responsibilities. Logan's six-year-old antics were equally endearing and convincing.

The story earned good marks for commerciality by being not only realistic but also nicely upbeat. The warmth between Logan and Diana was a refreshing change from many of the harried housewife stories I read at *McCall's*. I especially enjoyed the easy give and take between them that the writer showed in this light-hearted scene, when Diana comes out of the shower and sees how pleased with himself Logan is for tidying up the living room:

Logan sat in the wing-backed chair beside the window looking for all the world like a child who had just been crowned the local king. His bowl-cropped hair was neatly combed, and he had changed into his most becoming, ironed, shirt . . .

"[You] look gorgeous." She stopped halfway across the room to grin at her cherubic son. Funny that he seemed so terribly grown-up sometimes . . .

"You're going to change, aren't you?" His smile faded as she stood in the middle of the room wondering whether to tell him what she felt. He'd probably find it horribly embarrassing.

"In a minute . . . I've got something important to tell you first."

"Can you tell me later? It's going to be slushy, isn't it?"

"Yes. It's going to be slushy." Diana caught him up and dragged him from his chair. "Now listen to me, kid, and listen good," she muttered in a gravelly voice, " 'cause if you don't listen, you're going to end up in the river wearing a pair of cement overshoes, see? The warden in this joint loves you to distraction. So there!" She planted a raspberry kiss against the giggling youngster's cheek.

"James Cagney, right?"

The voice came from the kitchen doorway, deep and masculine and every bit as amused as the brown eyes that met hers unexpectedly.

So David wasn't a figment of Logan's imagination after all! That sort of twist can be fun to come across in a story, but it's difficult to pull off convincingly. There's a fine line between having it seem to come out of nowhere and so clearly telegraphing it that the reader feels insulted the writer expected it to be a surprise. This writer had succeeded, however, and earned my respect in the process. Looking back, I could see that Logan's description of David had been too detailed, too idiosyncratic for even the most imaginative six-year-old to have conjured from thin air. But I'd been enjoying the friendly repartee between Logan and Diana so much that I was carried right along, unsuspecting.

Since I was as surprised as Diana, I could understand her puzzled dismay to be standing there, still in her bathrobe, face to face with a leather-jacketed stranger. Especially one who is so much more in command of the situation than she: "I found one beer and about half a glass of wine in your refrigerator," David tells Diana. "Plenty of apple juice, though. I think we're set for apple juice until the turn of the century. Do you want the wine or the beer?"

Taken aback, Diana warns David that he'd better leave, then marches off to the bedroom to change out of her bathrobe. David goes after her a few minutes later, hoping to talk her into changing her mind. But he aggravates the already tense situation by striding into the bedroom before she has finished dressing. Diana tells him she doesn't like the fact that her son has taken up with a total stranger—a scruffy-looking biker, of all things. But David finally wins her over in this scene (one of my favorites), explaining that, far from being a Hell's Angel, he's actually an investment counselor.

"I'm serious." He pulled out his wallet and handed her a card. "Here's my ID."

There he was, serious and reflective, dressed in a dark gray suit and impeccably correct blue tie. He certainly looked like a man who could be trusted with one's money.

He flipped through his wallet. "My driver's license. I'm licensed for everything except tractor trailer rigs and I don't need corrective lenses . . . My library card . . . I read occasionally. . . . My uniform donor's card. . . . If I drop dead in your living room, just call this number and they'll come divide me into my most useful parts. . . . Do you think I can stay for supper, or do I have to show you my credit cards, too?"

Diana relents, and while the three of them eat dinner, David spins silly stories that give further evidence for why Logan adores him.

After Logan goes off to bed, David and Diana talk for a while. Finally David gets on his motorcycle to go home, but he stops at the end of the driveway to make a rambling, embarrassed speech about how much he's wanted to kiss Diana all evening. Here's how Diana responds:

> Something had to stop his idiotic flow of words. Diana kissed him. His arms hung loose for a startled half-second before he caught her up, taking her breath away with the ferocity of his embrace.
>
> "Yeah, well. . . . that's what I wanted to do," he whispered when he let her go. . . ." I own a sidecar. Have you ever seen a sidecar?"
>
> "No."
>
> "Well, you will. Tomorrow. I'll pick you both up at 10. Be ready. I like my womanfolk to be on time." He kicked down hard to start the engine.
>
> "David! There's just one more thing you've got to know if we're going to see each other," she shouted above the engine's rasping blare. "I will not be called a womanfolk. I'm nobody's womanfolk!"
>
> "The hell you aren't!" His triumphant voice was swallowed by the screeching gurgle of the engine as he soared down the street.

Now, I liked Diana and David, and I'd sort of hoped they would hit it off. But that conclusion seemed a bit much. They had decided they were going to be seeing each other after just one evening? Like most readers, I enjoy a little romance and a happy ending. But in this case (as in many of the stories I received at *McCall's*), I felt the writer was forcing the story to end on a more optimistic note than it warranted.

There were so many things I liked about the story—the zippy dialogue, Logan's exuberance, David's offbeat sense of humor, Diana's rapport with her son. Where had the story lost me?

Advice Well Taken

To get a clearer sense of why I had trouble swallowing that ending, I went back to the scenes that led up to it. In some places, I felt the story lacked sufficient motivation for the character's actions. In others, I saw that the writer had provided more explanation than necessary. Two scenes in particular I found awkward and unconvincing: One was right after David's appearance, where Diana tries to get him to leave. The other was when David goes into her bedroom to talk.

Now, I could understand Diana's being startled to discover that David was real. But she seemed to be over-reacting to the situation. David was such an amusing, good-natured fellow that I couldn't see why she was so determined to get rid of him. And since Logan was so proud of himself for inviting David to dinner, it seemed out of character for Diana to go against his wishes.

The impropriety of David's barging in on Diana also struck a sour note. He was a bit outrageous, but nothing else in the story suggested he was ill-mannered. If he really wanted to gain Diana's good graces (and I believed he did), he certainly seemed shrewd enough to pick a more comfortable setting for their conversation.

Despite its problems, the story exhibited a freshness that I didn't come across often in the manuscripts I read for *McCall's*. These basic situations and relationships the story dealt with were certainly appropriate for our audience, and Logan, David and Diana were people I thought our readers would find especially appealing. I thought the story had promise. So I passed it on to Helen DelMonte, the fiction editor, for another reading.

She shared my feeling that the story had spark, and agreed that it didn't yet live up to its potential. We discussed the elements of the story we liked, as well as those that made us uneasy. Our job was not simply to point out the story's faults, but to figure out concrete ways they could be corrected. How could individual scenes be made to work better, and how would these changes affect the overall shape of the story.

The main problem was that the story tried to cover too much emotional ground. I couldn't believe that a reasonably level-headed woman like Diana would undergo such an abrupt change of heart in the course of one evening—and one short story. On page nine, she was trying to throw David out of her house. Just ten pages later, she was falling head over heels in love with him. The story didn't seem to demand either of those extremes of emotion—both Diana's initial antagonism toward David and that extravagantly romantic conclusion seemed false. If, on the one hand, the writer would temper Diana's hostility (and cut that scene where David makes matters worse by bursting into her bedroom) and, on the other, tone down the certainty of their love affair, the story wouldn't have to travel so far to get where it was going. And it would be much more convincing. We decided to ask the author to revise the story with those things in mind.

The writer, Sharron Cohen, didn't have an agent, and she'd never published fiction. In fact, this was the first time we'd seen her work. Encouraging a writer to rework a story and then let us see it again wasn't terribly uncommon. But we knew that, unfortunately, only a small percentage of those revisions would find their way into the magazine. What made us think that it would be worth our time—and Sharron Cohen's—to work on revising this story?

It offered a lot of material to work with, and contained certain essential ingredients, like vivid, sympathetic characters. (It's much harder for an editor to guide a revision of a story that has shadowy characters—you can raise questions that such a story begs to have answered about the people in it, but that's no guarantee the writer will succeed in making them come alive.) Sharron Cohen had conveyed such a strong sense of the kinds of people Diana, David and Logan were that we could pinpoint places in the story where their actions were out of character, throwing the story off track. As a result, we could offer her specific suggestions for making the characters more consistent and believable, and the story, as a whole, more satisfying.

We also decided to pursue this story because it gave indications the writer was capable of making the kinds of changes we would ask for. Essentially, we wanted her to pull back a bit, to be more subtle. The light touch she had brought to those first pages (in drawing Diana's relationship with Logan, for instance) gave us hope that she could accomplish what we thought the story needed.

So I wrote Sharron Cohen a letter that included these comments:

"Nobody's Womanfolk" is fresh, charming, and full of wit and humor. Logan is a cute kid and there's a nice quality to the relationship between mother and son. But rather than make this a full-blown love story, the *suggestion* of an attraction between David and Diana is really all that's needed, and that's what the story should build toward.

Diana shouldn't be so hostile when David turns up—maybe just puzzled and flustered—and she shouldn't try to throw him out of the house. (After all, she's too sensitive to her son's feelings to be mean to his "best friend.") You should also avoid having David come into her bedroom—it's just not convincing that he would barge in on her like that.

Of course, there has to be some initial tension here, and a resolution of it. You should emphasize David's humor and their common consideration for Logan's feelings in easing Diana's reluctance toward David and in making her willing to make the best of an awkward situation . . .

All you need after Logan goes to bed is to bring the story to conclusion—the reader should get the idea that Diana and David are interested in each other, that romance is in the air, but they shouldn't be diving headlong into a relationship quite so obviously.

I sent the letter off, not knowing what sort of response I would get. I had given the writer a general outline of what I thought the story needed. It was her job—if she was willing to entertain my suggestions—to figure out how, specifically, to implement them.

When I received Sharron Cohen's revision a few weeks later, I was delighted to find she'd taken my advice . . . and run with it. She had seen what I was getting at and, without diminishing the spark and vitality of the original version, had reshaped the story to make it much more persuasive. She hadn't been afraid to substantially alter problem scenes, yet she had been careful to weave those changes into the fabric of the story. She had done some cutting, some adding—and she had sometimes taken elements from the first version and recast them for a subtly different effect. Here, for instance, you can see what a different turn she gave to that final conversation between Diana and David, right down to the sidecar references:

> "You've raised a fine, well-mannered boy," David said as Diana followed him to the porch.
> "So I'm discovering. Thank you for being so nice to him."
> He retrieved his helmet . . . and turned it nervously in his hands . . .
> "It's a nice motorcycle," Diana said, searching for something to say in the awkward silence. And searching too, she realized, for some way to prolong the moment before he said good night and drove away.
> "Do you know about motorcycles?"
> "No. Just what Logan tells me."
> He shifted his weight from one foot to the other and frowned down at the helmet in his hands. "I have a sidecar, too. Have you ever seen a sidecar?"
> "Only in the movies."
> "They're worth seeing, sidecars," he murmured as he pulled on his helmet and backed down the walk. "I use it to do my grocery shopping. I should be coming down this street about 10 tomorrow morning. In case Logan wants to see the sidecar."
> He kicked down hard to start the engine, then turned back to shout above the motor's rasping blare. "Maybe I can repay Logan for the supper invitation some night . . . And you. Good night."
> "Good night."
> She locked the kitchen door behind her, catching sight of the widening shimmer of her smile in the mirror inside the pantry door. She'd remember to tell Logan. David would be by at ten.

A Little More Polish

I was impressed by the solid, thoughtful work Sharron Cohen had put into the story. It worked much better now. Best of all, I still found the story charming and fun, although I had long since lost track of how many times I'd read it. But I knew my enthusiasm alone wouldn't get the story published. It would have to receive approval from the fiction editor, several senior editors, and finally the editor-in-chief. All of those people except Helen DelMonte would be reading the story for the first time. Now that the contours of the story were in place, I had to try to imagine what it would be like to read this story for the first time. Were the details presented in a way that was easy to read and follow?

Rereading those first three paragraphs, I realized they might confuse a reader coming to the story cold. It was hard to tell when or where the action was taking place, and it took a while to figure out what the relationship between the people were. I knew that a reader who had to work too hard to figure out what was going on in a story would likely put it down. Although those opening paragraphs contained important information—*and* were fun to read—they would have to be modified for the sake of the story.

The main action began almost three pages into the manuscript when Diana approaches the house on the night David will turn up for supper and calls out to Logan "Hey, Slugger!" Three pages was too long to expect a reader to wait. Since most of the first two pages seemed to refer to remarks Logan had made about David in the last month, why not open the story with the "Hey, Slugger" scene—which was firmly anchored in the present and would immediately orient the reader to the story's action—and then have Diana flash back to what she'd heard Logan say about the motorcycle man?

As I experimented with rearranging the manuscript, I realized that to begin in the present and then flash back all at once to the first two pages would pull the reader too far away from the story line. Because the first two pages consisted of snippets of several different recalled conversations, I decided to use a series of flashbacks and to intersperse them with the ongoing scene when Diana gets home that evening.

The reorganization I had in mind would require occasional bridges between past and present. And I was sure the writer could provide transitions that would be far more graceful and better suited to the story than I could. As a rule, we didn't send an unpurchased story back for a second revision. If it didn't overcome our objections after one rewrite, it probably wouldn't be worth our time—or the writer's—to ask for a second. But the substantial work Sharron Cohen had already put into the story did solve its major problems. Now it needed fine-tuning. So I wrote her a letter that included these comments:

> You've done an excellent revision of "Nobody's Womanfolk." The story is much stronger now, and you've turned the romance between Diana and David with a very nice touch. But we would like you to do a bit more polishing.
>
> I've already done some editing and am enclosing my working copy of the manuscript. None of this is graven in stone, of course, but it will give you some idea of what we think needs to be done. Your introductory paragraphs are a bit confusing. It's not quite clear what's happening or when the action takes place. We think it would be better to start right off with Diana's arrival at home on Friday night. I've reorganized the first four pages, interspersing present and past in a way that gives the reader

the essential background information without getting too far away from the scene at hand. In many cases, as you'll see from my marginal comments, all we're asking is that you supply a line or two of transition or stage directions to get the characters from place to place.

Sharron Cohen went to work on the story again. Our combined efforts produced an opening that in part read:

"Hi, Slugger!" Diana waved at the dark-haired child who waited expectantly beside the gate.

"Hi, Mom! You're finally home! We've gotta hurry." Logan came at his mother like a wheeling, dark-eyed crow. "David will be here at six. We've gotta get his supper!"

David, David, David. Logan talked of nothing else these days. "David told me this great joke today, Mom . . ." "David says I can go fly-fishing with him some day . . ." "David thinks Jane Fonda's prettier than Kathleen Turner . . ." And now this. David was coming to supper. Never mind that Logan had invented him from the whole cloth of his mind. David was coming, and that was that.

"David said he'd come over on his motorcycle." Logan's eyes glittered with excitement as he slipped his hand into his mother's to tug her along.

"C'mon, Mom. Hurry up. David likes his womanfolk to be quick with his supper."

"Womanfolk?" He says things like *that*?

"He says womanfolk are meant for cooking and nursing. He's real pleased you're a nurse. And pretty. He says he likes pretty, green-eyed nurses. Almost as much as motorcycles . . ."

Sold: A First Short Story

Our final job was to cut the story. At a magazine like *McCall's* where limited space is allotted to fiction, almost every manuscript must be shortened somewhat. Cutting this story wasn't something Helen and I relished, but we knew we had to do it if the story were to have a shot at publication. By the second revision, every scene had an important function. So we couldn't remove whole chunks of text without damaging the story. Some scenes could be speeded up, though. And from there on out, it was a matter of trimming a nonessential word or phrase here, an occasional sentence there. The idea was to tighten the story throughout, without losing anything that was especially fun to read or necessary to lead the reader through the story. I had asked Sharron Cohen to do as much cutting as she could, and she'd done quite a bit. But, as she wrote me when she returned her second revision, "I went at 'Nobody's Womanfolk' with grim determination and managed to cut only half of what you wanted, so I'll leave the rest of the cutting to your discretion. I'm also enclosing a copy of the story before my cuts, in case you disagree and think some parts should be restored." Helen and I thought most of her cuts worked just fine. Then we found places where we could make a few more.

All of the substantial changes to the story had been made by the writer herself. I had tackled the manuscript only to reorganize her material in the early pages and to do some cutting. Beyond that, I had offered her suggestions, but she had done the real work—the rewriting, recasting, reshaping.

Although the problems this story eventually overcame were typical of the kinds of things we might work with a writer to correct, we seldom asked a writer to do so much work on a single story. In many cases where a story needed this much work, we would simply write a letter explaining why the story didn't work for us and asking the writer to let us see more of her work. We felt that few writers would have the willingness or skill to rework a story so thoroughly, and we knew that it was asking a lot of a writer to put so much time into revisions when we couldn't promise that the story would be accepted for publication.

But I had seen something special in this story that made me willing to take a chance on it. My persistence and the writer's paid off. Sharron Cohen's story appeared as "The Man on the Motorcycle" in *McCall's*. She had sold her first short story.

Vera Henry

The Short Short

The short short story is like the heart of an artichoke. The incidents leading up to the event, the long passages of description, all the unnecessary words and gestures have been peeled away. What is left should be pure story.

It has a beginning which lures the reader like a sideshow barker. It has a middle which develops the story and a conclusion that should not leave the reader feeling he has been cheated. It should have not only form, but content. It is not to be confused with the anecdote. An anecdote or vignette is the sort of thing people tell at parties. It may be interesting enough, but it is incomplete. It is a fragment—the handle of a cup.

The short short story is exactly that—a miniature story that is a whole. Within the limits of two thousand words or less, it attempts to throw a bright revealing light upon a situation and the people involved in that situation. The conclusion curves like a ring back toward the beginning.

The short short must be compact. It covers a brief period of telescoped time. It uses as few scenes and characters as possible Every word must have a purpose. It does not need to be meager. The strong words, the vivid description and simile can say as much as paragraphs. Dylan Thomas did that with phrases like—"the snow-bandaged town"—"a small, dry, egg-shell voice"—"boys catlicked their hands and faces"—"trams that hissed like ganders."

It helps to envision the short story as if it were a play being produced by a director on a low budget. Without sacrificing quality, he tries to keep the action limited perhaps to a single set or two. He uses only absolutely essential characters. Two or three are perhaps most satisfactory. Too many can confuse the reader. There is not room for the sound development of several characters. For this reason the characters used must not be overly similar. Their traits should contrast or conflict. Even the names should begin with different letters and the sounds vary.

Which Subjects Are Best?

Not all story ideas are suitable to the short short. Some are too strong to be confined within such tight limits. The story with a complicated plot or one that depends on a detailed knowledge of the background does not belong here. The O'Henry surprise twist is not used as often now but it is sometimes effective in short short form, if the conclusion comes naturally and without distortion. Suspense stories that demand a fast, smashing pace can be done as short shorts. So can humor, or the warm story with strong reader identification but too frail a plot to spin out into a longer length.

A few years ago, Margaret A. Robinson wrote a short short story for *Redbook,* "At the Center a Memory." This is the story of a college student who is unable to accept the reality of her father's death. His funeral seems unreal. When she returns to college she keeps expecting a phone call or letter from him. She thinks she sees him on the street.

She goes home at Easter. The house seems just the same. She looks at her parents' big bed that had room for her brother, herself and the Sunday papers. She remembers her father would have only white sheets and shirts. She opens the closet to inspect his clothes. They are gone, his side of the closet empty.

At her cry, her mother hurries into the room. She says for weeks she couldn't get rid of the clothes, thinking somehow he would need them. Then finally she thought they weren't doing anyone any good there. "So—well I—"

She holds out her arms and the daughter runs to her and finally is able to weep.

The theme is one with which many readers can identify. This brief, short short form is very successful in throwing a brilliant light upon a warm family relationship and the devastation of grief. There is no action, yet it fulfills the definition of a story—something of importance has happened—something has been resolved. There is change. The main character is not the same at the conclusion of the story as at the beginning.

Since the story has no plot in the usual sense, if it had been dragged out to a longer length, the strong emotional impact would have been lost. Rather than share a powerful experience, the reader might have become numb with words.

This story, dealing with death and grief, would have had trouble finding a market a few years ago. The writer must at all times keep in touch with current trends. Story styles and content change constantly. The fiction writer must not only be familiar with the current market, he must be a prophet who senses a coming trend even before it happens. He does this by constantly reading newspapers and magazine articles and listening to the sounds and trying to interpret the vision of the world around him.

The short short is a good length for the beginning writer. Its form is relatively simple. The prospect of trying a full-length novel or even a twenty-page short story can be overwhelming. The short short running anywhere from four to eight pages seems as easy (though it's not!) as a letter to home. It has the advantage, however, of being easier to sell. There are a great many markets for this length, ranging from the high-paying slicks like *Redbook* through the various religious magazines and other specialized publications.

Where Does the Story Start?

The beginner's most serious problem seems to be knowing when and where to start the short short. Unless he has had considerable experience, a short short written in chronological order, commencing at the point where things begin to happen, is the simplest and most effective.

Writing rules are made to be broken but the writer must first know those rules and when and how they can be changed.

The flashback is seldom a satisfactory technique in the short short. It breaks the story unity and confuses the reader. Rather than distract attention with a large indigestible hunk of flashback, the writer can gradually feed in the needed background information. Dialogue can also eliminate the need for a flashback by furnishing information while giving immediacy to past events.

Here is the opening from an *Ellery Queen* story of my own.

> "How was the funeral?" Mr. Leary asked, putting down his cutting knife and surveying with distaste the fifteen dollar a yard white living room carpeting which he was listlessly installing.
>
> Estelle, the hefty maid, produced a bottle of gin and handed him a generous drink. "The way they rushed it through, you'd have thought the old lady had to catch a train to heaven, or wherever she went. They didn't waste no time or tears—cheapest kind of casket—no music—and had her cremated next day. If you ask me it shows a lack of respect."

This was a grimly humorous murder story. The cutting knife and the new carpet are important factors in the story, so they were introduced promptly.

It would of course have been possible to use a flashback. I might have written:

With a shudder Estelle remembered the strange happenings the day the rich old woman died. She remembered the way Margo, the daughter, had first called the contractor to order a new swimming pool and then phoned the doctor and the undertaker to say the old lady was dead.

Dialogue kept the story in the present. The use of a flashback and the necessary transition would have changed the entire mood.

A good many short shorts cover a single scene. Some cover a longer period of time, but use as few changes of scene as possible.

This story covered several weeks, but had only two scenes. Here again dialogue quickly covers the events concerning the second mysterious death.

"Cheers," said Mr. Leary accepting the proffered drink. "I just heard the news when I came back from vacation. How was *this* funeral?"

"It was real nice," Estelle said dreamily. "You should've seen the crowds and all those police and newspapermen. Margo looked as natural as life. She wore her second best wig, but you couldn't tell the difference in the coffin."

This suspense story depends throughout on characterization and dialogue before it reaches its biter-bit conclusion, with Harry, the husband, convicted, not for the murder he did commit, but for the accidental death of his wife.

"What They Don't Know Won't Hurt Them" was a short short. It had a plot. Something of importance was resolved and there was a revelation of character.

If it had been an anecdote it might have read something like this:

Sampson was perhaps the luckiest beagle in the world. Certainly he was much luckier than his master. Harry was in jail, charged with the murder of his wife, Margo. Margo had been an heiress who recently inherited from her mother.

Ordinarily the police would have sealed up the house where a crime had been committed. This would have left poor Sampson homeless. The court therefore decided to allow Sampson to remain in comfort in his old home with the maid, Estelle, to care for him.

So, while Harry led a dog's life in jail, Sampson and Estelle were living up the life of—the life of Harry.

While this little anecdote contains most of the information that was in the short short, it obviously would not have sold. There is no plot or conflict. It has no theme and nothing of importance has been resolved.

What About the "No-plot" Story?

A good many young writers are confused by *New Yorker* stories. This is a highly specialized, limited field, that contradicts much of what the beginner has been told about short story writing. The plot situations are not strong in the conventional sense. It is as if the reader is a passenger on a train that has paused on a siding. He can see into a brilliantly lighted room. He hears the dialogue and knows the thoughts of its occupants. He probably does not know what has happened to these characters in the past nor what will become of them in the future. For one brief, blinding instant he has witnessed the interplay of human relationships, a revelation or development of character. Many *New Yorker* stories seem to be fragments of novels. The reader may not know the past and future of the characters, but the writer knows all about them. It is this and the excellent writing that make them noteworthy.

The Plotted Short Short

The short short must get off to a fast start. Mystery writer Dan Marlowe says it is necessary to jump off the gangplank right into the middle of the story. He says he has never written one yet in which it hasn't developed that on the second or third draft, he finds himself eliminating the three or four introductory paragraphs which at first seemed necessary.

Summed up then, the short short is a true story form dealing with an event that matters. It is compact, uses few characters and scenes and starts as close as possible to its conclusion. It springs from the heart of the situation rather than goes into detail to explain. It deals with the problem of the moment.

Its characters should be vivid and vital—dull characters make dull stories. The self-pitying spinster, the neglected parent, the unfortunates dying of incurable diseases, deserve our compassion in real life, but they are not good story material.

The short short may mystify, shock, amuse, inform and entertain. It must never bore nor meander vaguely along.

It knows where it is going and it gets there fast.

Ben Nyberg

The Serious Business of Choosing Literary Fiction

To take, or not to take: That's the bottom-line question we editors are always asking. When I first became a practicing editor back in 1966—picking stories, poems, and essays for *Kansas Magazine*—I had no complicated set of criteria to help me answer that question, and fortunately, I didn't need many. If something was publishable, *Kansas Magazine* wanted to publish it. Not that we didn't reject plenty of stories. We had our standards. But they were like a homeplate umpire's—a story was a strike or a ball; if a strike, we took it.

A year later, Harold Schneider and I found ourselves editing *Kansas Magazine's* successor, *Kansas Quarterly,* with four times the space to fill. I don't think we've ever "widened the strike zone" to make up our quota of pages. From the start, I believe *Kansas Quarterly's* standards have been consistently high (or at any rate consistent). But I know that at first it was still possible to make editorial decisions largely on the toggle basis of printworthiness: publishable, green light; not publishable, red light. Sometimes I yearn for those good old days, when I could feel that every deserving submission we screened saw print.

But only sometimes. Most of the time I'm happier being an editor besieged by deserving writers, deluged by worthy material. I like knowing there's so much good stuff out there, so many wordsmiths crafting diligently away, quite a few of them eager to be published in our magazine. I'm also glad I've had to become a better editor. When you can print only a few of many deserving submissions, you have to refine your critical sensitivity and establish your esthetic priorities beyond the simple toggle level. You have to know—well enough to explain and justify it to fellow editors—why you value one publishable work over another.

Special Affects

You ask: What *are* the standards literary magazine fiction editors try to apply to the steady, welcome stream of unsolicited mss? As a fairly representative literary editor, I can explain. But before getting down to criteria, a disclaimer: No matter how hard I, or any other editor, may try to make purely objective judgments, there are always X-factors muddying our objectivity. This doesn't make our decisions less just, only more human. When the late John Gardner judged *KQ*'s fiction awards for 1977, he admitted candidly: "My fifth standard is pure blind prejudice." Meaning that he, like the rest of us, had his quirks. I know we editors sometimes seem to behave like soul-less robots, handing down death sentences with icy indifference. But we're really pretty normal humans with a full set of personal passions and phobias, and a fair measure of fallibility.

These X-factors are the main reason magazines need editorial boards. Without X-factors, we could simply codify selection guidelines and hire a technician to screen submissions. A few magazines do operate with a single editor as judge-jury-executioner. This eliminates all the wrangling sessions and speeds the waiting author's trial. But editors are too scrupulous a lot, generally, to like one-man shows. Consensus judgment rather than individual taste holds sway. That means more hurdles for your ms to leap, but less chance you'll be rejected (or accepted) because of X-factors.

One other thing to keep in mind: a publication's "special interests." Of course, some of them are obvious enough. *Ellery Queen's Mystery Magazine,* not surprisingly, "accepts only mystery, crime and detective fiction." *Rod Serling's Twilight Zone* is interested in "experimental, fantasy, horror, psychic/supernatural." A waste of time and postage to send mainstream fiction to either of them. But most general-interest magazines have a slant, too, and you'll have to dig beneath their names to find it. Reading a magazine before you submit to it is the only way to know for sure what its editors want. But descriptions of objections and needs, like those in this directory, can help narrow your list. You'd think *Road King Magazine,* for instance, might be every bit as macho as *Hustler,* but its editors warn: "Remember that our magazine gets into the home and that some truckers tend to be Bible belt types. No erotica or violence." *Modern Maturity,* whose audience is 55 and over, prefers not to see stories about coping with retirement, entering nursing homes, dealing with tired marriages, etc. So be sure you really know the special needs of any magazine before you ship your work off to it.

Some magazines also strive for some kind of thematic unity in each of their issues, so that unless your story has the particular focus they're featuring it will be returned unconsidered. But keep your eyes open and you can also take advantage of such special topics. I've heard of magazines doing issues that featured epistolary fiction, Edgar Allan Poe spoofs and parodies, stories about children, rural fiction. The best thing about submitting to such "specials" is that there's just not as much competition. It won't mean a better chance of getting shoddy work published, but good work won't have so far to rise to the top. Invitations to submit to features are normally found in the magazines themselves. But most editors seek variety rather than unity of effect, so that once they've taken several stories with a similar theme (like marital infidelity), tone (brightly comic, steely grim), or even setting (shopping mall, darkest Africa) they're unlikely to want another until they've seen the accepted one into print.

Baited Breadth

Still, after all the X-factors and special interests, it's the literary excellence of your work more than anything else that brings acceptances. Regardless of our individual whims and cranks, we editors are all looking for the same thing—fiction masterpieces. No wonder the commonest piece of advice to writers in sourcebooks like *Fiction Writer's Market* about "how to break in" is: Send us your best. Now we know, given the choice, you'd rather have your story appear in, say, *The New Yorker* than in *Boondocks Review;* you get more visibility and the pay's better. But don't suppose the editors of *Boondocks* will be any easier to satisfy than *The New Yorker*'s. Rumor has it that name writers send out their junk to *Boondocks,* whose editors snap it up because they'll do anything for a little status. But of course name writers don't want trash published under their name, in *Boondocks* or elsewhere, and *Boondocks* doesn't want condescension from anyone. So send only your best to any magazine and hope the editors are discriminating enough to appreciate it.

And keep sending it. Even if your work deserves print, given the odds against you on any one submission it probably won't make the grade if you don't persist. You've heard of shrinking violet geniuses who never showed their stuff to anyone and left a trunkful of masterpieces in the attic of posthumous publication. Such pathological modesty is no virtue for you to imitate. Better model yourself on the old fisherman who baited up a dozen poles along the bank, and when he was accused of taking unfair advantage of the fish, replied, "Hell, I'm just giving myself a fighting chance!" Use your own poles and bait, but keep as many hooks baited as you can to keep yourself in circulation.

Your best stuff, and only your best stuff. But that really presents the tough question—what is your best stuff? And how do you know when it's good enough? Maybe that's not even something a writer should ponder much. You can start brooding about "actualizing your creative potential" and wind up spooking yourself right out of the game. But you do need to have a firm grip on just who you are and what you know that merits a reader's attention. If you don't know your own mission, vision, habits, scruples, and quirks, you're not on familiar enough terms with yourself to self-criticize. Only if you're a "conscious artist," working from technique rather than "inspiration," can you use any advice about how to improve.

Playing God

Now to those criteria. Mine work like a system of screens, from coarsest to finest or, in another sense, most basic to most refined. To be acceptable, stories need to pass the first two screenings. To be actually accepted, probably three or four. The first, most fundamental screening must be for the most essential virtue:

Honesty. What, honesty in a craft dedicated to artifice? Yes, because only sincere lies will do. Your imaginary details must come from an alternative environment so real that you're not alibiing when you talk about it. Building air-castles is fine, but unless you create the ground they stand on and the beings that live in them as well, you're not going to convince anybody that they exist. Your first duty as a fiction writer is to know that other place like a native, not just an occasional visitor. Trollope was so well acquainted with Barsetshire that he knew what its people were doing even when they weren't in the story. Faulkner "lived" in Yoknapatawpha County as surely as he did in Jackson, Mississippi. You've got to do the same. Being familiar with the setting is the only way to cover the doings and sayings, goings and comings of your imagined world's residents accurately and thoroughly enough to take us there with you. That's the essence of honesty—giving the reader a direct view of the lives of people who exist only in your unique mindland.

Obviously all the stories *KQ* has printed over the years felt honest, at least to us. Probably half our submissions have this basic virtue. But that still leaves half of them "dishonest" in one way or another. How does an editor know when a story is dishonest? The same way you'd spot any con-job—it smells fishy. As an example, let me recap my first attempt at fiction writing. Twenty-five years ago I knew little of fictional honesty. What I did know was that I could give *Good Housekeeping*'s readers a better story than they were used to getting. I'd have to sacrifice some seriousness and subtlety, but with just a little scaling down of my lofty standards, I'd treat them to a real gem of a yarn. So I went and wrote a slanderously false account of a gawky high school intellectual's helpless infatuation with a glamorous cheerleader. The story bore no resemblance to life as it is lived. Worse, it was insufferably patronizing, strutting and swaggering, casting snide glances at a presumed throng of enchanted admirers. The sad moral of this bad fable: Don't write out of pride or greed, and don't write about what you can't believe in. In short, be honest.

Efficiency comes right after honesty. I mean the principle that in fiction, nothing's there for nothing. Fiction may look like straight life, but the resemblance is superficial. Scratch a story and you get, not blood, but contrivance: structure, logic, symbolism, all sorts of synthetic goodies. Events happen only because some author-god makes them happen. In the real world, we seem to enjoy a measure of free will, but the world of fiction is driven entirely by the will of author-gods. Authors can literally make anything happen. They can say, "Let there be light," and there will be light. Because they are all-powerful, author-gods have an absolute responsibility to play fair with both their puppet characters and their show's spectators. And the basic rule of fair play is: Give readers as much as, but no more than, they need to know to get the point of the story. So the presentation of evidence in fiction is highly selective— what helps the reader *get it* belongs; what doesn't, doesn't.

3-D Efficiency

I've returned hundreds of potentially strong stories that failed mainly because of inefficiency. Every year I read dozens of narratives that seem to be nothing but records of actual experience. The raw data can't be doubted, but I always have to wonder why a reader should be curious about the random episodes of somebody's personal life he doesn't know from Adam or Eve. Such a confessional ego trip is a waste of editorial time. We try to pretend it's really fiction and so to make sense of the authorial persona's spiritual journey, only to find that in the end the joke's on the reader, there's no real point after all.

Of course nothing done by fallible humanity is ever perfectly anything. So no story is ever perfectly efficient. But some *KQ* stories have come close. I recall with a shudder the stern, cruel efficiency of James Hashim's "The Party" (*KQ*8.1.), that John Cheever praised for its total control. Or Phil Schneider's sure-footed, closely felt "Traps" (14.3.), a saga of self exile and isolation that won both our *KQ* (national) and Seaton (Kansas only) awards. As Lee Zacharias said, "It is a rare story which can so successfully close in on itself." Or Jack Matthews' "Quest

For an Unnamed Place" (13.3/4), which Natalie Petesch called "an exquisitely-rendered story of the yearning for lost innocence and the days of our youth, with a gently-heroic ending that is unforced and honest." Honest and efficient both! What makes me cite these stories for efficiency is their refusal to waste a single moment of the reader's attention. They never quit pushing ahead, never relax their search for answers to the questions they raise. The result is a rich, dense illusion of life that manages to pack large meaning into a few pages.

Few, but not necessarily very few. Efficiency isn't simply brevity. The shortest of these efficient stories needed nine *KQ* pages. And some of the classical masterpieces of efficiency like Joyce's "The Dead" and Chekhov's "The Lady With the Pet Dog" would take 30 or more. Efficiency isn't pure velocity either. For sheer speed Ian Fleming's spy novels are hard to top, but for real pace—that feeling of powerful purpose unfolding, surging inevitably on like a great river to spill finally into a vast resolving sea—give me Conrad's *The Secret Agent* any day. Pace is set by the rate a story's central idea develops, not by the noise level of the plot. So if you're tempted to introduce some sex or violence just to liven things up, ask yourself instead why your story's so dull. If it's not going anywhere anyway, no amount of gratuitous hype will save it.

Complexity is the third screen I sift stories through. Eudora Welty says a good story is a "continuing mystery." That means, no matter how often your read it, a story worth reading will always be larger than your comprehension of it. You can't wear it out because its central question is the question life itself asks. Life gets more profound the more we know of it, and so does the expanding universe of serious fiction. What gives a story this quality of complexity is its author's determination to accept no easy fixes, to settle for no less than the depth and range of actual experience. Specifically, this means 3-D characters involved in 3-D predicaments.

It's so tempting to sell out. Human nature yearns for simplicity, because life's so complicated. We want fairy tale solutions—"and they lived happily ever after." It's tough enough to live problems, we feel. Why should we have to face them in our stories too? Because stories, the best stories, are the finest life-problem decoders and life-crisis stabilizers available. Of course there'll always be escapist fiction too, for those times when we really need to run rather than cope. Nobody's up to fighting trim every day. But nobody with any gumption wants to spend more time running than coping. Hence, the mission of serious fiction: to see life steadily and see it whole (thank you, Matthew Arnold).

Authority, Authority

When I was trying to work myself up to read *The Lord of the Rings,* I asked those who'd read and liked it what there was to get interested in. Fan after fan told me, without hesitation. I'd be fascinated by Gollum. When I got into it, I saw why: Gollum is Tolkien's little go at Dostoevsky. No Raskolnikov, but still a truly tormented soul that makes us ponder Faulkner's everlasting problem of the human heart in conflict with itself. Stories that fail the Complexity test do so because they try to deny human nature, to tell us life is a bowl of pitless cherries. Good fiction gives us the cherries, pits and all.

Of the many *KQ* stories deserving blue ribbons for complexity, the first to come to mind is Winston Weathers' "The Man Who Was Tricked By God" (2.1.). There is a magical resonance about its narrator's spiritual journey that moves me, just thinking of it now, some 15 years later. Even longer ago, George Blake's "A Modern Development" in 1.1, a natural microcosm complete with Everyman trying to fight off the inevitable, was an O.Henry Prize winner. Natalie Petesch's allegory, "The Bathhouse & Leprosarium" (8.3/4.), returns to haunt me with dismal regularity. As David Madden wrote, "Ms. Petesch approaches perfection in her handling of all this story's elements." Which hints at the essence of complexity: quality workmanship throughout, uniformly top-of-the-line components, no skimping on characters or theme or plot or setting. Henry James recommended that you try to be one on whom nothing is wasted. If you practice that kind of sensitivity, and add honesty, you've got complexity.

Authority, my fourth screen, is hard to define, but easy to feel. The honest story that lacks authority may well be the single biggest category of rejected fiction. Because poor authority is so tough to describe, writers often think editors capricious, arbitrary, or evasive when they report, "Your story didn't quite come off," or "Interesting, but not quite compelling." Such remarks usually mean, "Close but no cigar"—a compliment. If you're new to the craft, be encouraged. A little more experience should bring the authority you need.

But what is this mysterious "authority" and where does it come from? I'd call it a wise and easy authorial confidence that both guides a reader's attitude and spurs his thinking. How to get it? Exercise. Practice. I mentioned earlier that you had to be able to live in the elsewhere of your story. The air of that elsewhere is words, and you've got to breathe words. When you've made and remade enough sentences that the scribal act is the most natural and familiar routine of your life, you ought to feel comfortable enough with words to write with authority. Not that the verbal flow ever turns smooth or steady, but its trickle/gush can become as mundane as heartbeats.

Original Drumbeat

The common name for authority is, of course, *style*. But style is really authority in action, authority showing itself verbally. Or concealing itself: The best style is usually invisible. When writing calls attention to itself, ordinarily it's a case of words upstaging ideas, which puts cart before horse. Poor style of any kind—from "purple" to sloppy—is a distraction, and so an enemy of concentration, and so an enemy of good writing, fiction or otherwise. Of course there are exceptions to this rule. H. E. Francis' stories, several of which *KQ* has had the good fortune to publish, are always very gaudy stylistically. But only because they reflect the tortured minds of their main characters. Rodney Nelson used poetic diction in "John Root Is Gone" (9.1.) to capture the aura of his Roethke-like central figure. Stephen Dixon's "Cy" (8.1.) can't very well keep his strangeness from showing itself in his narrative voice. But the rule stands: *Good style* is normally a colorless, odorless, textureless medium of conveyance. What's conveyed may have color, odor, texture, but style shouldn't be a distorting lens the reader has to correct for.

When a reader's under the influence of style/authority, it's like following the Pied Piper. About Jerry Bumpus' "A Morning in Arcadia" (9.3.) John Gardner wrote, "it wears its learning with a beautiful indifference, wastes not a word, not an image, convinces me against my will." That's authority. He went on, "Bumpus can lay down a line of prose—his sentences have the authority of a Zen painting or a Mozart transition." That's style. Anne Tyler said of H. E. Francis' "Two Lives" (11.1/2.), "I felt I was not so much reading [it] as becoming absorbed into it. Returning from it took hours." No finer tribute to authority than that.

Originality is the ultimate test of worth. Nothing is rarer than genuine originality, nothing artistically finer. Of course it's very easy to be different. Anyone can perform a weird masquerade and get folks to point at him. What's hard is to be different and still get folks to hear and believe. That takes genius. Meaning it's out of reach for most of us? On a daily basis, probably yes. Beethoven, Shakespeare, Michelangelo—a handful of creative giants seem to have enjoyed steady runs of original vision. But for most of us garden-variety specimens it's a case of now-and-then, off-and-on flashes of "inspiration."

The most important thing to remember about originality is that it absolutely can't be forced. Try to force it and you'll get nothing but oddity. The most you can actively do is to cultivate your eccentricity. Don't let your natural uniqueness die of neglect. If you spend your life imitating others, socially or artistically, you can't expect to turn out very original. It's not even necessary to be a recluse in some isolated garret. Just don't lose your identity in the crowds. Hold fast to your observer status, to that perspective that sets you apart. You needn't look down on people or think you're a privileged character. But you can't hop on the bandwagon and also march to a different drumbeat.

Some young fiction writers worry about a lick of freshness in their plots or unusualness in their characters or novelty in their style or format. Remind yourself that Shakespeare's plots were all derivative and his dramatic technique was conventional, and quit worrying. If you have the potential of originality, be yourself and it will show through.

Cool the Coffee

Having claimed so much for originality, I'm not suggesting that most *KQ* stories achieve it. But we have printed several that convince me anew each time I read them that they really do break fresh ground. I'll mention only two of them: first, yet another H. E. Francis gem, "A Chronicle of Love" (7.1/2.), our most "prized" and anthologized story, of which William Gass wrote: "a splendidly ambitious piece, full of emotional power, real song, and impressive verbal energy. One is at once aware of a writer going somewhere very special in a high-performance vehicle." It is indeed a trip worth taking. The other story I'll credit with originality went largely unnoticed, so far as I can tell, except by *KQ* editors—"Mary" (2.1.) by J. Johnson, who may have published nothing before or after, but who made her indelible mark on our consciousness with this eerie tale of a transfigured reality as potent as a black-and-white Bergman film.

From originality you can only go back to honesty and start over. Originality is simply the highest avatar of honesty, the ultimate expression of authority. True complexity is possible only within a context of full efficiency, which must be practiced upon a groundwork of honesty. And so it goes, up and down—and around—the scale. Five benchmarks of quality, five gradations. You must be honest to pass. Honest and efficient gets you a C. Add complexity for a B. And authority for an A. Originality is that exceptional A+ that's really off the scale.

In closing, let me give you the one criterion that sums up all the descriptive ones. One final bit of personal history. I recall the Sunday afternoon I finished reading the submitted ms. of Steven Allaback's "It's Never Bad in the Mountains" (14.1.) and turned to find a full cup of cold coffee beside me. The neglected cup of coffee: not too bad a figure for the subjugating mesmerism of strong fiction. The intensity of this experience a powerful story inflicts on us comes, I am convinced, from our being forced to face its issues so directly we adopt them as our own. We are, in a word, *implicated* in the depicted action. In the Allaback story I was caught up superficially on the level of adventure, wondering if anyone was going to fall to his death, and if so, who. But I was more surely held by the battle of wills, the moves and countermoves of its three conflicting quests. I was made to care so deeply about the lives of these imaginary beings that I forgot they were only performers on a stage and took their case to heart.

That's always the way with working fiction. No wandering idly through a zoo, noting with detached amusement the alien oddities of some other species. Rather, listening for dear life to crucial news about humanity's struggle for high ground. We don't so much escape into great fiction as come home to it. We don't lose ourselves in some exotic adventure, we find ourselves challenged by our own uncertainties, disturbed by our own cussedness, supported by our own determination. And when we're all done, our coffee's gone cold. Make an editor forget his coffee and you're a long way toward making him take your story.

George Edward Stanley

Mastering Editorial Requirements for Writing Young People's Stories

What do editors of young people's stories want? Well, according to some of my editor friends, it depends on the time of day, or whether or not they've had their morning coffee, or whether they've just been chewed out by the editorial director, or many, many other things that may cause you to gasp. You may be wondering how in the world you'll ever be able to publish a short story if this is what you're going to have to deal with. Actually, what it should help you realize is that editors are human, a condition that very few writers ever even consider attributing to them. Editors often don't really know what they want, even though they'll send you nicely printed editorial guidelines for their magazines. What you should always remember, though, is that editors know exactly what they want when they see it!

Many editors will tell you that they want stories in American settings about today's young people who are able to solve problems suitable to their years. That's true. But for a number of years, I had young characters in foreign settings who often solved problems no adult could have solved. The point here is that almost anything you write that's within the bounds of good taste is marketable *as long as you find the right market for it*. My stories fit perfectly the magazines they were published in. In fact, many of them were developed specifically for certain magazines. I once had an editor ask me to change the setting of a series from America to France, because he thought the main character of the series (who was absolutely brilliant!) would be more acceptable as a French girl than as an American girl. It was his opinion that American young people don't accept *brilliant* American young people as readily as they accept brilliant foreign young people.

Often editors will tell you they want fresh ideas or fresh approaches to old ideas. The readers of the magazines change, but not the age the magazine is written for; that means that each magazine will continue to be written for a certain age group but that the members of that age group will constantly change. The age groups are always concerned with the same developmental information, which means that the magazine must deal with the same information over and over. This is a very difficult situation for a magazine to be in. The editors don't want to reprint the same stories year after year after year, even though they have a new audience almost every year. They want new stories about the same information. This, then, is your job as a writer: to write a story with a fresh approach to an old idea.

Editors are also on the lookout for current themes that the writer can treat realistically. But don't confuse current with faddish or popular: I'd never suggest that you write a story on anything popular or faddish unless an editor has specifically requested you to do so. If you do do this, chances are by the time your story gets to an editor, it'll be out of date. There's less of a problem with this in writing short stories than in writing books, but you're still taking a chance that you'll be wasting your time.

If the subject you want to write on is controversial, write on it. Don't try to outguess an editor. Don't waste your time wondering if it'll be rejected. Write the story, send it out, and if it comes back, then send it out again. If it's a good, well-written story, it'll probably eventually find a home, because there really are editors out there willing to take chances—almost to lay their jobs on the line—for a story they think should be published.

Magazine Editorial Requirements

Editors usually like stories that are interesting to read, fun to read, exciting to read—anything except what they've just read that they don't like! You may be wondering how you're supposed to know what it is that they've just read. You can't know this, of course. You're just supposed to write the best possible story you can write and then send it out. If you're lucky, it'll get into the hands of "your" editor right away. If you're unlucky, then you might have to wait a while to be published. But there are some guidelines you can follow that will help you get published sooner.

In order to master editorial requirements, you must have an understanding of:

1. Categories of stories
2. Age groups, reading levels, and story lengths
3. Point-of-view
4. English grammar and usage

While magazines come and go, most editorial requirements stay basically the same. Of course, they may from time to time move from magazine to magazine. I'd now like to look at some specific editorial requirements as they exist for short stories in publications for young people. I have purposely *not* listed the names of the publications, because, as I've said, the publications may come and go, but the requirements remain basically the same. If you can master these editorial requirements, then you can use them for any publication they happen to fit at the moment you're seeking a home for your short story.

In *Writer's Market* and *Fiction Writer's Market,* you'll find the editorial requirements for young people's publications that accept short stories. You need to pay very close attention to these requirements. You may be able to change some of them later on, but certainly not until you've sold the publication a number of stories and the editors know you well. Don't tamper with the requirements in your first short story.

Here are some samples of editorial requirements that you might encounter and some ways I think you should go about mastering them:

1. *Stories and articles must have a Christian frame-of-reference.* This means that the stories this publication will accept must entertain first and foremost but be set in a home, a church, or a camp where Christian religious teachings are a part of everyday life. You may not even have to mention religion in your story, but ideals of religious training must be adhered to. These stories may be in almost any category.

2. *All stories published are geared toward entertaining the reader.* Humor is probably tops here. But exciting, action-filled stories would also have a place. Serious themes and well-developed characters would probably be wasted.

3. *Adventure, nature. No science fiction, talking animals, or religious stories.* These people are interested only in realistic stories, preferably stories set in the great outdoors. Animals in these stories would probably be welcomed, but stories featuring them should be about the finding of a hurt animal or about how man and animals co-exist in the environment. The feeling that all the beauty in nature is created by a supreme being would be accepted, too, but this should come through indirectly, not from something that anybody would say directly.

4. *Short stories for beginning readers. Humorous stories, holiday themes.* Almost any category of story for beginning readers will be considered, but the special needs are for humorous stories and for holiday themes. You need to remember, too, that there's at least a six-month lead for holiday stories. If you're not familiar with the vocabulary of beginning readers, do some research before you start writing.

5. *Honesty; selflessness; bravery; adventure; true or true-to-life stories; stories that portray problems encountered by the use of drugs, alcohol, or tobacco; and stories related to parent-child and boy-girl relationships.* Within the confines of good taste (and I know this is rela-

tive), this publication will accept very straightforward stories about problems that confront America's young people. You'll find no dodging of issues here.

6. *Parables that are written in modern style and that teach Christian principles.* In order to write for this publication, you must have a very secure knowledge of the parables of the Bible and the ability to translate the parables into modern terms.

7. *Authentic historical and biographical fiction, adventure, retold legends relating to monthly themes.* The first thing you'd want to do here is to get a copy of the monthly themes, which the editors have probably developed more than a year ahead. Stories for this publication would have to be thoroughly researched, because you would be teaching as well as entertaining, but the entertainment element would probably be what would sell the story to the editor.

8. *Realistic, historic, fantasy, science fiction, folk tales, fairy tales, legends, myths, picture stories.* Be careful. Any publication that would list all these areas would probably demand the highest of professional standards. Why? Because many of these are areas that beginning writers want to write in and in which they very often produce a lot of unpublishable material. Make sure that you're quite familiar with all the classic fairy tales in order to know what the masters have written and in order to make sure that you aren't retelling badly someone else's tale. A course in mythology probably wouldn't hurt, either.

9. *Fast-moving stories that appeal to a boy's sense of adventure and/or sense of humor. Avoid preachiness, simplistic answers, and long dialogue.* It's best to be familiar with what young boys are doing today before you attempt to write for this publication. If you don't know any young boys, then get to know some. Humor changes with each generation, as does what constitutes adventure. Short sentences—usually no more than one sentence per character each time a character speaks—is what this publication is looking for. Problems should be solved in these stories, but the solution must come from what happens within the story, not from a solution you impose upon the story. The story should definitely not read like a lecture from a parent.

10. *Adventure, mystery, action (a Christian truth must be interwoven into the story). Avoid moralistic and trite writing.* These stories should read like the Hardy Boys told from a Christian viewpoint. All religious information should be integrated so that it's a normal part of the boy's life. What the boy does in the story, how he behaves in different situations, should indicate his Christian viewpoint, rather than having somebody spout at him or read him quotes from the Bible.

11. *Action, fantasy, mystery, West Indian and African folklore, set*

in the past, present, or future. Informs and tries to instill the heritage of black culture, history, and pride into lives. I don't subscribe to the opinion that you have to be black to write for black publications—I know too many white writers who've written for primarily black publications. But you most certainly have to be aware of what black publications are trying to do. This publication must be studied carefully.

12. *Stories with universal settings, conflicts, and characters; children of other lands and cultures and religions; adventure stories; parables; moral building stories. Stories should focus on character-building qualities and should be wholesome without moralizing or preaching.* This publication will accept a very broad range of story types, as long as each story promotes indirectly a positive attitude toward traditional family life and ways to solve life's problems by living a wholesome life. This publication would also be a very good place for stories in which religions other than Christianity are the focus.

13. *Stories in rhyme, easy-to-read stories for beginning readers, seasonals with holiday themes, realistic or fanciful plots, folktales, read-aloud stories. Avoid stereotyping. Characters should appear realistic. Stories about working mothers, single-parent homes, changing times.* This would be a very challenging publication to write for. On the one hand, it seems very attractive to a lot of beginning writers who want to write stories in verse, but who often turn out very dated stories, using information from their own childhood. The secret to success here is to make the subject matter as current as possible. A good story in good rhyme about a child's relationship with his working mother or his life in a single-parent home, for instance, would probably find immediate publication here.

14. *Stories that appeal to both boys and girls, which the eight-to-twelve group will read, which will capture their interest in the first few sentences. Need stories for beginning readers that have strong plot and suspense, with short sentences and lots of action. Need stories with female leads, humorous, urban settings, adventure, other cultures and religions. No war, crime, or violence.* Pay very close attention to the taboos here, because almost any mystery or suspense/adventure story will have some crime or violence, so it'll take a lot of effort on your part not to include these in your story. This particular publication might accept a crime or mention of a crime *offstage*, but never anything in which the main characters are involved. Crime and violence must never seem to touch the main characters—a very tall order. This publication would be a good place to send stories about religions other than Christianity.

15. *Experimental, mainstream, mystery, suspense/adventure, sci-*

ence fiction, fantasy, humorous, religious, and historical fiction. If you're interested in writing category short stories, this should be one of your first markets, since it's very open. *Experimental* is the key word here. It means that the editors will be willing to look at less traditional approaches to writing stories, even category stories.

16. *Realistic stories, fantasies, adventures set in the past, present, or future. Want good plots, strong structure, action, and humor.* Here, the type of story you write is less important to the editor than the fact that you have unique characters, settings, and plots. These stories should be strongly written. You must pay very close attention to the structural development of the story. This publication would also be a good place to send your historical short stories.

17. *Adventures that present characters working out their problems according to Biblical principles; adventures with religious, spiritual lessons or applications. No fictionalized Bible stories or events.* A good story for this publication would be a suspense/adventure set in a church camp where problems are worked out with direct references to passages in the Bible.

18. *Christian adventure . . . no mention of dancing, drinking, smoking, divorce, mixed swimming, use of television, sports of a professional nature, wearing of shorts or slacks for women.* Don't be put off by these editorial details. In fact, this would probably be an excellent market for a writer of religious fiction who's interested in writing about things he remembers from ten, twenty, or thirty years ago. These stories would be similar to those found in publications in the '40s and '50s, or even earlier.

19. *Nautical and oceanographic adventure, historical, humorous.* Don't think you have to live by an ocean to write for this publication. Books from your local library can help, but also remember that this publication will probably also accept stories involving boating on a lake in your area. Talk to some of the local boat owners and listen to their tales of adventure, then gear their tales to young readers.

20. *Stories of heroism, adventure, nature; should stress principles of living right, such as good health habits, temperance, honesty, truthfulness, courtesy, purity, respect and love for parents and God.* Very seldom do you see the word *heroism* in editorial requirements, so I'd zero in on that if I were you. This publication would be interested in young people's rescuing other people from burning buildings or from tornado-ravaged homes. The editors would probably also be interested in a story about a young person who found a purse with lot of money in it and returned it to the owner. The story should probably indicate that the young

hero or heroine is putting to work the values instilled in him by his parents.

21. *Christian character-building but not preachy; the hero or heroine should be eleven or twelve, in situations of one or more of the following: mystery; sports; adventure; school; travel; relationships with parents, friends, and others; animal stories (preferably dogs or horses).* A story in a wholesome setting would work here. A good bet would be a mystery or an adventure in which a horse or a dog played a prominent role. Any time you see animals listed in the editorial information, you can usually assume that the editors don't get many such stories.

22. *Stories that provide patterns of forgiveness, respect, integrity, understanding, caring, sharing; God; Jesus; the Bible; prayer; death; heaven.* A publication such as this would be interested in a story about the death of a young person and about how the other young people around this young person come to terms with it. Such a story could start with the diagnosis of an illness and carry the main character and his friends from that point to the death of the young friend. As such, it could almost be a blueprint of how young people can handle such situations.

23. *Profiles of scientists and children; topical stories about animals, the environment, astronomy, and other areas of science.* A lot of research would have to go into a story for this publication. But it must still be an entertaining story. A good story would be one about the life of a famous scientist as seen through the eyes of his children. How were their lives affected by their father's work? How were their lives different from those of other children? What was their attitude toward their father? Another type of story would be one in which a young person develops an interest in a particular area of science and decides to make this his career.

24. *Picture stories, bedtime, naptime, easy-to-read stories, stories with educational value, health-related stories, and anthropomorphic animal stories.* This would be a very good market for stories that teach as well as entertain. I've discovered that most editors of magazines for young people are always interested in coordinating the contents of their publications with school curricula.

Many editors of magazines for young people have on hand the curriculum guides for major school systems, such as those in Florida, Texas, California, and New York. They know at a glance what's being taught in those systems. The editor can consult the curriculum guides to see if the story he's interested in can be promoted as a supplement to a particular curriculum.

While it would be possible to write a curriculum-related story in all the categories I've discussed, it does seem to me that the mystery and suspense/adventure categories offer the best possibility for success.

Some of the school subjects around which mystery and suspense/ adventure stories could be centered are:

a. *English.* English grammar holds some intriguing possibilities, especially for mystery stories. Why, for instance, do we use the forms *who, who-m,* and *who-se?* You could let grammatical *case* become your detective's *case!* Students would be much more likely to care about grammar if they could first read about it in a mystery story rather than in a grammar book.

b. *Health studies.* Phobias are a good source for mysteries in the area of health. Most phobias have long, complicated-looking names, but a mystery story giving the symptoms, then asking what causes the phobia, can simplify phobias, creating an interest in solving phobia-related problems that young people often have.

c. *History.* History, too, can be the basis for interesting mystery and suspense/adventure stories for young people. Did Richard III really kill the Little Princes? The debate still rages. You can search history books for mysteries that remain unsolved or hidden treasures that haven't been found and turn the information into entertaining *and educational* short stories.

d. *Science.* This subject offers one of the greatest possibilities for solutions to mysteries. There's especially a tremendous amount of material available in the area of forensic science, which is very much a part of crime-solving in most cities around the world. Almost every library will have at least one book on forensic (or police) science, that is, how police use science to solve crimes, but it might well pay you to invest in your own copy of a book on general forensic science so it'll always be handy.

Police contacts, while not necessarily a must, certainly offer you a depth of information. Now I must admit that I have family connections to the Detroit Police Department, but even if you don't have similar connections, you can always find somebody who knows somebody who knows somebody who knows a policeman. Get them to introduce you. In my home town in Oklahoma, not only have I become acquainted (professionally!) with members of the local police department, I've also become acquainted with members of the F.B.I. and the Oklahoma State Bureau of Investigation. Things I've learned from these contacts have allowed me to give my stories authenticity. If you're a serious writer, almost any policeman will be glad to let you in on a few tricks of the trade.

Get to know teachers in the elementary schools in your area and find out from them what problems really bother their students in the area of science (or other school subjects, for that matter), then do research in those areas to try to find the plot for a story.

25. *Short stories that motivate Jewish children toward learning about Judaism and help them find a place in the Jewish community as productive members.* Editors are always interested in stories that celebrate Jewish holidays. You could have a non-Jewish friend visiting a Jewish friend during the holiday season and have the Jewish friend explain the significance of the holiday. Historical stories would find a home here, especially those that emphasize keeping alive Jewish beliefs.

Most published writers have been published because they've learned to master editorial requirements. If you master them—if you study the requirements, pay very close attention to them, and learn to read between the lines—then you, too, will be a published writer.

Laurie Henry

Submitting Your Short Story— The Waiting Game

Once you've written a short story that you're proud of, it's time to think about submitting your work for publication. Most writers find the submission process a little confusing—and disheartening at first, especially when the rejection slips start coming in. Taping a couple of turn-downs to your refrigerator may seem a novelty at first. But as they begin to cover the entire door you realize the idea is a masochistic one—and that it's time to study or review the important steps to follow in finding publication for your work. With a little care, and just a little extra effort, you can save time (and frustration) and multiply your chances of having a story accepted more quickly.

Making Your List

If you're not at all sure where to send your story, your first step should be a trip to the library. Check the main branch of the public library in the largest nearby city to learn more about commercial periodicals, and a college or university library for literary magazines. Spend a day browsing through the stacks, reading stories, and making notes.

Write down the names, addresses, and fiction editors of magazines that interest you. If there's a particular magazine in which you'd really like your work to appear, read (or skim) all of the stories that have appeared in it for the past two or three years. Even if you write fiction about an obscure subject (like flyfishing) it may pay to look also at magazines that don't usually accept fiction but do publish nonfiction about the subject (like *Flyfishing News, Views and Reviews*). Then you could query the editor to see if he might like a short story with flyfishing as a part of it.

One way to ascertain who the magazine's "target" readers are is to note the kind of advertising the magazine carries. A magazine with cigarette advertisements, for example, will not accept a story with an anti-smoking theme. Even within a single category of magazines, you'll find tremendous differences. You wouldn't send the same story to *Cosmopolitan* and *MS*—and *Mademoiselle* would probably not be interested in a story about a young mother; but *Family Circle* might jump at it.

Some writers have a list of 100 or so magazines and routinely send a story first to the most prestigious or best paying magazine on their list, and, if the story is rejected, continue submitting to the next best, and the next-next best, and so on until the piece is accepted. Other writers have much shorter lists and set stories aside for rewriting if they are not taken after ten or twelve tries. How many times you send out a story depends on how prolific you are, how willing you are to spend money on postage, how energetic you are about keeping your work in the mail, and how convinced you are of your story's value.

A Note on Literary Magazines

If you haven't seen many literary magazines in the past, you may wonder why anyone would bother to send work to a publication that paid little—or, indeed, nothing at all. But don't ignore them! There are many, and the range of style and format is great. Some literary magazines, like *The Paris Review, Antaeus,* and *Granta* carry much weight in academic and literary circles and will help your résumé as much as a publication in *Esquire* would. Agents and editors at commercial publishing houses also read literary magazines and sometimes solicit stories from writers whose work they see there. Many literary magazines also serve the valuable function of publishing experimental, idiosyncratic fiction that magazines with larger circulations eschew. Literary magazines are often open as well to stories much longer than those printed by commercial periodicals, and writers of fiction for literary magazines can generally count on a story being published just as it was written—without editorial revisions or concern for space.

Not all literary magazines belong to the elite category, of course; there are many that are published from one person's basement, kitchen table, or local copy center—this is one more reason to make sure you've seen a copy of a magazine before submitting your stories. It is possible, however, to find literary magazines that will accept almost anything you (or anyone else) submit—a valuable function, if you're anxious for publication.

Directories for Fiction Writers

There are a number of annual directories of fiction publishing opportunities available to help you narrow down your market search, and help you select those magazines you will want to examine.

Fiction Writer's Market (Writer's Digest Books, 1507 Dana Ave. Cincinnati OH 45207) lists over 1700 publishing opportunities for writers, including detailed descriptions and editors' comments on over 900 magazines that publish fiction, and a category index so writers can easily find magazines interested in particular types of fiction—science fiction, erotica, or mysteries, for example. *Fiction Writer's Market* also publishes original and reprint articles on various aspects of the writing and publishing process.

Writer's Market (also from Writer's Digest Books) includes a good list of commercial magazines that buy fiction—along with many more that accept fiction only rarely or not at all, and a small selection of literary magazines.

The International Directory of Little Magazines and Small Presses (Dustbooks, Box 100, Paradise CA 95969) currently includes listings of 4,400 literary magazines and small presses, among which many publish fiction. This directory is indexed by state, so writers will find it easy to learn about publishing opportunities in their own region, which are often more open to new writers than national publications.

The *Magazine Market Place (MMP)* (R. R. Bowker Co., 205 East 42nd St., New York NY 10017) offers very brief descriptions of a huge number of commercial magazines, along with a concise listing of the editors' names that appear on the magazines' mastheads, but there is no explanation of their needs and interests. Most libraries carry this expensive annual directory.

The Writer's Handbook (The Writer, 120 Boylston St., Boston MA 02116) is another all-purpose writer's directory, including many commercial periodicals that accept fiction and some literary magazines, as well as articles about writing and publishing by authors and editors.

There are also smaller, special-interest directories like *The Writer's Northwest Handbook* (Media Weavers, Box 19775, Portland OR 97219); *A Writer's Guide to Chicago-Area Publishers* (Gabriel House, Inc., 5045 W. Oakton St., Suite 7, Skokie IL 60077); *International Writers' & Artists' Yearbook* (includes many foreign publishers of English-language fiction, available from Writer's Digest Books); and *Grants and Awards Available to American Writers* (PEN American Center, 568 Broadway, New York NY 10012). National writers' organizations (e.g., Science Fiction Writers of America, Mystery Writers of America, Romance Writers of America, Western Writers of America) publish their own newsletters with up-to-date marketing information.

No matter what directory you use, make sure to use a current one, since editors move around a lot, and magazines—especially literary magazines—do move or go out of business from time to time.

Manuscript Mechanics

How you prepare your story is much less important than how well written the story is. But, chances are, the editor to whom you've sent your story will be choosing among many good stories, and a professionally presented manuscript will fare better than a sloppy one. Unlike nonfiction writers, you'll seldom need to send a query letter to an editor before submitting your manuscript. In general you only need to query (1) if the editor specifically requests it; (2) if the magazine publishes issues on special themes and you need to know what the themes of upcoming issues are before sending your story; (3) if you're not sure that the magazine in which you're interested is still in business, or that it publishes fiction at all.

Your story must be typed neatly on white, 8½″ × 11″ paper with a good ribbon. Always double space and leave margins of 1¼-1½ inches on all sides of the page. Your name, address, and phone number should appear in the upper left-hand corner. Proofread the story carefully before sending it out, whether you type it yourself or pay someone else to do it. (For a more thorough explanation on manuscript preparation of the short story, check *The Writer's Digest Guide to Manuscript Formats,* by Dian Dincin Buchman and Seli Groves.)

You should always enclose a self-addressed stamped envelope (SASE) with your manuscript. The SASE should be stamped, folded in half, and placed inside the envelope. Unless your story is four pages or fewer, you'll need to use an envelope around 9″ × 12″ in size. Choose the smallest size into which your manuscript will fit without being folded (which might well be an odd size like 9¼″ × 11½″)—there's less chance for damage in the mail if the manuscript doesn't slide around in an oversized envelope. You'll want to keep plenty of office supplies on hand so you don't have to return to the post office or supply store every week—buy as much typing paper, envelopes, stamps and typewriter ribbon at a time as you can afford.

If you're sending a story to a Canadian or another foreign magazine, you'll need to send IRCs (International Reply Coupons) instead of return postage. IRCs can be bought at most larger post offices—if you don't live near a large city you might want to stock up the next time you drive through one. Note that many postal employees don't run into IRCs every day and may not be familiar with them. Persist, though—they do exist! They currently cost 80 cents each—and how many you'll need depends on the weight of your manuscript and the country to which you're sending it.

It's almost always okay to submit photocopies nowadays. But it's also a good idea to say something like "This is a photocopy—but not a simultaneous submission" in your cover letter, if you know the editor takes a negative view of multiple submissions. In any case, *never* send out the only copy you have of a story.

You'll find that if you have to submit the same story several times to different magazines, the copy you're submitting will eventually come back looking worn and dog-eared. When this happens, throw it out and make a new one. Every editor wants to think that his/her magazine is the first one to which you've sent your work.

Keeping Track of Submissions

Once you've written more than four or five stories, you'll need some kind of system to keep track of where you've sent them. It's embarrassing to realize you've just sent out "Cold Running Water" to *The New Yorker* for the third time.

Many writers use lined note cards to keep their submission details straight. Type the name and address of the magazine and editor to whom you've sent your story on a note card and then write the name of the story you sent there, the date you sent it, and when you hear back from the editor on the first available line of the card. If your story is rejected and you need to send it out again, write the name of the next magazine on your list on the next line of the card.

You can keep a second note card file with the name of each of your stories on the top line of a card and note to which magazines you've sent them on the lower lines. This way you can tell at a glance which of your stories is out, and how many places each has been submitted. You'll also be able to tell if a particular editor is consistently slow to respond and should be removed from your list.

Waiting to Hear

The most common problem for a writer who has properly submitted a story is waiting a long time for a response from the editor. Generally, it's a good idea not to worry about your story until three months have passed. After that, you are free to send a follow-up letter, asking the editor if the story has been received. If this doesn't evoke response from the editor in a month or so, write another letter, stating that you are withdrawing your story for consideration. Then make a new photocopy of your original story to send along to the next place on your list.

Even if an editor loses your story, or holds onto it for a year before rejecting it, or spills battery acid on it, don't write in anger. It's not wise to send another story to a magazine whose editors treat you badly—but remember that editors do move on to other jobs, and there's no reason to alienate the entire staff of a magazine when you really object only to a single editor.

A Note on Agents

Submitting a story manuscript for publication may sound like a lot of trouble. New writers who are tempted to try to find a literary agent to do the work for them (in exchange for 10-15 percent of the magazine's fee), however, are likely to be disappointed. Literary agents are seldom interested in representing new writers who have written only stories—there's not enough money in it for them. After you've placed four or five stories on your own, you will probably be in a good position to find an agent if you want one.

Personalize Your Submission

It's always best to send your story to the magazine's fiction editor, whom you should address by name. If you find no fiction editor listed in the masthead or in a current directory, address your story to the name listed under "Editor in Chief."

Should you send a cover letter with the manuscript? Yes, unless a particular editor requests (in a directory listing) not to see one. State the name of the story you're enclosing, then mention any other publication credits you have that might impress the editor—don't include high school or college publications. If you have no previous publications, it's still a good idea to personalize your submission with a *brief* (one or two sentence), truthful statement of some kind. Say something like "I work as a veterinary nurse and have been writing about gravely ill zebras for some time," or "As the father of eleven children, I have a deep personal knowledge of the kind of sibling rivalry I describe in my story." Never be apologetic about your fiction, or hint that you're unsure of your craft.

If the editor rejects your story but writes a personalized note on the rejection slip asking to see more, by all means send another story within a week or two, and refer to the editor's note when you send it (e.g., "Thank you for requesting another story. Here's a copy of 'The Man Who Ate Harrisburg' for your consideration").

Short Story Collections

Your chances of selling a collection of short stories to a publisher are much greater than they were ten years ago—there's been a virtual renaissance in the form, and editors are open to collections by writers without previous book credits. Before you try to market your collection with a major publisher, however, you'll probably need to have placed at least half of the individual stories in commercial or prestigious literary magazines. Small presses are slightly more open to collections by previously unpublished writers, and contests like the AWP Award Series in Short Fiction, The Drue Heinz Literature Prize, and The Iowa School of Letters Award for Short Fiction are excellent bets. Check a directory (like *Fiction Writer's Market*) for information on how to enter.

Persistence

If you follow good submission practices, you can be reassured that your manuscript won't be tossed into any editor's immediate-rejection pile. What happens next depends on how closely your story matches the tastes and needs of the editor. Obviously, the more stories you have out at any given time, the more likely you are to get an acceptance. Don't let a story sit on your desk for a month before resubmitting it elsewhere!

As you keep writing, your skills will sharpen, and your stories will become more polished and publishable. This is inevitable, no matter how much knowledge of the craft of fiction writing you start out with, or how much or little market research you do. Many writers aren't dedicated enough to persist—and there's no sin, of course, in deciding you never want to touch a typewriter again; that's just the decision many people make if their work does not find quick recognition. But if your love of writing endures, and you're willing to spend the time it takes to submit a professional-looking manuscript, your chances for eventual success in placing your stories are very good indeed.

Adela Rogers St. Johns

Tips from a Master

All good short stories get published.

Writing is not writing until it is read any more than an airplane is an airplane until it takes off and flies.

The heaps of yellow paper are among the things I can tell you about how to.

There are others I have learned, some of them the hard way.

1. What you have to say is always more important than how you say it.

2. Anybody can learn to write, but there are very few writers and always have been.

3. Ninety-two percent of the elapsed time on a short story takes place before you ever put a word on paper.

4. The short story equivalent of a nose for news, the ability to know a story when you see it, is the one thing with which a writer of short stories must be born.

5. An absolute Must is the training and development of the writer's memory, which is different from any other, and unless the aspiring writer can recognize it he would be better advised to go looking for uranium direct.

6. The majority—I should say 85 percent—of short stories are in some degree reportorial, they are sparked by something the writer saw, heard, felt, or read.

7. Therefore it is necessary to have a nose like an anteater for everybody's business, a rubber ear that hears what people say, a spyglass that sees what's going on, a keen faculty of observation for little things, all motivated by a burning, unquenchable curiosity about people.

8. All successful short story writers are utterly ruthless about where and how they get material. Nothing can be inviolate to them. Change it around so it won't be recognized, use it to benefit mankind, but the story comes first always. Get it.

9. Read, read, read, read. Read all the short stories ever published.

10. Right now, check your own story reactions to these ideas . . . A

boy's blue suit with two pairs of pants . . . A borrowed diamond necklace . . . A mechanic's afternoon off . . . An old lady whose most treasured possession is a moth-eaten fur tippet . . . A young man and woman who, as children, had the same dreams . . . A son who took his inheritance and skipped . . . A girl whose stepfather kept snakes . . . The longest walk in the world . . . If you do not within a couple of days react with some kind of a yarn about at least one of them, give up the whole idea. All of these made very, very popular and well-known short stories. Good ones, too.

11. There are no new plots. There are only new people, new treatments, new reactions, new locations, new times. But it is necessary to invent a good story to tell, because a short story writer must be a storyteller.

12. A professional writer will starve if he waits for inspiration, he must learn to combine spontaneity of emotion with sound techniques to make the result read like inspiration.

Summing Up

I would like to sum up here the few things I have found it possible to say honestly about the technique of writing a short story. There are not many, but I believe those I do know are sound.

Spend most of your time before you start to write, in the sense of putting anything except notes down on paper.

Know your characters well. *Know* them. In the same way that Kipling made me as sure as I was at nine, and still am, that Mowgli was real, as sure as Mary Roberts Rinehart made Tish part of my acquaintance, or Steinbeck made me know Jody, you must know your characters before you start. Live with them. Pay no attention to what other people think of you as you blithely or gloomily inhabit a world where you converse with and watch these people you are painting from life—putting together. Live with them until one day you hear yourself laugh out loud at something one of them said to you or find you have to wipe away a real tear because one of them said to you, "It's—all over. So *quick.*" Then you can begin to plot.

Plotting, then, is working out those things which could and would happen to a particular character or characters. This is a combination of reporting, memory, and invention. But you have to do it.

This most vital technical point in any short story is where you start it. Spend any amount of time needed to measure this one. In the end it will be time saved.

Stick to the point.

One minor story maybe, interwoven to prove a point. No more.

Art grows. It is a living thing. Writing must be a living thing, growing from the heart and soul of the writer. Many will never achieve it. But to produce any honest, real writing is a great career, a fine profession, a service to mankind, and a magnificent life.

So let's take up the one about your best being too good.

And then my conviction that there never is a time, never has been, never will be, when good short stories will not find publication. The only thing that could shadow this would be failure to get enough good stories.

There is one last word. Always, always, always give it everything you've got. Otherwise, it's not worth doing. Reach, and every time reach for the moon. Try with all your heart to write a great story.

About the Authors

Michael A. Banks has published twenty-one books, including three science fiction novels (most recently, *The Odysseus Solution* with Dean Lambe) and one interactive novel. His short fiction — some forty science fiction and detective stories — has appeared in magazines such as *Analog* and *Isaac Asimov's Science Fiction Magazine*, as well as in magazines in Japan (where he writes a monthly "how-to" column for SF writers), Argentina and other countries. He has judged a number of fiction writing contests and served as associate editor of *Far Frontiers/New Destinies*. Among his more than 1,000 published articles are numerous pieces on writing technique for *Writer's Digest* and other magazines. He is co-author (with Ansen Dibbell) of Writer's Digest Books' *Word Processing Secrets for Writers*.

Lawrence Block is a prolific writer in and on fiction. The author of more than 100 novels, including his two mystery series with popular heores Matthew Scudder and Bernie Rhodenbarr, Block has also written short story collections and several books on fiction. His latest is *Spider, Spin Me a Web: Lawrence Block on Fiction*. Block writes a monthly column on fiction for *Writer's Digest*. His most recent Scudder book is *A Ticket to the Bone Yard*.

Hal Blythe and **Charlie Sweet,** professors of English at Eastern Kentucky University, have collaborated for fifteen years on everything from tennis to novels. In addition to teaching creative writing, they have published nonfiction in *Writer's Digest*, *College English*, and *Poe Studies*. Their fiction has appeared in magazines ranging from *Home Life* to *Ellery Queen's Mystery Magazine*. Currently the two are working on a mystery novel.

Paul Darcy Boles wrote his first novel at eighteen, the beginning of a long and illustrious career. He went on to publish eight novels — including *The Limner* and *Mississippi Run*, plus more than 150 short stories, which appeared in *Saturday Evening Post, Ladies' Home Journal, Playboy,* and *Cosmopolitan*, and won him numerous awards and honors. Boles died in 1984. *Storycrafting*, from which "Sensing Extra Perceptions" and "Mastering the Short Story" are excerpted, was his last work.

Hallie and **Whit Burnett,** well-known fiction experts, drew on their long experience as co-editors of *Story Magazine* in their varied careers. Whit Burnett was a reporter, city editor, instructor in advanced short story writing at Columbia University, and writer and editor of more than thirty-five books. Hallie Burnett is the author of seven books and co-editor of twelve anthologies. She has taught creative writing at Sarah Lawrence College and Hunter College.

Janet Burroway has written a dozen books, including novels (*The Buzzards, Raw Silk, Opening Nights* and the recently completed *Cutting Stone*); poetry (*But to the Season, Material Goods*); a children's book (*The Giant Jam Sandwich*); and numerous short stories that have appeared in magazines in this country and in England. Formerly a teacher at the University of Sussex in England and the Iowa Writers' Workshop, Burroway is currently McKenzie professor of English literature and writing at Florida State University. Her teaching experience as director of the F.S.U. Writing Program is the basis of her acclaimed and successful writing text, *Writing Fiction: A Guide to the Narrative Craft,* from which "Call Me Ishmael: Point of View" is taken.

Orson Scott Card swept the 1987 science fiction and fantasy awards, winning the Nebula, the Hugo, and the World Fantasy Award. In addition to science fiction, he is the author of fantasy and historical novels and stories. His novels include *A Woman of Destiny* and *Ender's Game,* and more recently *Seventh Son* and *Red Prophet.* Card, a frequent contributor to *Writer's Digest,* is the author of *Characterization and Viewpoint,* one of six books in the Elements of Fiction Series from Writer's Digest Books.

Robyn Carr is the author of eleven historical novels, including *By Right of Arms* (winner of the Golden Medallion Award for the best historical novel of 1986), *The Everlasting Covenant,* and *Woman's Own.* Carr also writes popular contemporary fiction, nonfiction articles, and is a popular speaker at writers' conferences. She lives with her family in Arizona.

R.V. Cassill has taught writers' workshops at Columbia, Harvard, Purdue, Iowa, and Brown universities. He is both a novelist and a short story writer. His most recent novel is *After Goliath;* one of his short stories, "The Biggest Band," was the basis for the musical comedy "The Music Man." Cassill is also the editor of the *Norton Anthol-*

ogy of Short Fiction, which appeared in a third edition in 1986, and *Writing Fiction,* from which "Notebooks and Lists" was excerpted.

Robert Cormier left his fulltime newspaper writing career after twenty-five years to write fiction. A favorite author of young adults, Cormier has reached hundreds of thousands of readers with his warm and touching, often controversial but highly-acclaimed, realistic and honest novels: *The Chocolate War, I Am the Cheese, After the First Death, The Bumblebee Flies Anyway, Beyond the Chocolate War* and *Fade.* A popular speaker at conferences and in classrooms, Cormier has also written short stories—*Eight Plus One* is a collection.

Ansen Dibell is the pen name of Nan Dibble, Senior Editor with Writer's Digest Books, who has written the internationally acclaimed five-book science fiction series, *The Rule of One.* A former freelancer and college English teacher, Dibble continues to keep in touch with beginning writers' problems and concerns through her involvement with writers' groups and college-level writing classes. She is the co-author (with Mike Banks) of *Word Processing Secrets for Writers* and is also the author of *Plot,* one of the Writer's Digest Books' Elements of Fiction Writing series. Her newest book of writing how-to is *20 Plots and How to Build Them.* She's at work on a science fiction trilogy, *The Sidewise Chronicles.*

Barbara Wernecke Durkin sold her first short story to *Seventeen* in 1981, and since, her stories and articles have appeared in *Lady's Circle, Woman's World, Grit, Young Miss, Boston Globe Sunday Magazine,* and other publications. In 1984 she published her first novel, *Oh, You Dundalk Girls, Can't You Dance the Polka?,* cited as one of the "Best of 1984" by the American Library Association. She has completed another novel, and enjoys writing op-ed essays which she hopes to publish someday as a collection.

Judith Ross Enderle and **Stephanie Gordon Tessler** collaborate on books for young people under the pseudonym of Jessie Ross Gordon. Together they have authored fourteen books, including *Jacquelyn, Nord,* and *A Touch of Genius.* Separately, Enderle and Tessler have published seventeen and fourteen books respectively. The two also write for children's magazines and professional and educational periodicals, as well as speaking and teaching at schools and writing conferences. They are partners in Writers Ink, a critique service specializing in children's literature, and co-edit *Totally Kids, The Fox Kids Club Magazine.*

Esther M. Friesner specializes in fantasy and science fiction. Her short stories have appeared in *Isaac Asimov's Science Fiction Magazine, Amazing Stories*, and others. Her full-length fantasy novels (thirteen in print, three more in production) include *Harlot's Ruse, Spells of Mortal Weaving, The Silver Mountain, Elf Defense, Here Be Demons, The Water King's Laughter, Druid's Blood, Demon Blues, Hooray for Hellywood, Mustapha and his Wise Dog, The Witchwood Cradle, New York by Knight* and *Sphynxes Wild.*

James Gunn has written plays, screenplays, radio scripts, articles, verse, and criticism, but his major interest is science fiction. He has been writing it for forty-three years. The author of nineteen books, the editor of seven, and the recipient of many awards, Gunn is currently a professor of English at the University of Kansas. He specializes in teaching fiction writing and science fiction, and is the director of the Center of the Study of Science Fiction. His latest novel is *Crisis!* and latest volume is *The New Encyclopedia of Science Fiction.*

James B. Hall, the author of more than twenty books—novels, short stories, poetry, and literary texts—has been called "America's most anthologized short story writer." His fiction and poetry have appeared in *Esquire, Omni, Atlantic Monthly, Sewanee Review*, and many other magazines, and have been represented in anthologies such as the O. Henry Collection and the Pushcart Prize Anthology. Hall has taught writing and English at Cornell and the University of California at Santa Cruz, where he is currently Professor Emeritus of Literature. A short story expert, he frequently conducts writing workshops and seminars, and enjoys working with new writers.

Laurie Henry is a graduate of the Johns Hopkins Writing Seminars M.A. program and holds an M.F.A. in fiction writing from the University of Iowa Writers' Workshop. Her work has appeared in *The Missouri Review, The Antioch Review, Poetry, The American Poetry Review, Kansas Quarterly, Silverfish Review*, and other magazines. She is currently teaching composition at the Universtiy of Cincinnati, and working on a novel.

Vera Henry contributed over 300 short stories and articles to major magazines, many of which have been reprinted in anthologies and translated into foreign languages. She also wrote adult and juvenile novels, which were made into TV and radio plays. Mrs. Henry was a teacher of creative writing, lecturer at writers' conferences, and an instructor with the Writer's Digest School. She died in 1987.

Rust Hills is a specialist in the short story: He was fiction editor for *Esquire* magazine for almost 30 years and a teacher of the short story at New York University, The New School, and Columbia. Hills also edited *Great Esquire Fiction: The Finest Stories From the First 50 Years* and *Writer's Choice: 20 American Authors Introduce Their Own Best Story*. He authored *The Memoirs of a Fussy Man* and *Writing In General and the Short Story in Particular*.

Will C. Knott writes every day. The author of more than 100 novels, westerns, young adult novels and two texts, and a man of multi-pseudonyms, he has written for the Long Arm Series (Tabor Evans); a World War II Series (Bryan Swift); The Trailsman Series (John Sharpe); and the Stage Coach Series (Hank Mitchum). He has also authored a historical novel, *The Texan*. He writes The Golden Hawk Series under his own name and he is working on a detective novel series.

Rega Kramer McCarty enjoyed a lifelong interest in the written word. She published poetry, short stories, confessions, and two career-romance novels, plus many magazine and newspaper articles and a weekly newspaper column. For years she worked as an instructor with the Writer's Digest School and wrote instructive articles on the writing process. Rega McCarty died in 1986.

Ben Nyberg, a professor of English, has been a member of the Kansas State University faculty for twenty-five years. In 1968 he founded (with Harold Schneider) *Kansas Quarterly*, the successor to *Kansas Magazine*, which he had also edited. Nyberg's fiction has appeared in *South Dakota Review*, *Quartet*, *Interstate*, *The Texas Review*, and elsewhere. His short story primer, *One Way to Write a Great Short Story*, was published in 1988.

Jean Z. Owen has written long and short fiction for years. She has critiqued fiction for the Writer's Digest School and lectured at writers' seminars and conducted workshops. She has also written and edited medical material on a freelance basis. "Trouble-Free Transitions" is excerpted from her book, *Professional Fiction Writing*.

Gary Provost has been called "the writer's writer" for his work as contributing editor of Writer's Digest and his Writer's Retreat Workshop in Bristol, Connecticut. A longtime freelance, prolific and versatile, Provost has authored, co-authored, and ghost-written 16 books, including novels, children's books, sports, and books for writers. He has also published over a thousand articles, stories and columns. His novel for children, *Good If It Goes,* co-authored with his wife, Gail, won the National Jewish Book Award for Children's Literature, 1985. His most recent true crime books is *Without Mercy: The True Story of the First Woman in South Florida to be Sentenced to the Electric Chair.* In 1987 Provost was one of seven national finalists to replace advice columnist Ann Landers.

Kit Reed has published eleven novels and three collections of short stories as well as two books for people who want to write fiction. A Guggenheim fellow and the first American recipient of the Abraham Woursell five-year literary grant, she has published *Story First: The Writer as Insider* and, for the Writer's Digest Books Elements of Fiction Series, *Revision.* She works with student writers at Wesleyan University, Middletown, Connecticut and is a frequent reviewer of fiction for, among others, *The New York Times Book Review* and the *Philadelphia Inquirer.* Her most recent novel is *Catholic Girls.*

Sharon Rudd has worked on the editorial staffs of *McCall's*, St. Martin's Press, *Writer's Digest* magazine, Writer's Digest Books and the *Cincinnati Business Courier.* Her work has appeared in *McCall's* and *Writer's Yearbook.* Currently she is a college textbook production editor for Macmillan.

Darrell Schweitzer is the author of two novels, *The White Isle* and *The Shattered Goddess*, and two story collections, *We Are All Legends*, and *Tom O'Bedlam's Night Out.* He has published stories in *Twilight Zone*, *Amazing Stories*, and *Night Cry*, and a number have appeared in various anthologies. Schweitzer, formerly an editorial assistant for *Isaac Asimov's Science Fiction Magazine* and *Amazing Stories*, reviews books for the *Philadelphia Inquirer* and writes a column for *Aboriginal SF.* He is also a literary agent and partner in Owlswick Literary Agency, and is co-publisher and co-editor of the revived *Weird Tales.*

Roy Sorrels is the author of *Kiss/Kill* and *Visit To Death,* two recent suspense-thrillers. A full time freelancer, he has also written numerous short stories, the most recent of which were published in *Twilight Zone, Woman's World,* and *Ellery Queen's Mystery Magazine.* He and his writer wife, Donna Meyer, divide their time between New York City and their home in San Miguel de Allende, Mexico.

Adela Rogers St. Johns began as a reporter, and her writing career spanned more than six decades. She taught short story writing at Stephens College and the University of California "on the theory that accomplishment in the subject taught was equivalent to the degrees I didn't have." Her last of many delightful and acclaimed books was *No Good Byes: My Search Into Life Beyond Death.*

George Edward Stanley is Professor and Chairman of the Department of Languages and Communication at Cameron University in Lawton, Oklahoma, where he has taught romance languages, Albanian, linguistics, and creative writing. He is the author of twenty children's books and more than one hundred short stories for young people. His adult stories have been published throughout the English-speaking world and his radio plays have been broadcast over the BBC World Service in London.

Dwight V. Swain, a freelance writer and former newspaperman and magazine staffer, holds Professor Emeritus status at the University of Oklahoma, where he taught for more than twenty years in the School of Journalism's Professional Writing Program. More than a million words of Swain's fact and fiction have appeared in national magazines; and his *Techniques of the Selling Writer, Film Scriptwriting,* and *Scripting for Video and Audiovisual Media,* are highly acclaimed and universally accepted texts on their respective subjects. Swain is currently working on a book on characterization.

John Updike has received most major awards for his prolific literary work—short story and essay collections, volumes of verse, one play, and his well-known and critically acclaimed novels, including the best-selling *Rabbit* trilogy, the two Bech books, *Roger's Version, The Witches of Eastwick* and *S. Trust Me* is his latest short story collection.

Index

Action stories, 213-214
Adventure stories, 212, 213, 215, 216
Alcott, Louisa May, 40
Allaback, Steven, 208
Anderson, Sherwood, 168, 171
Antaeus, 220
Antagonist, 17
Anticlimax, 18
Arnold, Matthew, 205
Asimov, Isaac, 138
Atlantic Monthly, 146
Auden, W. H., 24
Auerbach, Erich, 3
Austen, Jane, 3, 40
Authorial intrusion, 61

Background, of story, 14-15
Baldwin, James, 86
Balzac, Honoré, 1, 173
Barthelme, Donald, 173
Barthelme, Frederick, 4
Beattie, Ann, 2
Beginning, of story, 89-94
Bellow, Saul, 1, 172
Benchley, Nathaniel, 2
Benchley, Peter, 50
Benchley, Robert, 2
Benét, Stephen Vincent, 5
Bible, 5, 11, 60
Bierce, Ambrose, 118
Blake, George, 206
Bowen, Elizabeth, 12
Bradbury, Ray, 48, 127
Brand, Max, 112, 117
Brand-name realism, 148
Brett, Simon, 92, 93
Brontë, Charlotte, 1
Brontë, Emily, 1
Bumpus, Jerry, 207
Bunyan, John, 4
Burgess, Anthony, 163
Butler, Samuel, 171

Cain, James M., 6
Caldwell, Erskine, 173
Camus, Albert, 69
Capote, Truman, 1, 46, 117
Carver, Raymond, 4

Cather, Willa, 130, 173
Céline, 3
Character, dialogue and, 79-85; fiction and, 141; heroic, 39-40; hierarchy of, 32-34; jeopardy of, 38-39; motivation and, 53-54; pain in, 37-38; recognition of, 32; sketching of, 89-90; specific names and, 149; stereotypes of, 34-37; story ending and, 106, 108
Cheever, John, 7, 86, 87, 204
Chekhov, Anton, 6, 24, 205
The Chicago Manual of Style, 182
Christian stories, 212, 213, 215
Clayton, John Bell, 127
Climax, or crisis, 17; scene and, 115-116
Closure scenes, 118
Colwin, Laurie, 2
Complication, or rising action, 17
Conflict, 42, 44
Connolly, Cyril, 24
Conrad, Joseph, 66, 87, 116, 205
Coover, Robert, 64
Crane, Stephen, 86
Cutting your story, 159-167
"Cy" (Dixon), 207

The Decline and Fall of the Roman Empire (Gibbon), 138; language of the historian and, 138-140
Defoe, Daniel, 111
Description, eliminating, 164-166; and setting, 88, 141
Deus ex machina, 104
Dialogue, characters and, 79-85; describing, 71-72; direct references in, 70; in fiction, 141; heavy-handed, 73-74; plot and, 80; repetition and, 75-76; scene and, 115; short short story and, 198; tension and, 76-78; unnecessary, 74-76, 161
Dickens, Charles, 1, 31, 40, 48, 111, 129
Dixon, Stephen, 207
Dreiser, Theodore, 3, 112

Easy-to-read stories, 214
Editorial omniscient author, 59-62
Eisenberg, Deborah, 2
The Elements of Style (White), 168, 172, 182
End, of story, 104-109; character and, 106, 108; foreshadowing and, 107-108; place and, 107, 109; predicament and, 107-108

Epic, 60
Epistolary novel, 68-69
Esquire, 1, 111, 220
Exposition, 17

Fatal Dosage (Provost), 75; dialogue in, 75
Faulkner, William, 1, 7, 9, 65, 66, 87, 112, 117, 127, 129, 168, 169, 171, 203, 206
Fiction Writer's Market, 202, 212, 221, 225
Fiction, facts vs. experience in, 140-141; historical, 138-140; importance of, 1-4; selling the story and, 184-194; short story elements of, 17-18; viewpoint and, 140
Fielding, Henry, 40, 111
First person point of view, 64-67
Fisher, M. F. K., 129
Fitzgerald, F. Scott, 1, 7, 42, 66, 86, 124
Flashback, 153-158, 197
Flaubert, Gustave, 1, 4, 168
"The Flower Lady" (Sorrels), 93; analysis of opening lines and, 93-94
Foreshadowing, 107-108
Foreshortening 113
Forster, E. M., 8, 61
Francis, H. E., 207, 208
Frost, Robert, 172

Gallico, Paul, 128
Gardner, John, 201, 207
Gertler, T., 2
Gibbon, Edward, 138
Godwin, Gail, 60
Gogol, Nikolai, 48
Golding, William, 42
Goldman, William, 39, 40
Granta, 220
Grants and Awards Available to American Writers, 221
Greene, Graham, 4, 116

Hailey, Arthur, 117
Half scene, 118-119
Hardy, Thomas, 3, 6, 87, 88
Harris, McDonald, 113
Hashim, James, 204
Hawthorne, Nathaniel, 24, 112
Haycox, Ernest, 112
Health-related stories, 217
Heller, Joseph, 48
Hemingway, Ernest, 1, 7, 62, 86, 112, 123, 128, 149, 163, 168, 169, 171, 172
Historical stories, 213, 217
Huxley, Aldous, 127

Ideas, development of, 29-30; plot and, 45-51
The International Directory of Little Magazines and Small Presses, 221
International Writers' & Artists' Yearbook, 221
Italics, use of, 157-158

James, Henry, 23, 86, 88, 112, 206
Jewish stories, 218
Johnson, J., 208
Jolas, Eugene, 173
Joyce, James, 8, 23, 25, 168, 173, 205

Kafka, Franz, 173
Kesey, Ken, 2
King, Stephen, 36, 40, 148, 149
Kipling, Rudyard, 7

Lee, Andrea, 2
Lee, Harper, 41
Lewis, Sinclair, 1, 112, 128
Liberty, 150
Limited omniscient viewpoint, 60
Lists, and writing, 24-28
Literary magazines, 220
London, Jack, 112
Lovecraft, H. P., 44

McCall's Magazine, 184, 186, 188, 189, 193, 194
McCarty, Rega Kramer, 143
Magazine Market Place, 221
Magazines, editorial requirements of, 210-218; literary, 220; selling fiction and, 219-225
Mailer, Norman, 1
Malamud, Bernard, 86
Mann, Thomas, 50, 173
Mansfield, Katherine, 123
Manuscript mechanics, 222-223
Marketing, 219-225
Márquez, Gabriel Garcia, 4
Mason, Bobbie Ann, 2, 4, 148
Matthews, Jack, 204
Maugham, Somerset, 5
Maupassant, Guy de, 10
Means of perception, 60
Melville, Herman, 1, 86, 116
Metaphor, 122, 174

Middle, of story, 95-105; building up of, 98-99; conflict in, 96-98; distractions and, 100-101; reader interest in, 102-103

Mitchell, Margaret, 40, 45

Moody, R. Bruce, 65, 66

Moore, Brian, 113

Motivation, 44; character, 53-57; consistency of, 55-57

Nabokov, Vladimir, 25

Names, real, in your story, 148

Narrative-hook (N/H), 18, 116-117

Narrative style, 171-172

Narrator, 64-67

Narrator's voice, in fiction, 39-40

Nathan, Robert, 126

Nautical stories, 215

Nelson, Rodney, 207

Nonfiction novel, 2

No-plot story, 198-199

Notebooks, and writing, 23-24

Objective author, 62-63

O'Connor, Flannery, 8, 113

O'Hara, John, 122

O'Henry (Porter, W. S.), 196

Omniscient author, 59-62

Opening scene, 118

Peripheral narrator, 65

Person, definition of, 63

Petesch, Natalie, 206

Picture stories, 216

Plot, 14-15, 17; characters and, 41-42; definition of, 41; motivation in, 44, 52-57; scene and, 43-44; story ideas and, 45-51

Plotted short short story, 199

Poe, Edgar Allan, 50, 175, 202

Point of view, another character and, 68-69; first person, 64-67; the reader and, 67-68; second person, 63-64; third person, 59-63

Powers, J. F., 113

Protagonist, 17, 42

Proust, Marcel, 3, 9, 171, 173

Reader, entertaining the, 212; fiction, 17-18; orientation (RO), 114-115; point of view and, 67-68

Realistic stories, 215

Resolution, or falling action, 17-18

Revising, rewriting, 175-194

Rice, Ann, 44

Rinehart, Mary Roberts, 227

Robbins, Tom, 63

Robinson, Margaret A., 196

Romance, in fiction, 40

Roth, Philip, 1, 172

Runyon, Damon, 9

Salinger, J. D., 7, 173

Sayles, John, 2

Scene, climax in, 115-116; common denominators in, 112-113; definition of, 43-44; dialogue and, 115; effectiveness of, 117-118; half, 118-119; literary virtues of, 111-112; narration or, 113-114; narrative-hook (N/H) in, 116-117; opening and closing of, 118; reader orientation and, 114-115; set, 119; visual element of, 110-111

Schneider, Phil, 204

Scientific stories, 216, 217

Scott, Sir Walter, 6, 11, 88

Second person, point of view, 63-64

Selling fiction, 184-194; authority and, 206-207; complexity and, 205; directories for fiction writers and, 220-221; efficiency and, 204-205; finding the right magazine, 219-220; honesty and, 203-204; important tips on, 206-208; literary magazines and, 220; magazine editorial requirements and, 210-218; manuscript mechanics and, 222-223; originality and, 207-209; patience and, 223-224; personalizing your submission and, 224; persistence and, 225; short story collections and, 224-225; special interests and, 201-202; submission details and, 223, 224; structure of, 7-10

Sensory perceptions, 122-131

Sentences, use of short, 174

Sequence transitions, 135-136

Set-scenes, 119

Setting, 86-88

Shakespeare, William, 115

Shaw, Irwin, 113

Shelley, Mary, 46

Short short story, opening lines of, 197-199; plot and, 198-199; subject of, 196-197

Short story, anticlimax in, 18; the beginning reader and, 212; classical elements

of, 18; climax in, 17; collections, 224-225; complications in, 17; definitions of, 5, 195-196; editing of, 175-183; limits of, 159; motivation and consistency in, 53-57; resolution of, 17-18; situation in, 17; what to eliminate in, 160-166; tips on selling the, 226-228
Sillitoe, Alan, 65, 68
Simile, 122, 174
Specific names, communicating atmosphere and, 149-150; creating a false reality and, 150-151; defining character and, 149; establishing time/place and, 150; restrictions on, 151-152
Stein, Gertrude, 173
Steinbeck, John, 1, 11, 227
Stendhal (Marie Henri Beyle), 3
Stereotypes, in fiction, 34-37
Stevenson, Robert Louis, 4, 6
Story, background and character of, 14-15; beginning of, 89-94; characterization, 31-40; depth, 13; description in, 12; dialogue in, 70-85; editing of, 175-179; end of, 104-109; middle of, 95-105; motivation in, 44, 52-57; narrator in, 64-67; plot in, 10-12, 41-57; point of view, 58-69; polishing up of, 108-183; romance in, 40; scene in, 43-44, 110-119; selling of, 200-209; sentences in, 7-10; setting in, 86-88; specific names and, 148-152; symbolism in, 143-147; transitions in, 132-136; use of flashback in, 153-158; viewpoint of, 90-91
Stowe, Harriet Beecher, 1
Style, combinations of, 172-174; individual writing, 168-171; narrative, 171-172; punctuation and, 174
Suspension of disbelief, 100
Symbolism, paralleling the story action and, 145; as a resolving device, 143-145; and the surface story, 145-146
Synopsis, 137

Tallent, Elizabeth, 2

Third person, point of view, 59-63
Thomas, Dylan, 195
Tolstoy, Leo, 3, 60
Tours de force, the climax, 118
Transitions, in a story, 132-136
"Traps" (Schneider), 204
Trilling, Calvin, 2
Twain, Mark, 1, 40, 113
Tyler, Anne, 207

Unexpected voice, and character, 83

Viewpoint, of fiction, 140
Voice, in narrative, 58-69
Vonnegut, Kurt, 69

Wagner, Esther, 146
Weathers, Winston, 206
Welty, Eudora, 9, 173, 205
Wharton, Edith, 86
White, E. B., 168, 172, 182
Wolfe, Thomas, 113
Wolfe, Tom, 2, 86
Woolf, Virginia, 3, 24
Wouk, Herman, 117
Writer, dialogue and the, 123-126; smell and the, 126-128; taste and the, 128-129; touch and the, 129-131; visualization and the, 122-123

The Writer's Digest Guide to Manuscript Formats (Buchman and Groves), 222
A Writer's Guide to Chicago-Area Publishers, 221
The Writer's Handbook, 221
Writer's Market, 212, 221
The Writer's Northwest Handbook, 221
Writing, characterization in, 31-40; dialogue and, 70-85; ideas in, 29-30; lists and, 24-28; mechanics of, 19-22; notebooks and, 23-24; setting in, 86-88; style, 168-174; what to eliminate in, 160-166

Young people, stories for, 210

More Great Books for Writers!

The Writer's Digest Dictionary of Concise Writing—Make your work leaner, crisper and clearer! Under the guidance of professional editor Robert Hartwell Fiske, you'll learn how to rid your work of common say-nothing phrases while making it tighter and easier to read and understand. *#10482/$19.99/352 pages*

The 30-Minute Writer—Write short, snappy articles that make editors sit up and take notice. Full-time freelancer Connie Emerson reveals the many types of quickly written articles you can sell—from miniprofiles and one-pagers to personal essays. You'll also learn how to match your work to the market as you explore methods for expanding from short articles to columns, and even books! *#10489/$14.99/256 pages/paperback*

How to Write Attention-Grabbing Query & Cover Letters—Use the secrets Wood reveals to write queries perfectly tailored, too good to turn down! In this guidebook, you will discover why boldness beats blandness in queries every time, ten basics you must have in your article queries, ten query blunders that can destroy publication chances and much more. *#10462/$17.99/208 pages*

1996 Novel & Short Story Writer's Market—Get the information you need to get your short stories and novels published. You'll discover listings on fiction publishers plus original articles on fiction writing techniques; detailed subject categories to help you target appropriate publishers; and interviews with writers, publishers and editors! *#10441/$22.99/624 pages*

Writing the Short Story: A Hands-On Program—With Bickham's unique "workshop on paper" you'll plan, organize, write, revise and polish a short story. Clear instruction, helpful charts and practical exercises will lead you every step of the way! *#10421/$16.99/224 pages*

How to Write Fast (While Writing Well)—Discover what makes a story and what it takes to research and write one. Then, learn step-by-step how to cut wasted time and effort by planning interviews for maximum results, beating writer's block with effective plotting and getting the most information from traditional library research and online computer databases. *#10473/$15.99/208 pages/paperback*

Writing for Money—Discover where to look for writing opportunities—and how to make them pay off. You'll learn how to write for magazines, newspapers, radio and TV, newsletters, greeting cards and a dozen other hungry markets! *#10425/$17.99/256 pages*

Write Tight: How to Keep Your Prose Sharp, Focused and Concise—Discover how to say exactly what you want with grace and power, using not only the right word, but also the right number of words. Specific instructions and helpful exercises explain and demonstrate the process for you. *#10360/$16.99/192 pages*

Writing the Blockbuster Novel—Let a top-flight agent show you how to weave the essential elements of a blockbuster into your own novels with memorable characters, exotic settings, clashing conflicts and more! *#10393/$18.99/224 pages*